BOOK 1
FOUNDATIONS of HAPPINESS

Also by Kevin B. Burk

Astrology: Understanding the Birth Chart

The Complete Node Book

*The Relationship Handbook:
How to Understand and Improve Every
Relationship in Your Life*

*The Relationship Workbook:
How to Understand and Improve Every
Relationship in Your Life*

Astrology Math Made Easy

*The Relationship Workbook:
How to Design and Create Your Ideal
Romantic Relationship*

*The Relationship Workbook:
The Secrets of Successful Team Building*

*Astrological Relationship Handbook:
How to Use Astrology to Understand Every
Relationship in Your Life*

*Astrological Relationship Workbook:
How to Use Astrology to Understand Every
Relationship in Your Life*

Anger Mastery: Get Angry, Get Happy

*Principles of Practical Natal Astrology:
Talented Astrologer Training Book 1*

Astrology and the Human Game

BOOK 1
FOUNDATIONS of HAPPINESS

Build a Foundation of Happiness with Astrology Stories and the Human Game

Kevin B. Burk

SERENDIPITY
P·R·E·S·S

ISBN 978-0-9864496-6-6

©2023 Kevin B. Burk. All rights reserved. No part of this publication may be reproduced, transmitted, transcribed, stored in a retrieval system, or translated into any language, in any form, by any means, without written permission of the author.

Printed in the United States of America

Published by
Serendipity Press
Houston, Texas

Book design, cover design, and illustrations designed by Kevin B. Burk

The Human Game, Tell Better Astrology Stories, and all related characters and clements ™ and ® Kevin B. Burk.

CONTENTS

PROLOGUE
What Do Stories Have to Do With Astrology?.... 1

PART 1
FOUNDATIONS

CHAPTER 1
Foundations of Stories 7

CHAPTER 2
Foundations of Astrology Stories.......... .25

CHAPTER 3
Foundations of Astrology............. .39

CHAPTER 4
Astrology Story Tropes.............. .55

CHAPTER 5
Astrology Story Maps............... .71

CHAPTER 6
Foundations of Happiness Stories .... .87

PART 2
THE QUEST FOR HAPPINESS

CHAPTER 7
The Story of Your Need Bank Accounts ...... .95

CHAPTER 8
The Story of Your Safety Needs 103

CHAPTER 9
Safety Need Astrology Stories 111

CHAPTER 10
The Story of Your Validation Needs 127

CHAPTER 11
Validation Need Astrology Stories 135

CHAPTER 12
The Story of Your Happiness Account 151

CHAPTER 13
Happiness Resource Astrology Stories 157

PART 3
OBSTACLES

CHAPTER 14
Obstacle Stories. 173

CHAPTER 15
Astrology Aspect and Planet Story Tropes. 179

CHAPTER 16
Outer Planet Aspect Stories and The Quest for
Happiness 193

PART 4
THE IDENTITY QUEST

CHAPTER 17
Overview of The Identity Quest 209

CHAPTER 18
Chart Ruler: Human Seeming 215

CHAPTER 19
Mars: Human Doing 227

CHAPTER 20
The Sun: Human Being 239

EPILOGUE

EPILOGUE
Where Do You Go From Here?. 249

PROLOGUE
What Do Stories Have to Do With Astrology?

One of my favorite stories comes from *The Hitchhiker's Guide to the Galaxy* by Douglas Adams. This story concerns a race of hyperintelligent, pan-dimensional beings who designed an immense computer called Deep Thought. The first assignment for Deep Thought is to find the answer to the Ultimate Question of Life, the Universe, and Everything. After thinking about the problem for 7.5 million years, Deep Thought reveals the answer to the Ultimate Question of Life, the Universe, and Everything.

Which is 42.

This story illustrates one of the great Universal Truths: If you ask a silly question, you get a silly answer. The corollary to this is that the quality of the answer depends on who you ask.

Instead of asking a computer, they should have asked an astrologer.

It doesn't take an astrologer 7.5 million years to find the answer to the Ultimate Question of Life, the Universe, and Everything. It doesn't take an astrologer 7.5 seconds. To an astrologer, the answer to the Ultimate Question of Life, the Universe, and Everything is obvious: astrology.

Astrology is how human beings have always answered the ultimate questions. Since the dawn of civilization, humans have looked to the night sky and told stories about the movements of the planets to answer questions about Life, the Universe, and Everything. This is the origin of astrology.

In the beginning, there was astrology.

But before there was astrology, there was story.

Astrology evolved from stories, and we use astrology to tell stories. So, the way to get better answers from astrology is to tell better astrology stories.

Until now, astrologers have tried to tell better astrology stories by focusing on the astrology. Modern astrologers look outward and incorporate new symbols in the chart, including asteroids, hypothetical planets, and minor aspects. Traditional astrologers look inward and explore long-lost tools and techniques from the Golden Age of astrology. The problem is that astrology is the *language* used to tell the story, not the story itself. Expanding the language of astrology is like using a thesaurus to write a story.

The curious paradox of this hypothesis is that an expansive, eclectic vocabulary fails to facilitate a significant or meaningful improvement *vis-à-vis* the structure, aesthetic qualities, or clarity of the story.

In other words, a bigger vocabulary doesn't make a better story.

You're reading this book because you would like to be able to tell better astrology stories. To do that, first you have to understand how stories work and what makes a better story. That's where the Human Game™ comes in. The Human Game is a philosophy based on the idea that the Universe is made up of stories. If everything is story, when you understand how stories work, you can understand anything—including astrology.

But you don't really care about understanding the story of astrology.

The only story you care about is The Story of Your Life.

You believe that if you understand the story of astrology it will help you to understand The Story of Your Life. You believe that astrology can help you find the answer to your Ultimate Question of Life, the Universe, and Everything. You believe that astrology can help you to find happiness and discover the meaning and purpose of your life.

Astrology can do all this and more—when you combine it with the Human Game.

Why Tell Astrology Stories?

Let's say that you recently ordered a thingamabob from Amazon.com. That thingamabob began its story in the thingamabob factory, probably in China because thingamabobs are just too expensive to manufacture locally. The thingamabob is shipped from China to the main thingamabob distribution center. From there, it's shipped to a regional Amazon warehouse, and then to a local Amazon distribution center in your city, as little as one mile away from your home. Your thingamabob has completed more than 95% of its journey. All that's left is what's known as the last-mile delivery, where the thingamabob leaves the local distribution center and arrives on your doorstep.

The last-mile delivery is the most difficult and the most important step. You won't be happy if your thingamabob is dropped off somewhere in your neighborhood and you have to go out and look for it. You won't even be happy if your thingamabob is delivered to your neighbor by mistake. All you care about is that the thingamabob is delivered directly to you.

Astrology works the same way.

When a client books an astrology consultation with you, instead of ordering a thingamabob, they're looking for an answer. They've encountered some kind of obstacle in their personal story, which is keeping them from feeling happy, and they expect you to give them an answer they can use.

You take the client's personal story and connect it to their birth chart. You analyze the chart and use your preferred tools and techniques to explore the question and identify strategies and solutions that could help the client to overcome the obstacle. You assemble the answers, package them up, and you're ready to deliver them to the client. This is more than 95% of the astrology required for the astrology consultation, and all of it happened before you sat down with the client. All that's left is the last-mile delivery: the actual consultation with the client.

You can't rely on astrology for the last-mile delivery. Your client doesn't understand astrology—and they don't care about astrology. You need to translate your astrology-based answers into a language your client can understand so they can use the answer to overcome the obstacle and move toward happiness.

You do this with astrology stories. Astrology stories are how you connect astrology and the birth chart to The Story of Your Life.

The objective of this program is to teach you to tell better astrology stories. The emphasis is on the stories, not on astrology. Astrology is the language you use to tell the story, not the story itself.

It doesn't matter how you work with the language of astrology. It doesn't matter how you approach natal chart interpretation, or whether you work with traditional or modern techniques. In this program, you will learn how to complete the last-mile delivery so your client will be happy.

To demonstrate how astrology stories work, we'll work with the natal chart and the most basic components of the language of astrology. We'll take a journalistic approach to astrology stories and explore how different components of the language of astrology—the planet, modality, element, and house—answer specific questions, including **What**, **What Else**, **How**, **Which**, and **Where**.

If you're already familiar with the language of astrology, you will discover new ways to work with the simplest components. And if you're new to astrology, this program includes everything you need to tell astrology stories.

Along the way, you'll experience a new, dynamic approach to natal astrology. You'll learn how to build a foundation of happiness and experience your Happily Ever After. And you'll use astrology stories to assemble a Happiness GPS that gives you turn-by-turn directions to the best possible outcome in any situation.

Welcome to Astrology and the Human Game. It's going to be fun.

PART 1
FOUNDATIONS

CHAPTER 1
Foundations of Stories

The Human Game™ is a philosophy built on the idea that the Universe is made up of stories. If everything is story, when you understand how stories work you can understand anything—including astrology. We're starting with a foundation of story because you need to understand how story works before you can tell better astrology stories.

Stories are how human beings make sense of the universe. Stories give shape and structure to facts and ideas and connect them to your personal experience. A good story takes new information and embeds it in your reality without the need to study or memorize anything. Not only can stories change your reality, stories also create your reality. This is the ultimate potential of the Human Game.

Your life is a story, and you are the main character of The Story of Your Life. Every choice you make in your life is intended to move you closer to your ultimate goal: to get everything you ever wanted. The reason you want everything you ever wanted is that you believe when you get everything you ever wanted you will live Happily Ever After.

This doesn't mean what you think it means.

Happily Ever After isn't the end of The Story of Your Life. Happily Ever After is the end of the story of The Quest for Happiness. Happily Ever After means your life goes on—ever after—and that happiness is taken for granted. Happily Ever After means you have a foundation of happiness. Happily Ever After isn't a happy ending. Happily Ever After is a happy beginning.

You care about astrology because you believe astrology can help you advance in The Story of Your Life so you can experience your Happily Ever After. This is also why your future clients care about astrology. That's why you will learn to tell better astrology stories by connecting those stories to the bigger story of The Quest for Happiness.

In the Human Game philosophy, everything is story. Every smaller story is a part of a bigger story. The bigger stories are the context that makes it possible to understand the smaller stories. The Quest for Happiness is a part of The Story of Your Life, and The Story of Your Life is a part of The Story of the Human Game.

The Story of the Human Game™

The Human Game is a *game*. Games are optional, and the point of playing a game is to have fun. If you're not having fun, you don't have to keep playing. You're free to choose a new game at any time.

You play the Human Game in your mind, using your imagination and your creativity. You work with the rules, shape, and structure of story to take charge of The Story of Your Life so you can establish a foundation of happiness and build on it. To understand the Story of the Human Game, imagine that it has a game board.

The Human Game board has three key elements: the **Lie (Duality)**, the **Truth (Unity)**, and **Reality (Story)** (see figure on next page). In the story of the Human Game, you operate within a bubble of reality that contains The Story of Your Life. The objective of the Human Game is to move your bubble of reality away from the Lie of Duality and toward the Truth of Unity by improving your story. As you advance your story toward the Truth, you experience **Fun**, **Happiness**, **Prosperity**, **Joy**, and ultimately find the **Meaning** and purpose of your life.

Fun is the most important prize of the Human Game because the Human Game is a game. Fun, almost by definition, is the opposite of serious. The more serious the situation is, the less fun it is. This means that the lower the stakes, the greater the fun. Games are fun only when the stakes are low—when losing the game doesn't cost you anything.

Foundations of Stories

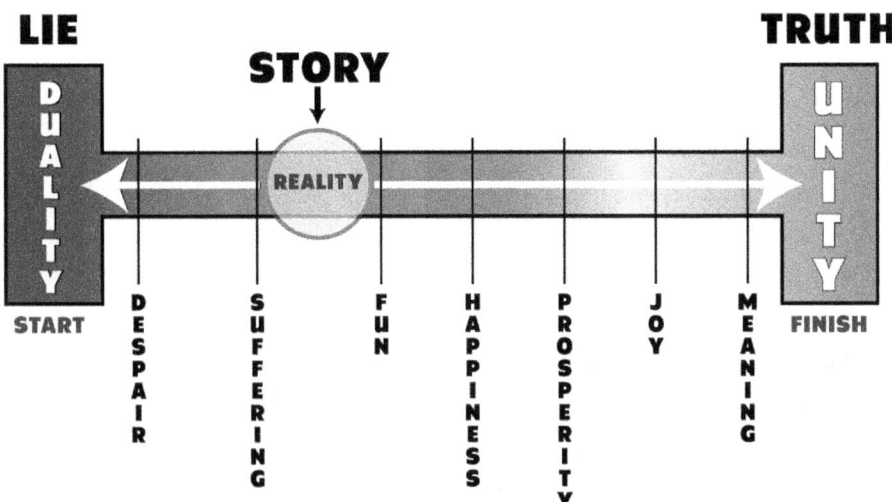

Fun is related to Happiness and Joy, but it's not the same thing. Fun is like the chocolate sprinkles on the top of the ice cream sundae. When asked, "Would you like fun with that?" the answer is always, "Sure!" But fun on its own isn't too satisfying: it's the chocolate sprinkles without the ice cream.

Happiness is the next most important prize, but it doesn't mean what you think it does. **Happiness is the feeling you experience when you are free from want and free from need.** Happiness doesn't mean that you feel *good*; happiness means you no longer feel *bad*. When you are happy, you don't have to do anything. You have unlimited options and you are free to choose any path that inspires you. Once you build a foundation of happiness, you can create prosperity and choose experiences that give you pleasure and enjoyment. But without a foundation of happiness, you won't be able to experience Prosperity, Joy, or find the Meaning of your life.

To advance in the Human Game and improve The Story of Your Life, you need to build a foundation of story to understand how story works. In a sense, the Human Game is a story about story. The foundation of story includes **The Rules of Story** and an understanding of story shapes, story levels, and story classes. Because your objective is to learn how to tell better astrology stories, this foundation will also include an introduction to story tropes.

These stories about story will probably feel abstract at first, and that's perfectly fine. Don't spend any time memorizing this information or struggling to make sense of it—but don't skip over it, either! As you advance through this program, you'll become more familiar with these concepts and they will begin to make sense to you. More importantly, these concepts will help you understand astrology stories in powerful and practical ways.

The Rules of Story

The Law of the Human Game is **The Best Story Wins**. This means that the best story immediately becomes the dominant story and completely transforms your reality. Not only does this change the future of your story, it also changes the past. This change is permanent. You can't ever go back to the old story or your old reality. You can't unring a bell and you can't unsee what you've seen.

You experience this change all the time without noticing it. When you encounter a new piece of information that shifts your perspective or opinion on something, the new piece of information is the best story, and it immediately changes the course of your original story. When the change to the story is significant, you experience a "light bulb moment." You flip a switch and see everything in a completely new way.

Think of this like a surprise plot twist at the end of a movie that changes your understanding of the story. Films like *The Sixth Sense* tell excellent stories up to the final moments when they reveal a new piece of information that transforms everything and makes the story even better. You can literally go back and watch the movie again from the start, knowing the big reveal, and enjoy it even more because you pick up on all of the clues you missed the first time. The new story is not only better, it's also bigger.

You can't simply replace your current story with a better story. The new, better story has to build on the current story for it to take over and change the course of the story. The easiest way to achieve this is to upgrade your current story. The more a story incorporates **The Rules of Story**, the better the story is. You can improve any story with **The Rule of Three**, **The Rule of Conservation**, and **The Rule of Compensation**.

The Rule of Three

The most important rule of story is The Rule of Three. Threes give structure to stories, and one of the easiest ways to identify the shape of a story is to spot the threes.

Consider how threes show up in popular children's stories. Threes are in the title of stories like *Goldilocks and the Three Bears*, *Three Billy Goats Gruff*, and *The Three Little Pigs*. Threes are implicit in stories like *Cinderella* (with her two stepsisters); *Sleeping Beauty* (with her three fairy godmothers), and *Aladdin* (with his three wishes). In *The Wizard of Oz*, Dorothy has three companions (Scarecrow, Tin Man, and Cowardly Lion), and in *A Christmas Carol*, Scrooge is visited by three Christmas ghosts (Christmas Past, Christmas Present, and Christmas Yet to Come).

The Rule of Three addresses the structure of stories and how that structure always involves the number three. Every story is divided into three acts, which roughly correspond to the beginning, middle, and end. Every story has three levels: **Plot**, **Character**, and **Theme**. And whenever you are faced with a choice between two options (the Lie of Duality), The Rule of Three tells you there is always a third option—you just need to find it.

The Rule of Conservation

The Rule of Conservation states that every detail of a story is essential. The more you recycle and reuse details in a story, the better the story is. The *deus ex machina* solution where the resolution to a story comes from a random, unexpected, and new situation is rarely satisfying. When you discover that everything you need to resolve the situation has been available to you from the start, and you solve the problem by seeing things in a new way, it's a much better story.

The Rule of Compensation

The Rule of Compensation states that every gift has a price and every price has a gift. The Universe is inherently balanced, even if it's not always fair. When you receive something, you have to give up something else in exchange. What you receive will always equal to or of greater value than what you give up, but that may not be obvious to you. Often, you begin the story grieving what you think you've lost. The Rule of Compensation reminds you that if you've lost something, you have received something else in exchange. It's up to you to find the gift and discover its true value.

Story Shapes

Think of a story like a clock. The face of the clock is the narrative of the story. The hands of the clock move around the clock face in one direction, and the story itself embodies multiple cycles: the hour hand, the minute hand, and the second hand. Taken together, this tells you where—or more accurately when—you are in time.

A clock face is divided into twelve segments, but stories need only three segments: one for each act of the story. The three hands of the clock relate to the three levels of the story. The hour hand is the Theme-level story, the minute hand is the Character-level story, and the second hand is the Plot-level story (see illustration on next page).

Like clocks, stories never end: they just complete one cycle and begin the next. When one or more of the clock hands points to the end of Act 3 of a story (indicating the end of one cycle and the start of a new one), you have the opportunity to choose a new story rather than to continue with the current story. But if you miss your exit window, you have to stay with the current story until the next window comes along.

You can't change the direction of the hands of the clock or disrupt the narrative of the story, but you can speed up the cycle so you can end one story and start a new one. To do that, you have to look inside the story clock and adjust the clockwork that drives it.

Clockworks consist of multiple gears that turn at different speeds. The gears move the hands of the clock and determine the speed of the

Foundations of Stories

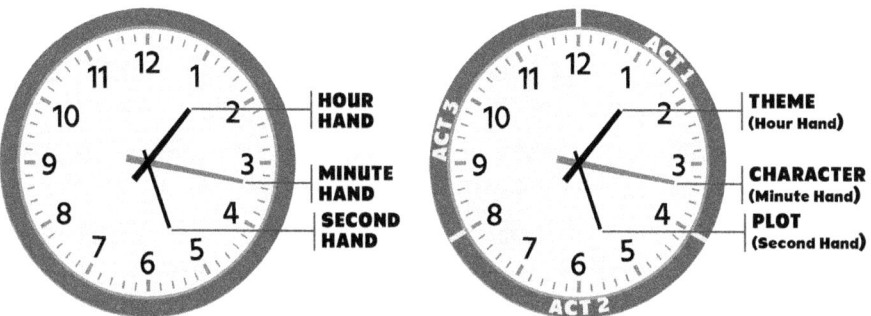

story. But each gear is itself a story. Each gear is a clock with its own narrative and its own cycles.

Stories are fractal: they are infinitely complex, never-ending patterns that are self-similar across different scales. A story—and reality itself—is an ongoing feedback loop. Once you start down that rabbit hole, it can be difficult to stop.

The key to taking control of your stories is to define which story you are exploring. Remember that whatever story you explore is also a gear that drives a larger story. Once you understand where the story fits in the bigger picture, you can explore the smaller stories that drive the main narrative of the selected story and make whatever adjustments you like. This is especially important advice when exploring astrology stories. If you don't stay focused on your objective, you will get lost in the chart and may not ever find your way out.

Story Levels

Every story operates on three levels: **Plot**, **Character**, and **Theme**. All three levels of the story combine to form a bigger story, just as you combine the hour, minute, and second to know the precise time. What you may not appreciate yet is that each level of a story is its own story. The Plot-level story is entirely different from the Character-level story, and the Theme-level story operates in its own dimension. Each level of story plays out over three acts, and each act of each story has a specific purpose. The simplest way to understand this is with the **Story Matrix**.

	ACT 1	ACT 2	ACT 3
PLOT	Goal	Obstacle	Resolution
CHARACTER	Want	Need	Choice
THEME	Lie	Truth	Test

Let's explore each level of story in more detail.

Plot-Level Story

The title of the Plot-level story is "Just the Facts, Ma'am." It's the objective sequence of events: what happened.

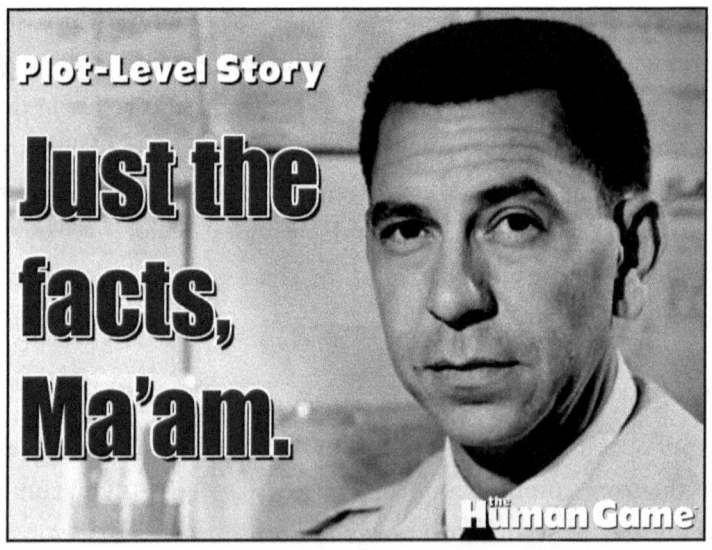

Act 1 of the Plot-level story identifies the **GOAL**: the objective that drives the story. **Act 2** of the Plot-level story is where you encounter the **OBSTACLE** you must overcome to achieve the **GOAL**. **Act 3** of the Plot-level story is the **RESOLUTION**, where you either achieve the **GOAL** or not.

You engage with The Story of Your Life from the Plot-level and believe that if you achieve your **Goal** you'll get what you **Want**, and then you'll be happy ... and then you'll find the meaning and purpose of your life.

Going back to the clock image, living your life from the Plot-level story is focusing on the second hand of the clock. You'll get to the end of the story eventually, but you're taking the longest route.

The problem with this approach is that it raises the stakes of the Plot-level story. Because everything seems to be connected in a cause-and-effect relationship, if you don't achieve your Plot-level **Goal**, it means you will never be happy, and your life won't have any meaning.

Your first objective in the Human Game is to lower the stakes of your stories by separating the Character-level story from the Plot-level story so the outcome of the Plot-level story no longer determines your happiness.

Let's begin with an example of a Plot-level story that most people can relate to.

The TPS Report (Plot-Level Story)

Your current **Goal** at your job is to complete the TPS Report and submit it by the end of the day on Friday. You have a countdown clock associated with this goal, and if you miss the deadline you will fail. The **Obstacle** is that you need input from Marketing and Sales to complete the TPS Report. If they don't give you those numbers by Friday, you won't be able to do your job and complete the TPS Report on time. To raise the stakes even more, you have a performance review coming up in a month, and your ability to complete the TPS Report on time is one of the most important parts of that review.

This Plot-level story (or one very much like it) can consume all of your attention, even outside of working hours. Completing the TPS Report becomes the single most important objective in your life. Every action you take and every choice you make is driven by your pursuit of the TPS Report. The TPS Report is your personal Holy Grail.

From a Human Game story perspective, the TPS Report is a **MacGuffin**. Alfred Hitchcock called the MacGuffin the thing in the story that the characters all care about but the audience doesn't. The MacGuffin exists to drive the plot and to motivate the characters to act, but on its own, it doesn't have any real significance.

Some famous MacGuffins include the Horcruxes in the *Harry Potter* series, the Maltese Falcon in *The Maltese Falcon*, Rosebud in *Citizen Kane*, Ryan in *Saving Private Ryan*, and the actual Holy Grail in *Indiana Jones and the Last Crusade*.

The TPS Report drives the Plot-level of your story because you believe that it's a necessary step on the road to happiness. But when you consider the Character-level story, you realize that you, personally, don't care about the TPS Report.

You think that completing the TPS Report will get you something you **WANT**. Getting what you **WANT** is the focus of **Act 1** of the Character-level story.

Character-Level Story

The title of the Character-level story is "What's in it for *Moi*?" The Character-level story is the story of the subjective experience of the external events. The Plot-level story is what happened; the Character-level story is what happened to me (and how I feel about it).

Foundations of Stories

You are the main character in The Story of Your Life, and the Character-level story is all about you. The Character-level story is your personal quest for happiness. The only reason you care about anything in your Character-level story is because you believe it will contribute to your happiness.

In **Act 1** of the Character-level story you identify what you **WANT**. What you **WANT** is closely related to the **GOAL** of the Plot-level story, but it's not the same thing. The **GOAL** of the Plot-level story is usually a MacGuffin. You pursue the MacGuffin because you believe that when you acquire it, you will experience something that matters to you. You care about getting what you **WANT** because you believe that when you get what you **WANT**, then you'll be happy.

Spoiler alert: this almost never happens.

In **Act 2** of the Character-level story, you become aware of what you **NEED**. When you get what you **WANT**, you believe that it will make a deposit in one or more of your Need Bank Accounts: your **Safety Need Account**, your **Validation Need Account**, or your **Self-Actualization Need Account**. Because happiness is the feeling you experience when you are free from **WANT** and free from **NEED**, when you manage the balance in your Need Bank Accounts, you experience actual happiness.

Act 3 of the Character-level story is where you make a **CHOICE** between what you **WANT** and what you **NEED**. The lesson is that you can receive deposits in your Need Bank Accounts (and experience happiness) without ever getting what you **WANT**.

The TPS Report (Character-Level Story)

You **WANT** to complete the TPS Report on time, but that's just a means to an end. You really care about what completing the TPS Report on time will do for the balance in your Need Bank Accounts.

You believe that if you complete the TPS Report on time, it will mean you get a good performance review, which will mean that you will feel secure that you will keep your job. That will make a nice deposit in your **Safety Need Account**.

And if you do well with the TPS Report, overcoming obstacles and not letting other people's incompetence stop you from doing your job, your boss will recognize you for that. In fact, you expect that you will be singled out as a shining example of excellence for heroically completing the TPS Report and celebrated for all of the extra effort you invested in it, which will make a big deposit in your **Validation Need Account**.

Finally, doing your job well and meeting your obligations is an important part of your identity. When you live up to that expectation, you receive a deposit in your **Self-Actualization Need Account**.

The problem is that you also believe that if you fail to complete the TPS Report on time it will make withdrawals from your Need Bank Accounts and limit your prospects of happiness.

This, of course, is silly. The TPS Report has no relationship to your happiness. When you realize this truth, completing the TPS Report is no longer a life-or-death scenario. If you achieve the Plot-level GOAL, it can still make deposits in your Need Bank Accounts, but that's a bonus. If you miss the TPS Report deadline, it won't take away anything from your Safety, Validation, or Actualization Needs, and it won't limit your happiness.

When you master the Character-level story and learn how to manage the balance in your Need Bank Accounts on your own, you build a foundation of happiness—and that's a wonderful thing to experience.

But happiness isn't the end of your story. You believe that once you are happy, then you'll find meaning in your life. You can find happiness at the Character-level of your story, but you have to look to the Theme-level story to find meaning.

Theme-Level Story

The title of the Theme-level story is "The Da Vinci Code." The Theme-level story is based on symbols and hidden clues contained in the Plot-level and Character-level stories. Nothing in the Theme-level story is about what it's about, and everything contains codes for you to decipher.

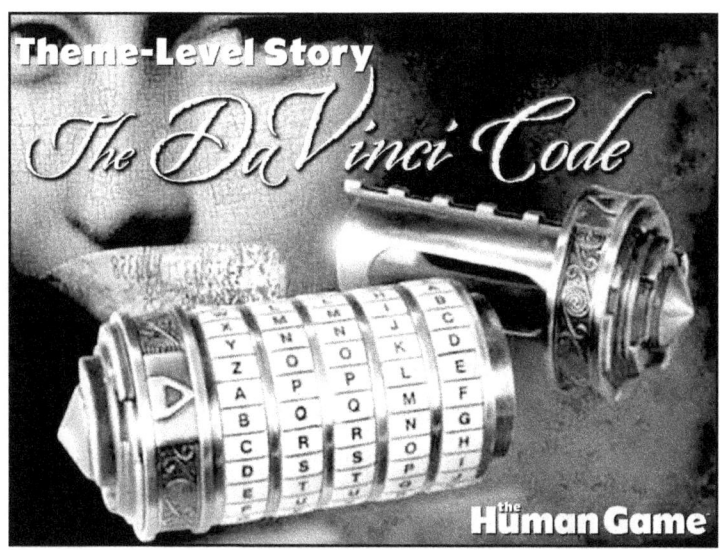

The structure of the Theme-level story is straightforward. In **Act 1**, you become aware that some aspect of your story you have always accepted is, in fact, a **Lie**. Discovering this **Lie** can be traumatic, and it may force you to question almost everything in your story. In **Act 2**, you set out to find the **Truth**—more specifically a Truth Key—that you can use to free yourself from the prison of the **Lie**. In **Act 3**, you face the **Test** where you find out if you can use the **Truth** to free yourself from the prison of the **Lie**.

The Theme-level story is the hour hand of the story clock. It's the slowest-moving hand, but when it does advance, it shifts the entire story. And when you're willing to confront the **Lie** and pursue the **Truth**—no matter the cost—that's when you discover the meaning and purpose of your life.

Nothing in the Theme-level story is what it appears to be. Everything is a symbol. Everything is in code. Everything is a clue and it all points you toward something bigger than you can easily imagine.

The TPS Report (Theme-Level Story)

The TPS Report in the Plot-level story could symbolize how you look for external solutions to make you happy—and in the Theme-level story, it might point you to the LIE that happiness exists somewhere in the outside world. The TRUTH is that happiness lives inside you and has nothing to do with the external world of the Plot-level story.

Alternatively, you could consider how important Validation Needs are in your Character-level story, and how you expect that the TPS Report will lead to approval and recognition from your boss. In the Theme-level story, your boss isn't your boss; in the Theme-level story, your boss may symbolize your father, and the deeper story may involve healing your relationship with your father and resolving deep childhood wounds.

The good news about the Theme-level story is that this is the level of story where you have absolute freedom and complete creative control. No matter what Theme-level story you create, it will help you to discover some aspect of the LIE that is limiting the Plot- and Character-level stories. When you confront that LIE with the TRUTH, it creates new opportunities at every level of your story.

The bad news about the Theme-level story is that you have absolute freedom and complete creative control. The Theme-level story is a blank page, and as any writer will tell you, there's nothing more intimidating in all of creation than a blank page.

The Theme-level story is optional, and it's very advanced. It's also where astrology enters the picture. Astrology is entirely symbolic, so astrology stories are Theme-level stories. When you assemble an astrology story from the different story components in the birth chart, you are constructing a Theme-level story.

Creating the Theme-level story is only step one. To be able to use that Theme-level story to advance the Plot-level and Character-level stories and give these stories meaning, you need to connect the astrology story to a personal story, and then you must activate that connection. This process involves a number of steps, but by the end of this program, you will understand how it all works and how to experience it for yourself.

Story Classes

Size matters when it comes to stories. The bigger the story is, the more meaningful it is. But stories can get too big to digest at once. Bigger stories often have to be broken up into smaller stories that, when taken together, tell a much bigger story. For example, the story of Harry Potter takes place over seven books and eight films—and that's not even the entire story of his life. The Story of Your Life is even bigger than that.

The Human Game model includes seven classes of story that range from F-Class stories of moment-to-moment experiences up to the A-Class story, which is the absolute Story of Your Life. G-Class stories are ghost stories that live in your past and haunt your character.

F-Class stories are the smallest stories: they're **forgettable, functional**, and **frequently frustrating**. Unless they connect to something bigger and play a critical role in an active E-Class story, you forget them as soon as you experience them.

E-Class stories are **events**. These are the main concerns and objectives you have in your life at any given time. E-Class stories include things like your weekend plans, your current project at work, or preparing your taxes. E-Class stories seem to happen one after the other. They don't feel meaningful because they're small and they rarely connect to a bigger life purpose.

D-Class stories are the **dreams** that you create in the Human Game Writer's Room. D-Class stories forge connections between the E-Class stories of your daily life and the more meaningful C-Class, B-Class, and A-Class stories. When you tell astrology stories and work with the Human

Game, you are creating D-Class stories. This program will explore two D-Class stories: **The Quest for Happiness** and **The Identity Quest**.

C-Class stories are **chapters** in your life. These are big and usually meaningful stories defined by major life events, such as where you live, where you work, or significant relationships in your life. C-Class stories often span a number of years and they always describe a linear sequence of time in your life. E-Class stories have meaning when they connect to a C-Class story.

B-Class stories are related to the different houses of your **birth chart**. Each B-Class story is the story of how you engaged with a particular aspect of your life—your money, your relationships, your creativity, your foundation, your career—over the course of your entire lifetime. Unlike C-Class stories, B-Class stories are not linear or sequential. A single B-Class story will intersect with multiple C-Class stories.

All of these stories serve to advance the **A-Class** Story of Your Life. The A-Class story is the **absolute** story. The more you're able to connect your experiences to the A-Class story, the more meaning and purpose your life has.

Story Tropes

The last piece of the foundation of stories involves story tropes. Stories are made up of stories. Story tropes are familiar story patterns that can be added to other stories to provide support and create structure. When you recognize the pattern of a story trope, you know what to expect in the story.

Some examples of story tropes include good guys wear white, bad guys wear black, and superheroes wear capes. Romantic comedy stories often begin with the "meet cute" story trope, followed by the "lovers initially hate each other" story trope. When you recognize the "three wishes" story trope, you know the first two will go wrong so the third wish can undo all of the damage.

Story tropes can be used over and over again without becoming clichés, as long as you understand how they work and can vary the details. A story trope is familiar, and when you recognize the pattern of a story trope, you

Foundations of Stories

know what to expect, which makes for a good story. When the story messes with your expectations and surprises you, it makes for a better story.

The symbols in astrology and the specific combinations of those symbols in your birth chart are story tropes. These story patterns play out over and over again in The Story of Your Life. You can't change these patterns and you can't escape them, and it's easy to focus on how limiting and frustrating that can be. But rather than focusing on the price, you can focus on the gift. When you can spot the story trope and recognize the pattern in your stories, you can use it to your advantage. You know what to expect because you know the shape of the story, and that means you can choose a better strategy and create a better outcome, which makes it a better story.

CHAPTER 2
Foundations of Astrology Stories

Before we can explore astrology stories, we need to consider your stories about astrology. Your current stories about astrology shape your understanding of what astrology is and how it works. The new stories you will learn here about astrology and the Human Game will build on the foundations of your current stories about astrology.

The challenge is that the Human Game approach to astrology won't quite fit with your current astrology stories. I need to upgrade your current stories and create a bigger story about astrology that can contain everything, while keeping your current astrology stories separate from the new Human Game astrology stories.

To do this, I need to make you aware of your current stories about astrology. Specifically, I need to introduce you to the major story tropes that shape everyone's stories about astrology. I'll introduce these tropes while telling a brief and biased story about the history of astrology. These stories will leave out quite a lot of detail, almost (but not quite) to the level of, "*The Lord of the Rings* is the story of a group of friends who take a road trip to recycle a piece of unwanted jewelry." With that in mind, I will divide the history of astrology into "traditional" and "modern" based on time, not on techniques. Traditional astrology describes Western astrology from the Hellenistic period (circa 200 BCE) to the 17th century, and modern astrology describes astrology from its rebirth in the late 19th century to the present day.

I promise you, it will be more fun than it sounds.

Traditional Astrology Stories

In *The Hitchhiker's Guide to the Galaxy*, the computer Deep Thought was created to answer the Ultimate Question of Life, the Universe, and Everything. Astrology was created for a similar purpose. The ancient civilizations that observed the night skies and built the language of astrology over thousands of years weren't that sophisticated, of course. For one thing, they had never heard of computers. They observed the movements of the stars and told stories and created the language of astrology to answer one question:

Why?

You ask **Why** only when you're unhappy. No one has ever fallen to her knees, looked to the skies and cried out, "Why? Why me?? Why did I win the lottery???" When you experience good fortune, you don't ask too many questions. When you're happy you don't need astrology to tell you **Why** you're happy.

Astrology can answer many questions. In this program, we'll explore the questions of **What**, **What Else**, **How**, **Which**, and **Where**. The question of **When** is limited to predictive astrology, which is beyond the scope of this program, and in the stories we'll explore in this program, **Who** is always you.

But the original question, the question that defines the shape of your stories about astrology, is **Why**.

When the programmers asked Deep Thought for the answer to the Ultimate Question of Life, the Universe, and Everything, Deep Thought warned them, "You're not going to like it."

There is an answer to **Why**, and you're not going to like it, either:

Because.

The only answer to "Why?" is "Because." Everything that follows "Because" is a story. The story might be true, but most of the time, the story is merely real.

When traditional astrology asks **Why**, the answer is, "Because fate." This introduces the story trope titled *As the Prophecy Foretold*, which is the foundation of your stories about astrology itself.

As the Prophecy Foretold

If creating a story is cooking, story tropes are spices: they're not the main ingredients, but they make the dish come alive. Some spices are more useful than others, and the same goes for story tropes. Prophecy story tropes are the salt of the story spice rack. Every good story benefits from a dash of prophecy.

Most of the time, prophecy shows up as foreshadowing, which, ironically, can be seen only in hindsight. This is an example of **The Rule of Conservation** where every detail is significant. Something happens in **Act 1** of the story that you don't appreciate until it blows up in **Act 3** of the story and you realize you should have seen it coming. In the world of theater, this is known as *Chekhov's Gun*[1], a story trope that states that if a gun shows up in **Act 1**, it must be fired in **Act 3**.

Much like salt, too much prophecy can dominate the story—and once it's in, you can't take it out. **The Rules of Story** are quite clear: every prophecy will be fulfilled. If a prophecy shows up in **Act 1**, it must be fulfilled in **Act 3**. When you are caught up in a prophecy story, it's not a question of *if*, it's a question of *how*.

Prophecy story tropes can play out in three different ways: you can **accept the prophecy**, you can **fight the prophecy**, or you can **beat the prophecy**.

The first option is to **accept the prophecy**. You surrender to your fate and give up without a fight. You take the path of least resistance, resolve the prophecy in the most literal and obvious way, and don't question the price you pay or how the prophecy has limited your options.

The second option is to **fight the prophecy**. You reject the prophecy and refuse to accept it. You run from your destiny and ignore the call. This never works out, but it makes for a much better story. **The Rules of Story** mean you can't escape destiny; still, the more you try to avoid your fate, the more satisfying it is when inevitably the prophecy is fulfilled.

The third option is to **beat the prophecy**. This option is available only when you play the Human Game because you need to know **The Rules**

---

[1] Anton Chekhov, Russian playwright whose works include *The Cherry Orchard, Three Sisters,* and *Uncle Vanya.*

of Story well enough to bend them without breaking them. You find the loophole so that you can fulfill the letter of the prophecy but not the spirit of it. You maximize the gift of the prophecy and minimize the price. This is the best story of all.

The *As the Prophecy Foretold* story trope is the foundation of your story about astrology itself. In your story, astrology can predict the future. That's not the *only* thing astrology can do, but it's the *first* thing astrology can do. And first impressions are lasting impressions.

From its origins in ancient Greece and Egypt through to the 17th century, astrology evolved as a way to forecast the future. Different branches of astrology use different techniques to answer different questions. Mundane astrology answers questions about world events and is perhaps the oldest branch of astrology. Horary astrology answers important questions of the moment, like "Did my ship arrive safely?" or "Will I win the lawsuit?" Even natal astrology used your birth chart to consider your personal destiny. As different as these branches of astrology appear on the surface, what unites them is that they all forecast the future.

Traditional astrology is prophecy.

In the late 17th century, astrology fell out of favor. Once an esteemed science taught in universities and practiced by all learned men (there were no learned women), astrology went underground for almost 200 years.

Modern Astrology Stories

Humanity continued to evolve while astrology kept a low profile. No longer content with simple questions, such as "Why?" we asked more complex questions, such as "Who am I?" and "What is my purpose?" These questions led to significant advancements in philosophy, spirituality, and science. Of course, these questions also led to Facebook ads and reality television, so the benefits of these questions have been, to put it mildly, mixed.

As profound as these questions are, another question is far more important. This question is at the heart of society, at the center of relationships, and easily within reach at all times:

What the hell is wrong with you?

Don't discount the value of this question. It's responsible for psychology, psychiatry, and sociology. When you strip these disciplines down to the studs, each one of them is dedicated to understanding and explaining in clinical terms (and often at a cost of more than $200 an hour) exactly what the hell is wrong with you.

Of course, this question doesn't apply to you, personally.

You, personally, are engaging and delightful. You're an open book. Your choices, preferences, insights, and perceptions are entirely appropriate. They need no justification because they're obviously correct, as any reasonable, well-adjusted, decent person would agree.

At least this is what you believe.

You can't test the theory because finding a reasonable, well-adjusted decent person is so hard to do when you're surrounded by lunatics.

Be honest. When was the last time you went more than an hour without a part of you wanting to scream, "What the hell is wrong with you?"

In his play, *No Exit*, Jean-Paul Sartre states, "Hell is other people." I think that's taking things to extremes, but let's face it: He has a point.

In Vienna in the late 19th century, Sigmund Freud explored a number of ways to explain what the hell is wrong with you. One of his most significant contributions was the invention of the modern idea of the personality. This meant that the problem isn't you, per se; rather, the problem is your personality.

Meanwhile, England was experiencing the first New Age movement. Along with an interest in spiritualism, theosophy, and the existence of fairies, came a renewed fascination with astrology. Alan Leo began to sell astrology lessons and became quite well known.

There was just one problem: fortune-telling was illegal in England. The practice of astrology may have deteriorated, but the story that astrology predicts the future remained.

Leo was prosecuted for violating this law, and to defend himself, he asserted that he wasn't teaching fortune telling; instead, he was teaching how to use astrology for personal development—you know, like Freud was doing in Vienna.

This defense worked for only a few years, and Leo was ultimately arrested and convicted of fortune telling in 1917. But between his first arrest in 1914 and his death in 1917, shortly after the second trial, Leo had revised his extensive writings about astrology, moving from what he called "event-oriented" astrology to a descriptive astrology of character analysis that became the foundation of modern natal astrology.

Modern natal astrology is based on the story of personality typing.

The Story of Personality Typing

Personality typing describes any system that sorts you into little boxes that seem to define who you are and why you do the things that you do. These include everything from BuzzFeed quizzes, like "What *Sex and the City* Character Are You?" to more complex tools like the Myers Briggs Personality Inventory, based on the work of Carl Jung.

We love the idea of personality typing because it assigns each of us to our own little box, and at least at first, that box makes us feel safe.

When you find your box, you understand something about your own personality and why you do the things you do. But more importantly, you can sort other people into their boxes, and that lets you believe that you can understand why *they* behave the way *they* do.

Astrology has significant advantages over other systems of personality typing because every other system of personality typing requires you to take a test to find your box. Astrology assigns your boxes based on the time, date, and location of your birth, which makes it much harder to cheat.

Personality typing is fun, and it has some real practical value. But it's also very, very limited.

The size and number of boxes is one of the limitations of personality typing. The bigger the box, the easier it is to sort people into it, but the less useful it is because it describes so many different people. The smaller the box, the better the fit, but the harder it becomes to sort people into the box.

But the biggest limitation of personality typing is that you are not your personality. You are a unique, complex individual, and you can't be

Foundations of Astrology Stories

described by little boxes. You start out excited by how comfortable you are in that little box, but soon feel trapped by the limits of that box.

Still, modern natal astrology is based on a story of personality typing.

When modern astrology asks **Why**, the answer is, "Because personality." This introduces a new story trope, titled *Here's Your Sign*.

Here's Your Sign

I've often argued that the era of modern astrology began in 1968 with the publication of *Sun Signs* by Linda Goodman. This book transformed astrology forever. It sold tens of millions of copies worldwide, and was largely responsible for the new pick-up line, "Hey, baby, what's your sign?" The problem (for astrologers, at least) was that Goodman's book presented a simplified, pop-psychology take on astrology. No longer did the practice of astrology require an accurate birth time and hours of complicated math to draw up a unique birth chart. According to Goodman, knowing your birthday was sufficient.

To be fair, in the Foreword, Goodman points out that merely interpreting the Sun Sign is no substitute for a complete analysis of your natal chart. She briefly mentions the functions of the other planets, and she also separates her work from the sign-based predictions in the horoscope columns of newspapers and magazines. But who reads the Foreword? Most of the readers who pick up this book turn directly to their own Sun Sign, followed by the Sun Signs of the significant people in their lives.

Here's Your Sign is a good story, but it's not a better story than *As the Prophecy Foretold*. It doesn't negate the prophecy story: it merges with it. You believe that astrology determines your personality, and that your personality is your fate. Personality is prophecy[2].

---

[2] This story is not limited to astrologers. "Personality is prophecy" is the defining story of psychology, although psychologists are rarely willing to acknowledge this. If your solution to a problem always involves altering the personality, this assumes the personality can't be avoided or ignored. In other words, personality is prophecy.

Many astrologers took this literally and claimed they could predict your future based only on your Sun Sign. This is an especially good story, and it resulted in an explosion of daily horoscope columns filled with vague and generalized prophecies. Most people had the good sense to enjoy these stories for their entertainment value and not take them too seriously.

Of course, a small minority of people liked these stories so much that they lived their lives based on these Sun Sign predictions. And then an even smaller minority of scientists got so upset about this that they felt compelled to haul out the pitchforks and denounce astrology itself.

This brings us to a hot take on the relationship between science and astrology.

Science and Astrology: a Hot Take

When it comes to the subject of astrology, scientists are neurotic, not psychotic. The difference between psychotics and neurotics is easy to understand. A psychotic *knows* that 2 + 2 = 5. A neurotic knows that 2 + 2 = 4, but *can't stand it*.

Scientists know that astrology works—at least some of the time—and they can't stand it. Specifically, they can't stand that their stories about astrology don't fit neatly in the context of their stories about science and how the universe is supposed to work. Scientists get upset because astrologers may come up with the right answer, but they can't justify how they got there, and in science, you have to show your work. This is a valid argument, and one that astrologers would do well to consider, but it's a symptom of the conflict, not the cause.

The root cause of the conflict between science and astrology is a story about perspective and statistics. Science looks at the big picture and considers the odds—the statistical probability—that something will happen. Objectively, the odds of winning the lottery are so minute that the lottery has been called a tax on the math-impaired. Science looks at something that is statistically improbable and dismisses it as impossible. This works until it doesn't. Eventually, someone wins the lottery. Winning the lottery is a million-to-one chance, but if you happen to be the one,

Foundations of Astrology Stories

your subjective, personal story about the lottery is quite different from the objective, scientific story about the lottery.

Scientists insist that astrology can't work from an objective perspective, and astrologers insist that it does work from a subjective perspective. Both are right, and both are wrong, and the only way to make sense of this is to find a bigger and better story to contain it all. The Human Game provides the framework for this story, but the full story of *The Science of Astrology* will have to wait for another book.[3]

The biggest obstacle in your astrology story is that astrology works some of the time, but it doesn't work all of the time. Astrologers take the reasonable position that if you got the wrong answer, you didn't consider all of the variables. Something is missing, and when you find it, you'll find the right answer.

This brings us to a story trope that influences how you learn astrology and how you use astrology. I call this story trope *More Cowbell*[4].

More Cowbell

It's important to recognize the *More Cowbell* story trope because it can make learning—and using—astrology more difficult than necessary. When you're not satisfied with the answer to your question, you think you need more astrology.

Astrology answers questions with a single sentence. A sentence in the language of astrology is something like, "Saturn in Leo in the Third House." This answer contains a tremendous amount of information and it can form the basis of any number of astrology stories. The challenge is that the simple sentence doesn't include all of the astrology.

Saturn in Leo in the Third House might also rule the Seventh, Eighth, and Ninth Houses. Maybe you need to consider the aspects Saturn makes to other planets in the chart. Or perhaps the issue is that Saturn in Leo is in Detriment, and the reason you got the answer wrong is that you didn't

---

[3] It's an epic story, and yes, I'm working on it.
[4] Google the *Saturday Night Live* skit if you don't get the reference.

consider how the dignity or debility of Saturn affects how Saturn might express.

These are reasonable considerations and they might be worth exploring. More astrology *might* make a better answer. But more astrology doesn't automatically make a better answer. And sometimes you don't need a better answer; you need a better story.

This is where the Human Game comes in.

Human Game Astrology Stories

In the beginning, there was astrology.

But before there was astrology, there was story.

The Human Game is much bigger than astrology. The Human Game explores the nature of story itself. Astrology is story, so understanding how story works with the Human Game will also give you a better understanding of how astrology works and what you can do with it.

When astrology asks **Why**, the answer is always, "Because prophecy." Even when the answer is, "Because personality," the full answer is, "Because personality is prophecy." Neither of these answers is satisfying or useful, and in either case, you're stuck with a prophecy that will limit your options in unexpected ways.

When the Human Game asks **Why**, the answer is, "Because story." This answer is both satisfying and useful. It's satisfying because it's true: *everything* is story. It's useful because when you realize that you're dealing with a story, you have additional options. You don't have to accept the limits of your current reality. You can use **The Rules of Story** to change reality itself.

Your prior experiences with astrology have embedded any number of astrology prophecies in your personal story. Without realizing it, every one of these prophecies limits your options and constricts your reality. For most people, these limits are barely noticeable and don't create obvious challenges. The more astrology you know, the more power these prophecies have in your reality. Some astrologers refuse to make any major decision without considering the astrological factors of the moment.

When you consider astrology on its own, you have to engage with the reality of the prophecy. Your only options are to **accept the prophecy** or **fight the prophecy**. When you combine the Human Game with astrology, you can engage with the story of the prophecy instead of the reality of the prophecy. This gives you access to the third option: you can **beat the prophecy**.

Beat the Prophecy

You beat the prophecy by leveraging **The Rules of Story**. The Rules of Story require that every prophecy be fulfilled, but they don't specify how. Unlike accepting the prophecy, which is passive, when you beat the prophecy, you take an active role. You engage with the story of the prophecy, you question it, and you use **The Rules of Story** to make it better.

You have three options to beat the prophecy. The simplest option is to **find your hole**; a more complex option is to **claim your gift**; and the most challenging (and the most rewarding) option is to **exploit the loophole**.

Find Your Hole

It's useful to remember that you are unique. Your personality contributes to that, and karma establishes some rigid guidelines, but you are not like anyone else in the world. During **Act 1** of The Story of Your Life, the fact that you are unique is a problem. It creates a sense of isolation and loneliness compounded by a need for approval and the desire to fit in.

The technical term for this is "Square Peg Round Hole."

You start out your story as a square peg in a world of round holes. As you live your life, overcome obstacles, and yes, experience difficulties and even trauma, the world chisels away at your identity. You're no longer a generic square peg—you are becoming a peg with a unique shape. And the more you change, the less chance there is that you will ever fit in a round hole.

You believe that if you could only fit in a round hole, you would finally be happy, and you spend the next phase of your life trying to change your shape—your very identity—so you can fit in the world.

Rather than changing yourself to fit in someone else's hole, you can choose to go out and find the hole where you fit perfectly. **The Rule of Conservation** means nothing is wasted: every peg has a bespoke hole. Take charge of your story, go out in the world, and find your hole.

Use the personality typing astrology stories to become conscious of your unique shape, and explore how people with other shapes behave differently than you do. The map of your birth chart can help you to find your hole and discover how you fit in the Universe.

Finding your hole addresses what makes you different. But what makes you different also makes you special. If you explore the story a bit more, you can claim your gift.

Claim Your Gift

The things that make you unique also limit you. Your karma, your destiny, and your personality make you unsuitable for many experiences. Chances are, you will never be a member of the Billionaires Club. You will never walk on the moon, win an Olympic medal, or give an Oscar acceptance speech[5]. No matter how hard you dream, you may never be as rich or as famous as you want. There are limits to what you can accomplish in The Story of Your Life, but there are no limits to the happiness you can experience.

The Rule of Compensation states that every gift has a price, and every price has a gift. When you focus on your limitations, you're focusing on the price. Since you've paid a price, you're entitled to a gift. However, you may need to find the gift and claim it.

The Rule of Conservation means that the qualities you value the least (and that cause the most problems for you) are also the qualities of your gift. Rather than suppressing those qualities, lean into them and see where they take you.

I'll share a personal example. My birth chart and my personality feature, shall we say, "issues" with authority. These "issues" created ongoing problems

---

[5] At least one that doesn't involve a hairbrush and your bathroom mirror.

for me in a series of unhappy employment situations over many years. Eventually, I discovered that the qualities that make me a lousy employee are also the qualities that make me a great consultant. As a consultant, I'm my own boss, and the "boss" at the company is my client, not my father. Did I say "father"? Sorry. I meant father. The point is that I get to run my own business the way I see fit, and provide support to other companies as needed, and I no longer experienced the original problems with authority. Claiming this gift improved my life and made me much happier.

Exploit the Loophole

The third way to beat the prophecy is to exploit the loophole. This option requires a level of mastery of the Human Game and The Rules of Story. Not only do you need to be able to view your life—and your current situation—as story, but you also need to be able to view the story from the perspective of the writer, not from the perspective of the protagonist. These are advanced skills, but they give you access to the full potential of the Human Game.

Every story element you've encountered in literature, movies, or television can be incorporated into your own story. Anything that makes your story better is fair game.

A popular way to exploit the loophole is with a quibble. A quibble is a plot device that allows you to beat the prophecy by fulfilling the exact and literal conditions of the agreement to avoid the intended meaning. One of the most famous examples of a quibble is in Shakespeare's *The Merchant of Venice*. Shylock rejects the merciful option and insists that he receive the pound of flesh to which he is entitled. Portia exploits the loophole in the contract and points out that the agreement does not include blood. Since it's not possible for Shylock to collect flesh without spilling blood, Antonio is saved.

When you're dealing with astrology-based prophecies, the prophecy you incorporate in your story is in English (or whatever language you speak), but that's not the prophecy itself: it's a translation of the prophecy. The prophecy itself is written in the language of astrology.

You don't need to quibble with the translation to find a loophole: you can go back to the original astrology and change the entire meaning of the prophecy with a new translation. Every symbol in astrology has hundreds of applications. You can choose the interpretation that works best for you and beat the prophecy by fulfilling it on your own terms.

You may be feeling a bit overwhelmed—I've taken you on quite a journey, and introduced some big and unfamiliar ideas. You don't need to understand these ideas yet. As you build on this new foundation, things will make more sense.

The good news is that now you're ready to explore the building blocks of astrology itself. We'll do that in the next chapter.

A Word of Advice...

The next few chapters contain quite a lot of new information. Please don't feel that you need to understand everything in a chapter before you can advance to the next chapter. Part 1 introduces you to most of the puzzle pieces you'll be playing with. Part 2 is where you'll learn how to fit the pieces together. Once you start to assemble the puzzle pieces, they will make sense.

CHAPTER 3
Foundations of Astrology

Now you're ready to build a foundation of the language of astrology itself. If you're new to astrology, this chapter will cover everything you need to be able to read a natal chart, recognize the different symbols, and assemble those symbols into astrology stories.

Do not skip this chapter, even if you're already familiar with astrology!

You need to build a foundation of astrology to tell better astrology stories. If you're new to astrology, this process is easy: just become familiar with the information in this chapter. If you're familiar with astrology, this process may be more challenging. You will need to set aside most of what you *know* (for the time being) so you can focus on what's *new*. While exploring the foundations of the language astrology, I'm also introducing you to the foundations of astrology stories.

Traditional rulerships play an essential role in the Human Game happiness stories, but you can tell astrology stories using modern rulerships.

How to Read a Chart

Reading an astrology chart is what's known as a "hard skill." In this context, "hard" doesn't mean difficult; it means objective. There may be a bit of "difficult" in the mix because you will need to study and memorize a few things, including the meanings of the astrology glyphs (symbols) that represent the planets and the signs, and the classical rulerships that connect the planets to the signs.

If you're new to astrology, you'll need to memorize the information in the following tables.

The Planets

The most important planets are the seven personal or inner planets. We'll meet the outer planets in Part 3.

INNER PLANETS	☉ The Sun	☽ The Moon	☿ Mercury
♀ Venus	♂ Mars	♃ Jupiter	♄ Saturn
OUTER PLANETS	♅ Uranus	♆ Neptune	♇ Pluto

The Signs

Each of the twelve signs is a combination of one of three modalities (**Cardinal**, **Fixed**, **Mutable**) and one of four elements (**Fire**, **Earth**, **Air**, **Water**).

♈ **Aries** CARDINAL FIRE	♉ **Taurus** FIXED EARTH	♊ **Gemini** MUTABLE AIR	♋ **Cancer** CARDINAL WATER
♌ **Leo** FIXED FIRE	♍ **Virgo** MUTABLE EARTH	♎ **Libra** CARDINAL AIR	♏ **Scorpio** FIXED WATER
♐ **Sagittarius** MUTABLE FIRE	♑ **Capricorn** CARDINAL EARTH	♒ **Aquarius** FIXED AIR	♓ **Pisces** MUTABLE WATER

Planets Ruling Signs

Rulership is an essential and widely misunderstood part of the language of astrology. In this context, Rulership defines the connection between the planets and the signs, which defines the connection between the planets and the houses they rule. The outer planets (**Uranus**, **Neptune** and **Pluto**) do not rule any signs or houses in the chart.

☉ ♌ The Sun Rules Leo	☽ ♋ The Moon Rules Cancer
☿ ♊ Mercury Rules Gemini	AND ♍ Virgo
♀ ♉ Venus Rules Taurus	AND ♎ Libra
♂ ♈ Mars Rules Aries	AND ♏ Scorpio
♃ ♐ Jupiter Rules Sagittarius	AND ♓ Pisces
♄ ♑ Saturn Rules Capricorn	AND ♒ Aquarius

When you look at a natal chart you need to be able to identify the planet that rules a house (based on the sign on the cusp of the house) and you need to be able to identify what house a planet occupies. The house cusps are the lines that divide the houses in the chart.

The position of each house cusp is indicated both by the sign on the cusp and the precise location within the sign, expressed as degrees and minutes. In the example that follows, the cusp of the First House is 01°51 Capricorn, and the planet that rules the First House is Saturn (which can be found in the Fifth House).

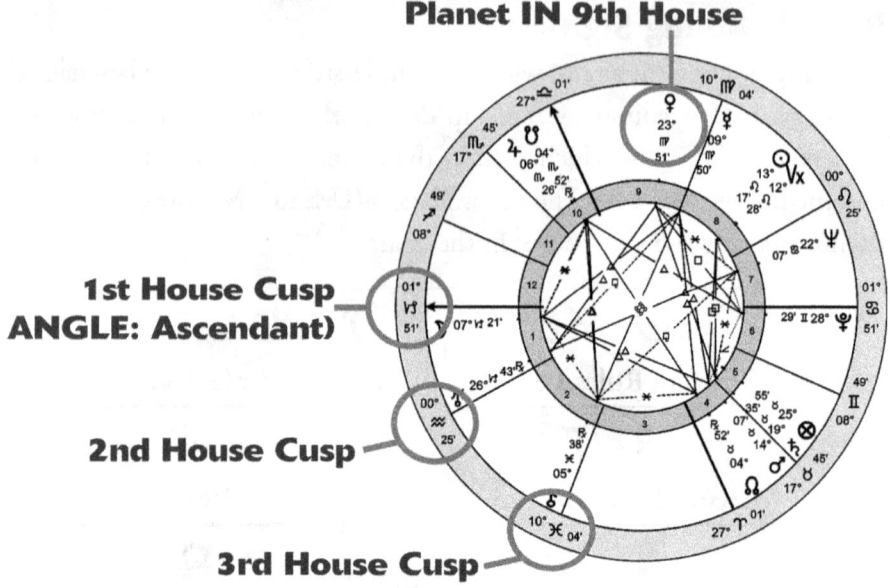

When you work with actual charts, you will need to choose a house system. This is almost entirely a matter of personal preference. The two most popular house systems for natal charts are **Placidus** and **Koch**. The cusps of the angles are the same in both, but the intermediate house cusps will shift from one system to the other. My personal preference is Koch houses, and that's the house system I use in my classes. You're free to use whatever system you like, but once you make your choice, you must stick with it[1].

Answering Questions with Astrology Stories

Good journalists are good storytellers. Journalists know that their news story must address the key questions the reader will have about the subject, and early on in their training they learn to structure their stories using the five Ws and H. Every article needs to answer the questions **WHO**, **WHAT**,

---

[1] When calculating charts for extreme latitudes, it's best to use an equal house system. Using Koch or Placidus houses for a chart based in Norway can give you houses that contain two or more signs and houses only a few degrees wide.

Where, **When**, **Why**, and **How**. We'll take a similar approach to building astrology stories and look to different components of the language of astrology to answer different questions.

We'll focus on building astrology stories that answer the questions **What**, **What Else**, **How**, **Which**, and **Where**. **When** questions apply to predictive astrology, so they're not covered here. In the stories we'll explore in this program, the **Who** is you (or your client).

What is the subject of the story?

By far, the most important question to answer is **What**. **What** identifies the subject of the story and has a direct connection to the **Goal** of the **Act 1** Plot-level story. The first objective when creating an astrology story is to connect the **What** of the personal story to a **What** in the astrology story. Most of the time we focus on the external, Plot-level **Goal** of our personal stories. In the language of astrology, the external **Goal** connects to a house.

This is a challenge, because in the language of astrology, the subject of a sentence—the **What** of the story—is always a planet. To make a house the subject of a story, you will use the planet that rules the house as the subject of the sentence.

The following descriptions will introduce you to the twelve houses in the natal chart so that you can connect a **Goal** in a personal story to the appropriate house.

First House: Happiness

The First House is your happiness. It contains everything that you enjoy and that gives you pleasure, including your hobbies and personal interests. It relates to your physical appearance, and affects how other people see you and whether or not they find you attractive. First House goals include all health, fitness, and appearance-related goals; goals that involve personal growth and overall happiness; and goals that involve your hobbies and interests.

Second House: Money and Prosperity, Skills and Talents

The Second House is your money and prosperity. It contains your finances and all of your possessions, and it relates to how you earn, manage, and spend your money. It also relates to your skills and talents. Second House goals involve money and prosperity; goals related to buying something (other than real estate); and goals that involve developing or expressing your skills and talents.

Third House: Comfort Zone

The Third House is your comfort zone. It's any place that is local, convenient, and familiar to you, where you are confident and comfortable, and where you know what to expect. It's also your habits and routines: your ability to automate behaviors and free up energy and attention for other things. Third House goals involve creating new habits, changing old habits, or automating routine tasks in your life; goals that involve building confidence and familiarity; and goals that involve expanding your comfort zone.

Fourth House: Foundation

The Fourth House is your foundation; it's the bedrock on which you build your life. Everything in your Fourth House has to be squared away for your life to function. It's also your private, personal life and your sanctuary where you take time for yourself to recharge your batteries. Fourth House goals include all home-related and real-estate goals (buy, sell, move your physical residence); all foundation-related goals, including anything that you believe will make your life more stable; goals that involve protecting your privacy and meeting your personal, individual needs; and goals that involve rest and relaxation.

Fifth House: Creativity, Recreation, and Risk

The Fifth House is your creativity, which is far more than just artistic expression. Every time you solve a problem, you access your creativity. It's also your recreation (entertainment, fun and games) and your tolerance for taking risks. Fifth House goals include all creative or artistic goals; goals involving dating, romance, and sex; goals involving your children; any recreation-related goal, including playing games and having fun; and goals related to gambling and risk-taking, including the stock market.

Sixth House: Job, Work, and Service

The Sixth House is your job. It includes everything that you *have* to do, and that requires effort and hard work. It's also service that you provide to others. Sixth House goals involve your job or your workplace; goals that involve improving relationships in your workplace environment; any goal that involves hard work that you have to do; goals that involve addressing the symptoms and underlying cause of sickness or illness.

Seventh House: Other People and Relationships

The Seventh House is all about other people. It's your relationships to other individuals, and it's your relationship to other people in general or in groups, such as when you go out in public. Seventh House goals include everything about romantic partnership, including finding a romantic partner and overcoming challenges in your romantic relationships; any goal that involves improving the experience and dynamic of a one-to-one relationship with another individual; and any goal involving contractual relationships or other kinds of partnerships.

Eighth House: Debt, Obligations, and Shared Resources

The Eighth House is your debts and obligations. These are not exclusively financial, and they include both debts you owe to others and debts other people owe to you. The Eighth House is really about how you give and receive support and engage with the Law of Circulation. Eighth House goals involve managing or paying off debts and obligations, especially financial obligations; goals that involve building or repairing your credit; goals that involve managing shared resources or other people's money; goals that involve giving and/or receiving support and engaging with the Law of Circulation.

Ninth House: Danger Zone

The Ninth House is your danger zone. It's distant, foreign, unfamiliar, and always a little bit unsafe. It's where you go to acquire new information and it's where you find all types of experts and authorities to help you to navigate the unknown. Ninth House goals involve learning or experiencing something new and include education-related goals (higher education, advanced degrees); goals that relate to becoming an expert or an authority in some field; travel-related goals, especially travel to foreign countries with different cultures and languages.

Tenth House: Reputation and Advancement

The Tenth House is your reputation and your advancement. It's your public image—how the world sees you—and it's the qualities that help you to advance personally, professionally, and socially. In today's world, it has quite a lot to do with your social media presence. Tenth House goals include all personal and professional success-related goals; any goal that involves raising your profile and becoming more public (or more famous); goals that involve the pursuit of advancement, promotion, awards, or honors.

Eleventh House: Ambitions, Aspirations, and Acquisitions

The Eleventh House is your aspirations and acquisitions: your personal dreams and ambitions that you believe you have to go out into the world to accomplish or attain. The Eleventh House is the pursuit of happiness because you believe that when you achieve your dreams, you'll be happy. But remember that true happiness lives inside you and belongs to the First House. Eleventh House goals relate to any dreams or ambitions that you have that you believe will make you happy, including your fantasies and daydreams (accepting an Oscar, winning an international singing competition, becoming an astronaut); and goals that involve achieving or acquiring something that you believe will make you happy.

Twelfth House: Blind Spot and Adversity

The Twelfth House is your blind spot. When you move something into your Twelfth House you become unconscious of it and it stops taking up attention or energy. This can be a problem if something in your Twelfth House becomes your responsibility or your business, because you may forget about it until it's too late. The Twelfth House is also your adversity and how you overcome challenges and setbacks. Twelfth House goals include the ability to move something into your blind spot so that you no longer think about it (or worry about it); goals that involve changing some kind of negative behavior pattern to create less adversity and limit your optional suffering; goals that involve making amends, taking responsibility for your mistakes, and cleaning up resentments that may turn your friends into hidden enemies.

What else is the story about?

A house can be the subject of an astrology *story*, but the subject of an astrology *sentence* can only be one of the seven inner planets. In the grammar of the language of astrology, the personal planets are both the nouns and the verbs. Everything else, including the element and modality of the sign and the houses associated with the planet answers questions about the planet and modifies its expression. When telling an astrology story, you can focus on the house a planet rules and overlook the planet itself, but the planet is still the nucleus of the story. The answers to the **How**, **Which**, and **Where** questions apply to the **What** of the house because they apply to the **What Else** of the planet.

Every story begins with **Act 1** of the Plot-level story and the **Goal**. The **Goal** is external and connects to the houses in the natal chart. Every **Goal** also connects to a **Want**, which is **Act 1** of the Character-level story. At the Character-level story, the thing you **Want**—and the thing you **Need**—corresponds to one of the seven personal or inner planets. One of the advantages of working with astrology and the Human Game is that once you identify the **Goal**, you also know the **Want**; the planet that rules the house of the **Goal** is always the planet that represents the underlying **Want**.

Character-level planet-based stories are more challenging because the objectives aren't as obvious or straightforward as house-based Plot-level stories. It's easy to see the structure of a story where your goal is to make extra money. It's harder to see the structure of a story where the subject is responsibility. To be able to recognize the pattern of the story, you must get more specific about the subject—for example, by determining what lesson you must learn about responsibility.

We will be working with several planet-based stories in this program. In each case, we'll focus on a small, specific expression of the planet to make it easier to recognize the patterns of the astrology story in your personal stories. What follows is a big picture introduction to the inner planets and the various needs they can represent.

The Sun

The Sun symbolizes your need for **integrity**, **authenticity**, and **vitality**. Integrity literally means being whole, unbroken, complete, and undivided; it's a personal quality of fairness that involves doing the right thing in a reliable way. Authenticity is the quality of being genuine, real, legitimate, and true; specifically, this is your need to experience your authentic "Big S" Self. We'll consider this expression of the Sun when we explore The Identity Quest in Part 4. Vitality relates to physical energy, health, and overall well-being; it's your need to express your life force.

The Moon

The Moon symbolizes your **Safety Needs**, your **feelings**, and your **emotions**. Safety is one of the fundamental human needs, and it's one of the fundamentals of happiness. We'll consider Safety Needs in detail in Part 2 when we explore The Quest for Happiness. Feelings are how human beings experience vibrations of consciousness; they are not the effect of anything, and ideally you use them to navigate away from the Lie of Duality and toward the Truth of Unity. Emotions are feelings with stories attached to them so that they appear to be the effect of circumstances rather than the cause of them.

Mercury

Mercury symbolizes your need for **understanding**, **communication**, and **story**. Understanding is how you orient your perceptions and experiences to your current reality; it reflects your need to know how you relate to your reality. Communication is how you seek confirmation of your subjective reality from other people. Story is how you create your reality, and in particular, it's the content of your reality.

Venus

Venus symbolizes your **Validation Needs**, your need for **approval**, and your **values**. Validation Needs encompass all forms of love and appreciation. Approval is a subset of validation, but it specifically involves external sources of appreciation from other people. We'll consider Validation Needs and the need for external approval in detail in Part 2 when we explore The Quest for Happiness. Values represent the things that you care about, personally; your values guide you to experiences of love and appreciation.

Mars

Mars symbolizes your **desire**, your **anger**, and your **ego**. Desire is an essential part of **Act 1** of every story; it's how you select a **GOAL**, and it's what gives you the energy to take action and pursue the goal. Anger is a valuable and misunderstood resource; the energy of anger makes it possible for you to overcome the **OBSTACLE** in **Act 2**, and to break through your limitations. Your ego is your "little s" self; it's the character you play in The Story of Your Life. We'll consider this expression of Mars when we explore The Identity Quest in Part 4.

Jupiter

Jupiter symbolizes your need for **growth**, **faith**, and **imagination**. Growth is an essential function of life; it's the need to fulfill your potential in every dimension. Faith is how you align with the Truth of Unity, even when it's not reflected in your current reality. Imagination expands the context of your story and makes it possible for you to create your reality.

Saturn

Saturn symbolizes your need for **responsibility**, **authority**, and **boundaries**. Responsibility includes your experience of duties and obligations, and your expectations of reward and punishment. Authority stories operate on multiple dimensions, including your "inner parent" (the voice of your internalized authority figure), external authority figures, and how you exercise authority in your story. Boundaries include all form, structure, and limitations, whether they are physical, mental, emotional, or spiritual.

How do you approach the Goal?

When you focus on the Plot-level story (as we generally do), the events of the story become the focus. The most useful question to ask about the events is **How**, because the answer to this question fills in critical parts of the plot. In the language of astrology, the three modalities answer the question of **How**.

Each of the twelve signs of the zodiac is comprised of two different parts of speech: modalities that function as adverbs and answer the question of **How**, and elements that function as adjectives and answer the question of **Which**. Adverbs modify verbs and describe the action, while adjectives modify nouns and describe the subject. A planet in Aries is influenced by both the Cardinal modality and the Fire element, but to fully appreciate this, you must consider the modality and the element individually. If you combine the two, the whole of the sign is always less than the sum of the parts.

We will take a much closer look at the modalities and explore specific examples of how they function as story tropes in the next chapter. For now, here's a brief introduction to the three modalities and how each represents different strategies and approaches to the GOAL.

Cardinal: Team Hare (Aries, Cancer, Libra, Capricorn)

If you have a Cardinal approach you are on Team Hare. The race to the GOAL is a sprint. You view the GOAL as an archery target that you must hit with a single shot. You invest time, energy, and resources to prepare for the shot and take careful aim, but once you release the arrow, you're done. If you hit the target you make remarkable progress all at once. If you miss the target, you have to start over again from scratch with a new arrow.

Fixed: Team Tortoise (Taurus, Leo, Scorpio, Aquarius)

If you have a Fixed approach, you are on Team Tortoise. The race to the GOAL is a marathon. You view the GOAL as an evolutionary process. You have faith that you will achieve the GOAL eventually, but you expect it will be a slow, methodical, lengthy process to get there. You must continuously balance your desire to achieve the GOAL with your desire to maintain the status quo and experience as little change as possible.

Mutable: Team Hummingbird (Gemini, Virgo, Sagittarius, Pisces)

If you have a Mutable approach, you are on Team Hummingbird. The race to the GOAL is a scavenger hunt. You focus on the individual tasks associated with the GOAL rather than the big picture. You care about what you can accomplish right now, and pursue the immediate gratification of being able to check items off your to-do list. This gives you the feeling that you are moving forward toward the GOAL but in fact, you may be running in circles.

Which kind of Goal is it?

In the broadest sense, the four elements describe the four different planes of existence. This is a big concept, and quite important, but it's also an idea that connects to the Theme-level story. Much like the planets, to consider the element we need a smaller, more specific story to use the elements to answer questions at the Plot-level story. In fact, we'll need a choice of stories. Depending on the situation, the element might describe WHICH of the four languages you speak to define a GOAL, WHICH of the four kinds of resources you need to accomplish the GOAL, or WHICH of the four kinds of fuel you need to pursue a GOAL.

We will take a much closer look at the elements and explore how they function as story tropes in the next chapter. For now, we'll consider the elements as the four languages you might speak to meet a NEED and define a GOAL.

Fire (Aries, Leo, Sagittarius)
Fire operates in the realm of life and spirit. The language of Fire expresses through action and activity, especially physical activity. The qualities of Fire include passion, intensity, and urgency.

Earth (Taurus, Virgo, Capricorn)
Earth operates in the realm of form on the physical and material plane. The language of Earth expresses through form, stability, and structure. Earth communicates through the physical senses, and through stillness.

Air (Gemini, Libra, Aquarius)
Air operates in the mental, social, and intellectual realms. The language of Air expresses through ideas and abstract concepts, and relies heavily on words and language. Air communicates by making connections and defining relationships.

Water (Cancer, Scorpio, Pisces)
Water operates in the emotional realm. The language of Water expresses through feelings, emotions, and intuition. Water sinks, seeking the lowest and deepest point, and the Water language seeks to express primal, non-verbal experiences.

Where is the Goal?
The final question, WHERE, considers the location, or setting of the GOAL. The setting of a story establishes the bigger context. The time and place of a story defines the resources available within the reality of the story. The setting can influence every aspect of the story, including the GOAL, the OBSTACLE, and the RESOLUTION, and yet the setting may not be WHAT the story is about.

Foundations of Astrology

The **What** of the story comes from the planet and the house or houses the planet *rules*. The **Where** of the story comes from the house the planet *occupies*. To identify the **Where**, describe the **What** of the house as a location or context.

A **First House** story takes place in your **happiness**, your **health**, or your **appearance**.

A **Second House** story takes place in your **money** and **resources** or your **skills** and **talents**.

A **Third House** story takes place in your **comfort zone**, or your **habits** and **routines**.

A **Fourth House** story takes place in your **private life**, your **home**, or your **foundation**.

A **Fifth House** story takes place in your **creativity** and your pursuit of **fun**.

A **Sixth House** story takes place in your **job**, your **workplace** environment, or your **sickness**.

A **Seventh House** story takes place in your **relationships** with **other people**.

An **Eighth House** story takes place in your **debts** and **shared resources**.

A **Ninth House** story takes place in your **danger zone** and your **beliefs**.

A **Tenth House** story takes place in your **public image**, your **reputation**, and your **advancement**.

An **Eleventh House** story takes place in your **ambitions** and **aspirations**.

A **Twelfth House** story takes place in your **blind spot** and your **unconscious**.

You now know the most relevant meanings of the astrology symbols and what role they play in astrology stories. What you have so far are definitions. In the next chapter, we'll convert those into stories.

How to Obtain a Copy of Your Birth Chart

If you don't already have a copy of your birth chart, you can obtain one online for free in just a few simple steps. I recommend Astro.com, because (at least at the time I'm writing this) you can get a copy of your chart without creating an account or providing any personal information.

From the landing page of Astro.com, click on the "Free Horoscopes" button, and then select Charts & Data. From there, I recommend the "Extended Chart Selection" because you'll be able to customize the free chart.

Your birth chart is based on the date, time, and location of your birth, and the birth time is essential. The birth time determines the degree of the Ascendant and the cusps of the houses. Without an accurate time of birth, you won't be able to use any of the house-based stories (although you will be able to use some of the features of the Happiness GPS to meet your Safety Needs and your Validation Needs). Enter this information when prompted.

I prefer the "Anglo" option for the Chart drawing style, and I use Koch houses for my natal charts, but you can adjust your preferences accordingly.

Once you display the chart, you will have the option to print it or email it. If you choose to register, you'll have the option to save the chart directly to a PDF file.

CHAPTER 4
Astrology Story Tropes

The most challenging part of creating an astrology story isn't the astrology, it's the story. The story is what makes the astrology relevant and practical. The previous chapter gave you information about the meanings of the different astrology symbols. The only way to use that information is to convert it into stories. To make this easier, I've created a library of astrology story tropes. You can use these story tropes to create your own astrology stories.

The story tropes help answer the questions of **How**, **Which**, and **Where**. When you combine a story trope with a subject—the **What**—you get a complete story. These story tropes may feel abstract or impractical because they lack a subject: they're answers without a question. You'll understand how to use them—and see them in action—in later chapters.

Modality Story Tropes: How

The modality tells you **How** you approach every **Goal** associated with the planet. The modality story tropes are extremely useful because they play out across all three acts of the Plot-level story. Each modality story trope explores how you approach the **Goal** (**Act 1**), identifies a specific **Obstacle** (**Act 2**) that results from that approach, and provides strategies for a successful **Resolution** (**Act 3**).

Cardinal Story Tropes

The story tropes for the Cardinal Signs (Aries, Cancer, Libra, and Capricorn) include *Archery Target*, *Fix the Past*, and *Jump the Gun*.

Archery Target

You view the GOAL as an archery target that you must hit with a single shot. All your energy goes into planning and preparation as you take careful aim at the target because once you let the arrow fly, you're done: you either hit the target or you don't. You expect to make multiple attempts where you miss the target before you hit the target. After each failed attempt, you evaluate what went wrong and make adjustments before the next attempt.

The OBSTACLE with this approach is because a near miss is still a miss. When you hit the target, you take a giant leap forward, but until you hit the target, you don't make any progress toward your GOAL. Each attempt wastes resources, and you may reach a point that what you gain from achieving the GOAL will no longer cover the cost of what it took to get there. This can cause you to abandon the GOAL and choose a new one.

The RESOLUTION strategy is to choose targets that are closer and easier to hit. You may not be able to achieve your ultimate GOAL with a single shot. Break the ultimate GOAL into reasonable milestones, so each time you hit a target you move closer to it. Consider setting time-based targets as well as task-based targets. Every time you hit a target, it gives you a sense of accomplishment that keeps you motivated.

Fix the Past

Not only do you expect the GOAL to create your future, you also expect it to fix the past. You need to recoup everything you have invested in pursuit of the GOAL before you can turn a profit. Each failed attempt adds to your expenses and makes the ultimate reward a little less attractive. When you selected the GOAL, you estimated the cost to achieve it and factored that cost into your expectations of the reward. As long as you don't exceed that budget, you will be satisfied with the reward when you achieve the GOAL.

The OBSTACLE with this approach comes from the perceived profit margin of the GOAL. When you exceed your original budget without achieving the GOAL, it raises the stakes. You become more concerned with how much of your resources you have already invested as the final reward seems to get smaller. This can trap you in the sunk cost fallacy, where you become even more determined to achieve the **GOAL** because of how much you've spent on it. It can also make you resistant to exploring different strategies to meet the **GOAL**.

The **RESOLUTION** strategy is to focus on your present **NEED**. Although the story may involve some tangible resources—money, for example—this isn't about your checking account. The resources you invest and the resources you expect to receive when you achieve the **GOAL** are tied to your Safety Need Account and your Validation Need Account. You can't be overdrawn in your Need Bank Accounts. It doesn't matter how long you've been low on safety resources. When you receive a deposit in your Safety Need Account, it's available immediately. And if you change strategies or abandon this **GOAL** completely, you won't be hit with any fees or penalties.

Jump the Gun

No sooner do you identify a **GOAL** than you're off in pursuit of it. You're so focused on the target that you don't always take the time to plan how to get there. This impatience is driven by the fear that you're falling behind. You skip steps, cut corners, and leap over obstacles so you can hit the target before time runs out. You expect to make adjustments along the way, and even to take a wrong turn or two, but the sooner you start, the sooner you finish.

The **OBSTACLE** with this approach involves avoidable mistakes that can force you to start over and cost you precious time. You may misunderstand something about the **GOAL** itself and aim for the wrong target. You may take an approach that has already proven unsuccessful. You may skip small but critical steps and have to go back and address them. In any case, you often end up lost and confused and in need of direction.

The **RESOLUTION** strategy is to read the instructions. Often, this means you will have to *find* the instructions, because you've probably tossed them aside in your eagerness to get started. The most successful strategy is to read all of the instructions before taking any action, but that's unlikely to happen. It might be enough to read the instructions that will help you figure out where you went wrong, but if you jump the gun again, there's no guarantee you won't make another mistake. Time spent reading the instructions is time well spent.

Fixed Story Tropes

The story tropes for the Fixed Signs (Taurus, Leo, Scorpio, Aquarius) include *Accounting Department*, *Fear the Future*, and *Start Tomorrow*.

Accounting Department

You view the **GOAL** as an ongoing process that requires planning, resources, and logistical support. You rely on your internal accounting department to coordinate everything and keep an eye on the big picture. This **GOAL** isn't the only project you care about, and your accounting department does its best to minimize disruptions and make sure that every active **GOAL** is advancing as planned. Once the **GOAL** is approved, you'll have to keep within your resource budget and meet your progress targets. If you go over budget and need to spend additional resources or if you won't be able to meet your progress target, you will need authorization from the accounting department before you can continue—and this can take some time.

The **OBSTACLE** with this approach involves becoming frustrated with how slowly things move because of the red tape and bureaucracy. The argument for careful planning and resource management is that it reduces the risk of failure and improves the quality of the results. If things change too much too quickly it can cause problems in the future. But if you don't meet your progress targets or at least see evidence of consistent progress, you'll want to cut your losses and pull the plug.

The **RESOLUTION** strategy is to measure everything and track incremental change across multiple dimensions. If possible, document everything about your starting position before you begin to pursue the **GOAL**, and then repeat those measurements at regular intervals. You won't notice significant progress between measurements, but when you compare where you are to where you were when you started, you will appreciate how far you've come.

Fear the Future

Just because you have enough available resources—such as time, energy, or money—to pursue your **Goal** in the present doesn't mean you'll have enough resources to achieve it in the future. You maintain resource warehouses with strategic reserves to protect against future lack, and when you acquire new resources, you would rather save them than spend them. Once your strategic reserves are full, you can spend whatever is left over. When a future crisis disrupts the supply chain, you'll be able to tap into your reserves and continue to advance toward your **Goal**.

The **Obstacle** with this approach involves not having enough in the present because you're worried about not having enough in the future. Sometimes there's a fine line between resource management and hoarding. Reserving a cache of resources for emergencies is a good idea: it can help you maintain a steady pace toward your **Goal** and ensure you have enough resources to complete the project. But if you focus too much on what you can save, it limits what you can spend. The perception that you don't have enough now makes you even more afraid of the future, which drives you to save even more.

The **Resolution** strategy is to remember that emergency resources are meant to be *used* in an emergency; they don't *prevent* the emergency. You don't have to wait for a full-blown catastrophe to tap into your reserves. If you have an unexpected expense, taking some money from your savings account to cover it minimizes the disruptions and allows you to keep moving forward. You can replenish your savings and rebuild your reserve when you've addressed the **Obstacle**.

Start Tomorrow

Setting a **Goal**, choosing a strategy, and getting the budget approved by your accounting department is often the easy part. The hard part is setting it all in motion. The **Goal** is a marathon, not a sprint, and the key to success is to maintain a steady, consistent pace. It's a good idea to clear the decks before you start so that you can give you full attention to the new project. If you can get caught up with everything today, you'll be ready to start the new project tomorrow.

The **Obstacle** with this approach is that the more you put off starting, the harder it is to start. Even though you've established the budget for the project, overcoming the inertia to get the ball rolling requires a big investment. It may demand time, energy, or other resources you expect to have available for your ongoing projects. The bottom line is that you don't entirely trust the accounting department. You're afraid that if you start the project, you won't have enough resources to keep it going, and if you abandon it, you'll have wasted your time, energy, and/or money.

The **Resolution** strategy is to free up more resources by pausing or ending inactive projects. You treat every project like a monthly subscription. Each month, you automatically set aside the budgeted resources assigned to the specific project. You may no longer care about that project, but if you don't inform your accounting department, you're still paying for the subscription. If you pause or end the project, you can allocate those resources to new projects. It's easier to begin a new project if you end an old one first.

Mutable Story Tropes

The story tropes for the Mutable Signs (Gemini, Virgo, Sagittarius, Pisces) include *To-Do List*, *Meet the Moment*, and *Multitask*.

To-Do List

You take a non-linear approach to achieving a **Goal**. Rather than identifying the sequence of steps to arrive at the finish line, you break the **Goal** into component tasks and organize them on a to-do list. You will achieve the **Goal** when you have checked every item off the list. Because you don't have to follow a linear sequence, you can avoid most obstacles and delays. You're willing to take the back roads if it means you can keep moving and not have to sit in traffic.

The **Obstacle** with this approach arises because some tasks are more important than others. Checking items off the to-do list gives you a feeling of accomplishment, but it doesn't mean you've made progress. Just because you've completed half of the items on your task list doesn't mean you're half-way to the finish line.

The **Resolution** strategy is to be conscious of how important each task is on the to-do list. The most significant tasks are often the most challenging: they take the longest to complete, and may even require your full attention. Prioritize working on the significant tasks, and then reward yourself by completing one or two easy but less significant tasks. That way you'll feel like you've made progress because you were able to check tasks off the to-do list, and you'll have made actual progress because you worked on a significant task.

Meet the Moment

When you pursue a **Goal**, you like to keep moving. You stay focused in the present so that you can respond to the current conditions and adapt as needed. If you encounter an **Obstacle** that makes it harder to complete your current task, you change course to bypass it. If that doesn't work, you might switch to a different task entirely because your main objective is to check something off your to-do list. Living in the moment also means you can take advantage of unexpected opportunities when they appear.

The **Obstacle** with this approach arises because if you focus only on the present, you can lose sight of the future. Feel free to enjoy the attractions along the scenic route, but don't forget your destination. If you stray too far from the path, you might get lost.

The **Resolution** strategy is to use the current **Goal** as a compass so you won't get lost. You don't need to avoid every **Obstacle** or seize every opportunity. That being said, the ultimate **Goal** is happiness. If you realize your current **Goal** isn't making you happy, look for one that does.

Multitask

You already approach each **Goal** as a collection of tasks so that you can avoid delays and make the most productive use of your time. You can accomplish even more if you multitask and combine items from different to-do lists. If you know you need to go grocery shopping, pick up your dry cleaning, go to the post office, and get your car washed, you could combine the four errands and check all four items off your to-do lists in a single trip. You can keep tabs on every GOAL and keep everything moving. The more efficient you are, the more you can accomplish.

The OBSTACLE with this approach can escalate quickly and be catastrophic. Multitasking is like juggling. It works as long as you know where each ball is and when to act to keep it in the air. It's easy to take on more balls when you find a groove, but the more balls you juggle, the less room for error. If you make a mistake and drop one ball, you might not be able to keep the rest in the air.

The RESOLUTION strategy is to know in advance which balls you can afford to drop. Prioritize the critical tasks for the important GOALS. Incorporate other tasks as long as they don't interfere with the critical tasks, and if you start to make mistakes, drop the extra tasks so you can manage the critical tasks. You may be able to save only one or two balls, but that's better than losing all of them.

Element Story Tropes: Which

The element tells you WHICH language you speak to meet the NEED of the planet and WHICH kinds of resources and fuel you require to achieve the GOAL. Element story tropes are more descriptive and less tied to the Plot-level story than modality story tropes. For each element, the first story trope describes the language itself and how you approach the GOAL; the second story trope describes what it means to be without the element; and the third story trope explores how to acquire the element.

Fire Story Tropes

The story tropes for the Fire Signs (Aries, Leo, Sagittarius) include *On Fire*, *Burn Out*, and *Heat it Up*.

On Fire

If you speak the language of Fire when you tell a story, expect passion, intensity, and urgency. Fire makes the story come alive and it provides warmth, but it also demands attention. When something catches on fire, you must respond immediately and contain the situation. If the fire is unwelcome, putting it out and limiting the damage becomes your top priority; other stories will have to wait for the all clear. If the fire is useful, you will need to keep an eye on it. Fire provides inspiration and motivation for you to take an active role in the story. You become fired up, and you have a personal, emotional stake in the outcome. If you don't feed and tend the fire, it will die and you will lose interest. If the fire gets too hot, your passion and urgency may do more harm than good. And if you don't contain it properly, it can spread to other parts of your life and wreak havoc.

Burn Out

Fire depends on fuel. The more fuel a fire has, the hotter it burns and the more energy it produces. However, the hotter the fire, the faster it consumes the fuel. The second you run out of fuel, the fire will die, leaving nothing but a pile of ashes. If you don't learn how to moderate your fire stories, this is how they will end. Your passion, intensity, and enthusiasm make you burn brightly and give you boundless energy, but when you run out of fuel, you burn out. It doesn't matter how much progress you made or what you accomplished, nothing will be left but ashes and you won't have enough energy left to care.

Heat it Up

If you would like to acquire Fire resources, you need to expend some energy and heat it up. Moving your physical body is a great way to start, and anything that gets your heart pumping will warm you up. You need a spark to light a fire, so look for something that excites or inspires you, and give it some attention. Find a personal connection to the story that gives you an emotional stake in the outcome. If all else fails, tap into your anger to light a fire—just be ready to direct that fire where it's needed.

Earth Story Tropes

The story tropes for the Earth Signs (Taurus, Virgo, Capricorn) include *Rock Solid*, *Shifting Sands*, and *Dig Deep*.

Rock Solid

If you speak the language of Earth when you tell a story, that story is built from the ground up with a practical structure meant to endure. Your stories are solid because they are firmly based in reality. You build with facts, not fiction. No amount of anger, argument, or emotion can move you because it can't change what objectively exists. You have little patience for fantasy or abstract ideas, but this doesn't mean you lack imagination or creativity. To build a castle in the sky, you have to start on the ground. Acknowledging reality doesn't mean you accept it. You can transform reality through hard work and consistent action.

Shifting Sands

The quality of the structure depends on the quality of the materials. Marble, granite, and stone create a solid foundation that supports your creations, but mining these resources takes time and leaves behind only sand. If you build too much too quickly, you will have to use cheaper materials and cut corners. Your creations will grow flimsy and collapse easily. They will not withstand the test of time. Whatever castles you build will be made of sand. They will crumble and wash away with the next tide. All construction must stop until you replenish your reserves of quality materials.

Dig Deep

If you would like to acquire Earth resources, you'll need to dig deep to extract them. Your first priority is to ground yourself to create some stability. Take a moment to become aware of your physical body and feel your feet on solid ground. Now consider your current environment and focus on the parts that remain constant and stable. If possible, spend some time doing a mindless physical activity such as folding laundry or cleaning out a closet. While you're moving your body, take a thorough inventory of the resources and tools you have right now that you can use to overcome the **Obstacle** and advance toward your **Goal**.

Air Story Tropes

The story tropes for the Air Signs (Gemini, Libra, Aquarius) include *Winds of Change*, *Out of Breath*, and *Bird's Eye View*.

Winds of Change

If you speak the language of Air when you tell a story, the words and ideas can take you anywhere. You fly through the realm of imagination, observing and cataloging everything, almost always in motion. You ride the wind and explore the surface of everything, from every possible perspective. You map a network of relationships and are able to find connections between distant ideas that can alter the nature of reality itself. You thrive in the realm of the abstract and the possible, but may struggle when it's time to give form to your ideas. You build your understanding of the story based on the external appearance, and that can create problems. As the story goes, you can't judge a book by its cover. Intellect alone is not sufficient. Sometimes feelings are more important than words.

Out of Breath

Nothing can equal the freedom you experience as you soar through the air. The higher you fly, the better the view, but if you fly too high, you'll run out of air. You won't be able to breathe, you'll have nothing to push against, and you will immediately fall to earth. Without air, you're a sailboat stranded at sea. Nothing moves without wind. You can't make connections, you can't communicate, and you can't find the words to make sense of things. You have no choice but to remain in the stillness and silence until you can catch your breath.

Bird's Eye View

If you would like to acquire Air resources, begin with a change in perspective. Set your personal feelings aside and focus on the bigger picture. View the story from the outside as the audience rather from the inside as the protagonist. Consider the situation objectively, and analyze the details. Use reason and logic to explore options and strategies. Pay particular attention to the words in all communication and agreements, and be certain you understand the most literal meaning. For the moment, listen more to your head than to your heart.

Water Story Tropes

The story tropes for the Water Signs (Cancer, Scorpio, Pisces) include *Still Waters Run Deep*, *Washed Up*, and *Test the Waters*.

Still Waters Run Deep

If you speak the language of Water, every story you tell contains hidden emotional depths. The surface of may appear calm and tranquil, but the only way to find out how deep it goes is to dive in. The watery realm of feelings, emotions and the unconscious is its own universe, and the experience of it can be powerful. Water embodies the truth of Unity as individual drops of water merge into the larger whole. Feelings can communicate more effectively than words, and you rely more on your empathy than your intellect. You might prefer to spend all of your time exploring the emotional depths, but this is not possible. You can't breathe under water, and if you don't return to dry land you could drown. The deeper the water, the more dangerous it can be. Some creatures that live in the depths of the unconscious are best left alone.

Washed Up

The realm of Water is wild and unpredictable. Without warning, the gentle stream can become whitewater rapids, a swell can become a tidal wave, and a storm can transform a calm sea into a whirlpool powerful enough to sink a fleet of ships. When the dam bursts and you are caught up in the flood of emotions, the only option is to ride it out. When the waters recede, you'll be washed up on the shore somewhere, battered, disoriented, and far from civilization. You are thirsty and need fresh water to survive, but first you need to wring out the water from the storm. In practical terms, you need some time away from other people's feelings so that you can gently reconnect to your own.

Test the Waters

If you would like to acquire Water resources, you need to get in touch with your feelings. Every active story in your life includes feelings and emotions, and the different streams combine and create a river of feelings. Sometimes the river gets muddy, which makes it harder to navigate. When that happens, you can test the waters, analyze your feelings, and create a story to clear things up. Tune in to a specific feeling, identify it by name, and then locate the story associated with the feeling. Repeat the process until you've untangled the different feelings and the waters are clear. When you understand what you are feeling and where each feeling comes from, you can make better choices in each story.

House Occupied Story Tropes: Where

The house occupied tells you WHERE you can find what you need to achieve the GOAL. These story tropes are designed to help you to move your current story to a different house. They have a more active focus than the GOAL-based descriptions of the houses in Chapter 3.

First House Stories

First House stories involve your health, happiness, and physical appearance. When you take care of your physical body with movement and exercise, make supportive choices around nutrition and rest, or even take a few moments for personal grooming so you look your best, you are in the First House. You're also in the First House when you're engaged in activities that you enjoy and that contribute to your happiness.

Second House Stories

Second House stories involve your money, resources, skills, and talents. When you engage with your money and resources by earning money, saving money, managing money, or spending money, you are in the Second House. You're also in the Second House when you're developing skills or using your talents.

Third House Stories

Third House stories involve your comfort zone, your habits, and your routines. The more familiar you are with your environment and the objectives in your current story, the more confident and comfortable you are, and this moves you to the Third House. You're also in the Third House when you can automate your life through habits and routines, so you can direct your attention to more interesting or important things.

Fourth House Stories

Fourth House stories involve your foundation, your sanctuary, and your privacy. When you take care of your foundation—the parts of your life that take priority and make the rest of your life possible—you are in the Fourth House. You're also in the Fourth House when you retreat to your personal sanctuary so you can enjoy your privacy and recharge your batteries.

Fifth House Stories

Fifth House stories involve your creativity, recreation, and risk. When you express your creativity, which includes everything from artistic expression to solving a problem, you are in the Fifth House. You're also in the Fifth House when you are having fun, playing games, experiencing pleasure, and taking risks.

Sixth House Stories

Sixth House stories involve your work and your service. When you spend time working, whether at your job or meeting some other responsibility, and you can't expect to be rewarded or appreciated for your effort, you're in the Sixth House. You're also in the Sixth House when you perform selfless service, and offer your time and energy in support of others.

Seventh House Stories
Seventh House stories involve your relationships with other people. When you interact with individuals who play supporting roles in your story, you are in the Seventh House. You're also in the Seventh House when you relate to the general public—non-speaking background characters in your story—and when you become involved in stories about people you don't know personally, such as celebrities or politicians.

Eighth House Stories
Eighth House stories involve your debts, obligations, and shared resources. When you engage with debts and obligations by accepting support from others, repaying that support, and following the Law of Circulation, you are in the Eighth House. You're also in the Eighth House when you combine your resources with others to create more opportunity for all.

Ninth House Stories
Ninth House stories involve your danger zone and your encounters with experts and authorities. When you leave your comfort zone behind and enter the danger zone, everything is distant, foreign, and unfamiliar. You are in the Ninth House, where you will find new experiences and a greater understanding of your story. You're also in the Ninth House when you seek out experts and authorities to help you understand the unknown.

Tenth House Stories
Tenth House stories involve your reputation, your advancement, and your public image. When you work for advancement in your personal, social, or professional life, and hope to create a reputation for success, you're in the Tenth House. You're also in the Tenth House when you engage with your public image through your social media presence.

Eleventh House Stories
Eleventh House stories involve your ambitions, aspirations, and acquisitions. When you engage with your ambitions, whether you create the story of

your dream or work to make it a reality, you are in the Eleventh House. You're also in the Eleventh House when you set out to acquire the things you believe will make you happy.

Twelfth House Stories

Twelfth House stories involve your adversity and your blind spot. Adversity takes many forms, but it always creates an **OBSTACLE** you must overcome to achieve your **GOAL** and advance in your story. When you experience adversity, you are in the Twelfth House, and you have the opportunity to discover hidden strength. You're also in the Twelfth House when you check your blind spot and discover things you have overlooked or taken for granted.

In later chapters, you will see these story tropes in action. I'll be creating a complete set of modality, element, and house occupied astrology stories for specific expressions of the Moon, Venus, the Chart Ruler, Mars, and the Sun, so you'll have quite a number of examples to consider.

But now, let me show you how it all fits together: how to use astrology story tropes to build an astrology story map.

CHAPTER 5
Astrology Story Maps

In this chapter, I'll tell the story of how to build astrology stories using astrology story maps. The best way to do this is to share my personal stories and how I can connect those stories to astrology stories found in my own birth chart. The content of my stories may not be relevant to you personally, but that's not the point. The intention is to demonstrate how to assemble astrology stories with astrology story tropes and connect them to personal stories.

This is the big picture blueprint for how you will work with astrology and the Human Game. This story includes any number of details and concepts that you may not yet understand, and it will raise any number of questions. The remainder of this book is dedicated to answering every one of those questions.

Story Maps

Let me begin with a story about maps. I have struggled with maps my entire life. My problem isn't with the maps themselves; it's that I don't immediately understand how the map relates to me. I'm slightly dyslexic, and I have a dreadful sense of direction. The only way I can follow a map is if I can orient the map to match my current position because I couldn't pick "North" out of a police line-up even if it were dressed in a Santa suit.

This is especially challenging for me in shopping malls, where the only way to orient myself to match the map is to stand on my head.

Every time I encounter a new map, I have to go through a process of orienting my actual surroundings to the map itself. This often involves taking what I like to call the "scenic route," but which others call "an endless succession of wrong turns."

When I explore a new environment, I make my own personal map. It's only when I can connect my personal map to the bigger, objective map that the objective map becomes useful to me.

This is how we will approach astrology stories. The birth chart is an incredibly detailed map of The Story of Your Life. But that map isn't much use until you can connect it to your personal experience of your life.

Using my own birth chart as an example, I'll demonstrate the process of building a personal and useful astrology story map.

Plot-Level Astrology Stories

Most personal stories begin as Plot-level stories that involve an external **GOAL**. The external **GOAL** relates to one of the houses in the birth chart, and the house becomes the **WHAT** of the astrology story. A house can be the subject of an astrology *story*, but only a planet can be the subject of an astrology *sentence*. The planet that rules the sign on the cusp of the house is the conduit that connects the modality, element, and house story tropes to the **GOAL**.

An ongoing **GOAL** for me has been to consolidate and pay off my credit card debt. Credit card debt belongs to the Eighth House, which includes debts (financial and otherwise) and shared resources. My personal story and my Plot-level **GOAL** connects to the symbolic Theme-level astrology story through the Eighth House. Capricorn is on the cusp of my Eighth House, so Saturn rules my Eighth House. My Saturn is in Aries (Cardinal Fire) and occupies the Tenth House.

Here's what the initial story map looks like. It connects the personal story to the astrology story.

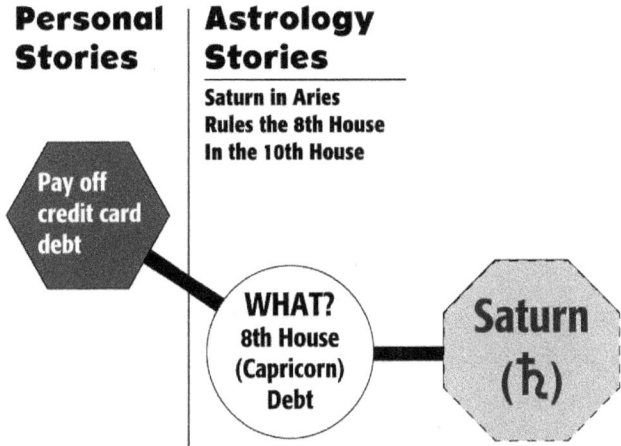

We're considering a Plot-level story in which I have a **Goal** to pay off my credit card debt. An excellent question to answer is **How** I approach that **Goal**, and we can find answers to that question by considering the modality of the planet that rules the house of the **Goal**. Saturn rules my Eighth House, and my Saturn is in Aries, so we add the Cardinal modality to the map and then consider what information it adds to the story.

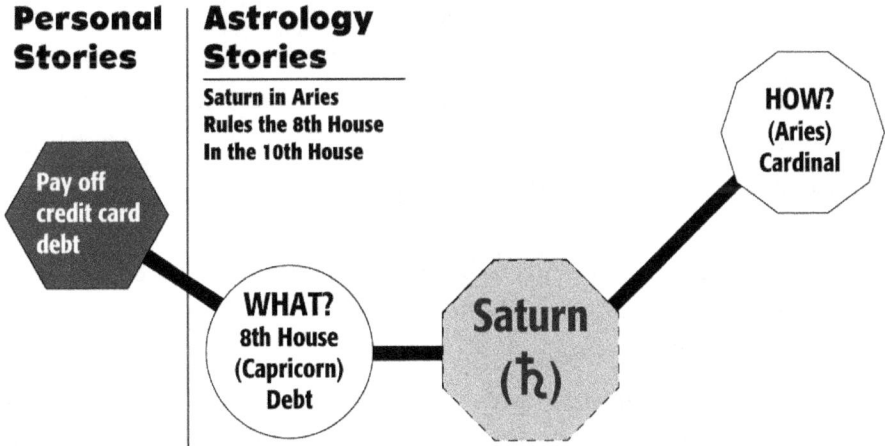

We'll begin with a single Cardinal story trope: *Archery Target*.

The *Archery Target* trope means that I view the objective of the **Goal** like an archery target that has to be hit with a single shot. I invest all of my energy and attention in preparation and strategy—taking aim at the target—but once I let go of the arrow, there's nothing more I can do. Either I hit the target and take a giant leap forward, or I miss the target, stay exactly where I am, and have to try again with a new arrow.

If we connect this trope with my personal story about paying off my credit card debt, it means that I view my debt like an archery target. I believe that I have to pay off all of my debt at once. I don't notice or appreciate incremental progress toward paying off my debts; I notice progress only when I hit the target and pay them off completely.

I've identified a pattern in the *astrology* story. I need to see if and how that pattern shows up in the *personal* story. When I find a connection between the astrology story and my personal story, it creates a light bulb moment. Without a light bulb moment, you (and your client) can't see how the astrology matters.

This connection created a big light bulb moment for me. This pattern perfectly describes how I approach my debts and financial responsibilities. I never thought about these stories in this way until I made this connection, but now it's obvious. I have *always* viewed my debts as archery targets, and I'm always looking for ways that I can pay off all of my debts at once.

I've activated the connection between my stories about debt and the *Archery Target* story trope, but I've only considered how it affects ACT 1 of the story: how I approach the GOAL. The *Archery Target* story trope influences ACT 2 of the story and can prepare me for the OBSTACLE I may face. It also offers strategies that can help create a successful RESOLUTION in ACT 3.

Let's consider what the ACT 2 OBSTACLE might involve. A tolerance for failure and wasted resources is built into the *Archery Target* story trope. I expect that each failure improves my odds of success on the next attempt. I adjust for errors and improve my aim. This is a reasonable strategy so long as the target is close enough to hit. If the target is out of reach, it doesn't matter how good my aim is.

A big source of frustration for me in my credit card debt story is that I rarely feel like I'm making progress. Paying down the balance on different cards doesn't give me a sense of accomplishment. I may have come closer to hitting the target, but close counts only in horseshoes and hand grenades. In an *Archery Target* story, a near miss is still a miss.

The Rules of Story mean that I will always view this **Goal** as a target; but no rule prevents me from moving the target closer. I'm free to break the big **Goal** into smaller targets and aim for those milestone targets in sequence. Each time I hit a target, I take a giant step toward the ultimate objective.

This gives me a better strategy to create a successful **Act 3 Resolution** to the story of my debts. I don't have to view my total debt as a single target. I can view each debt as its own target. I can set a new **Goal** to pay off one bill completely. When I hit that target and pay that card off, I not only get to feel like I've accomplished something significant, but I also take a giant step closer to my objective of paying off all of my cards.

We've reached the point in the process where the difference between *learning* astrology and *using* astrology matters.

We've barely started to assemble this map. There's so much more astrology to explore and so much more for you to learn. We've only considered one simple answer to one simple question.

But consider that *we already have a simple answer to a simple question*. I now have a much better story about how I approach my debts, and I have a new strategy I can adopt to achieve my **Goal** and pay off my debts. From a practical standpoint, I don't need any more astrology. This story map is more than sufficient.

At the moment, you're learning astrology, so I'll demonstrate how to add to the story map. But when you're ready to use what you've learned, remember that the point isn't to explore the whole map; the point is to find the shortest path to your destination.

Let's add to the story map and explore **Which** elemental language I speak when I tell these stories.

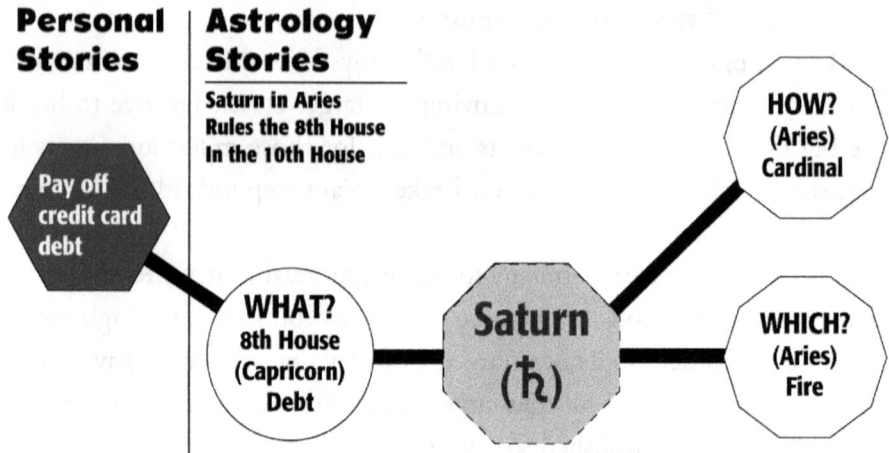

My Saturn is in Aries, which is a Fire sign, so let's incorporate the *On Fire* story trope. Everything about my Eighth House astrology stories, and by extension about my personal stories about my credit card debt, is metaphorically on fire. These stories are urgent and require my immediate attention, and the stakes are potentially high. Paying off my credit card debt is a priority because if I don't contain the fire, it could get out of control and burn my whole life to the ground. Every time I add to my debt or receive a new bill, it's like a new fire pops up that needs to be extinguished or contained.

The *On Fire* story trope can also provide insight and options to help me to navigate my personal stories. For example, it will be useful to recognize that the stakes of these stories can burn out of control, so I will need to know how to manage and lower the stakes. Just because something is on fire doesn't mean it's a crisis.

Next, we expand the map to include the house Saturn occupies to explore **Where** the story unfolds.

Astrology Story Maps

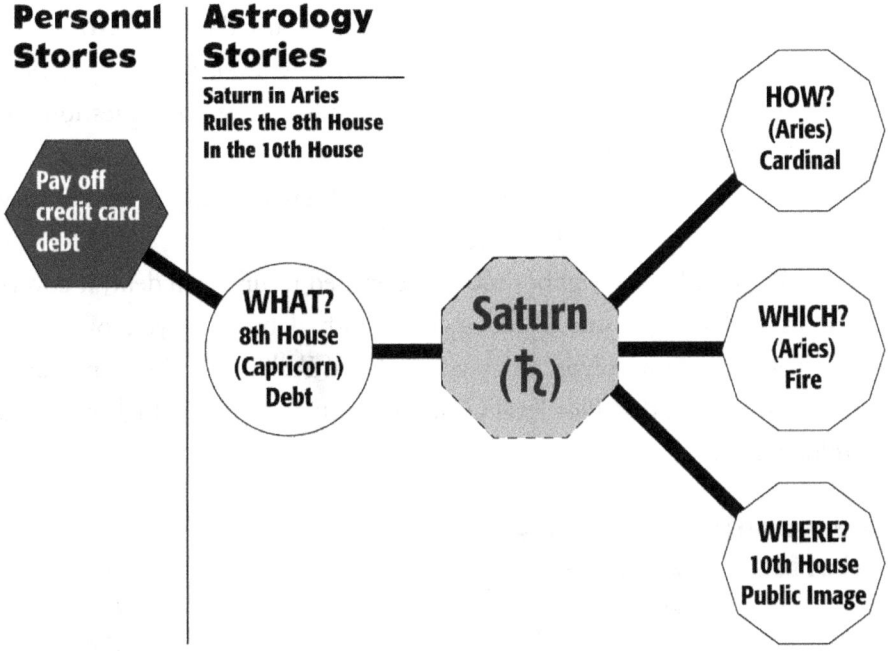

Saturn, the ruler of my Eighth House is in my Tenth House, which relates to my public image, my reputation, and my personal and professional advancement.

This suggests that my Eighth House astrology stories, and any associated personal stories, including stories about my credit card debts, are public. The world will know about these stories, perhaps because I post about them on social media. Or write about them in a book.

The house occupied by the planet not only describes **WHERE** the story unfolds; it also shows **WHERE** to find the motivation and resources for a successful outcome.

In my case, I can use the Tenth House connection as a positive incentive to keep me focused on my **GOAL** of paying off my debts. I can create a story that explores how paying off my debts will help me to succeed, both personally and professionally. I can use The Rule of Compensation, and rather than focus on the price I pay for having debts, I can focus on the Tenth House gift I can claim when I have paid them off.

On a personal level, I have upgraded all of my stories about credit card debt, and I have new strategies to help me achieve my Plot-level **Goal** and pay off my debts once and for all. On an astrology level, I have a practical map of my Eighth House that makes it easy to answer the questions of **How**, **Which**, and **Where**.

I can now use this map to understand and navigate any personal story that relates to the Eighth House neighborhood.

The Eighth House neighborhood isn't limited to financial debt; it covers all debts and obligations. Those include both debts that you owe, and debts that others owe to you. This means that if I'd like to collect on a favor someone owes me, that Plot-level **Goal** connects to the same Eighth House astrology map.

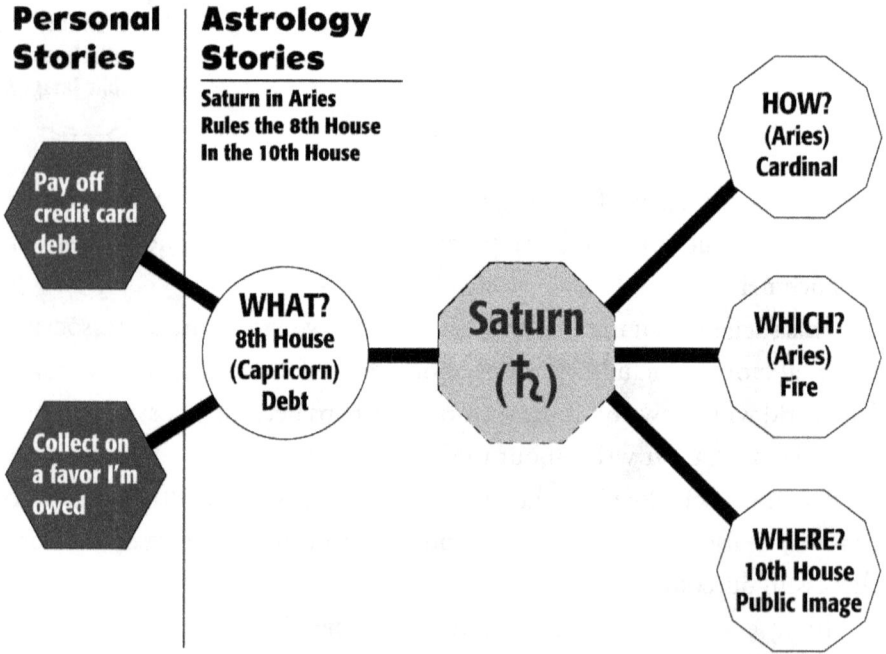

I already have answers to the questions of **How**, **Which**, and **Where**. The Cardinal story trope of *Archery Target* means I expect the entire favor to be repaid at once. The Fire story trope of *On Fire* raises the stakes and makes the situation urgent, so I probably need that debt to be repaid right now. And the Tenth House location suggests that I might expect the favor will help me to advance or succeed in a public or professional arena. It also suggests that if my friend doesn't meet my expectations and repay the favor, I'll probably post about it on Facebook (because social media is a big part of the Tenth House neighborhood).

At this point, I'm comfortable recognizing the patterns of these story tropes every time they show up in any personal story related to my Eighth House. These tropes aren't limited to my Eighth House stories, however. Aquarius is on the cusp of my Ninth House, so Saturn also rules my Ninth House. Ninth House stories about my beliefs, my experiences with the unknown, or my need for advice from experts and authorities follow the same patterns as my Eighth House stories.

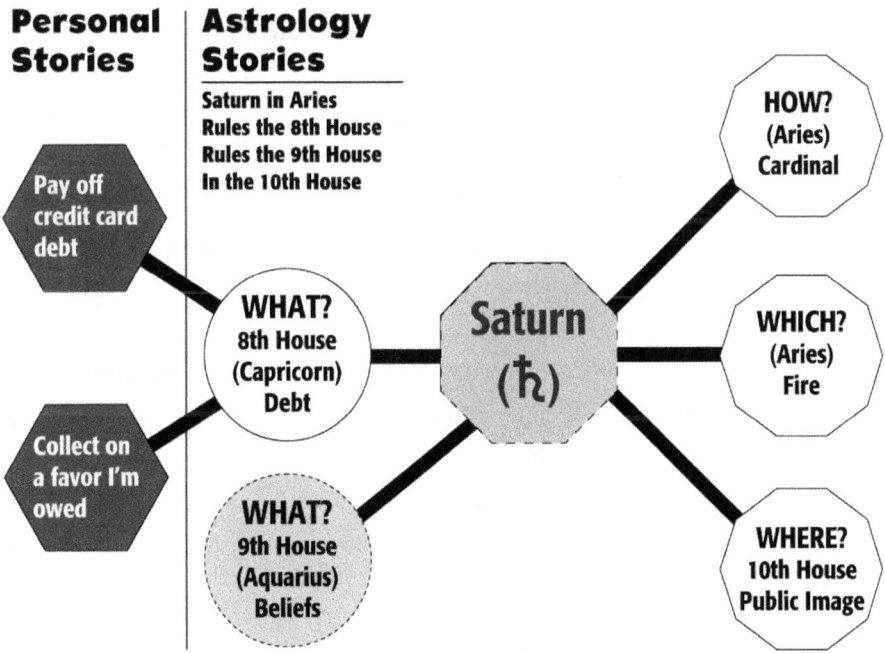

When I consider new information and form a belief about something, the *Archery Target* Cardinal story trope means that I form the belief in a single bound. I don't try out different ideas or consider alternative options; the belief shows up fully formed, all at once. The *On Fire* story trope of the Fire element means that my beliefs are often (quite literally) hot takes; they're subjective, personal, and expressive. And the Tenth House location means I'm public about my beliefs, and that my beliefs are integral parts of my brand and my reputation.

Adding additional story tropes can expand the story and uncover more options. If we add the *Fix the Past* Cardinal Story trope to the story about credit card debt, it highlights the fact that I'm literally dealing with the past by paying off purchases I made months or even years ago. When added to the story about collecting on a favor, the past is once again a dominant theme. The original favor I did for my friend, which created the debt owed to me, is in the past. When added to the story about how I create beliefs, it suggests that my beliefs may be more influenced by my past ideas and old information than I realize.

Not every story trope is useful or necessary. But the more story tropes you can recognize, the more options you have when you engage with a story. Each time you connect an astrology story trope to a personal story and recognize the pattern, it creates a new light bulb moment.

The light bulb moments are the point of this process. They're why the Human Game approach makes it so easy to learn astrology. When you connect the astrology story to a personal story and create a light bulb moment, that connection lives in you. You don't have to memorize it or study it: all you have to do is notice it. When you experience a light bulb moment, your story has been upgraded and your reality has changed. The light bulb comes on when The Best Story Wins.

So far, we've explored the Plot-level story, which relates to the house. From here, we can expand the map to address the Character-level story by considering the planet.

Character-Level Story

To connect the Plot-level story to the more meaningful Character-level story, simply add the ruling planet to the story map. The house is still the primary subject, and the main answer to the WHAT question; the ruling planet expands on the subject and asks **WHAT ELSE**. In this case, the **WHAT ELSE** is Saturn, and we'll begin with the idea of responsibility.

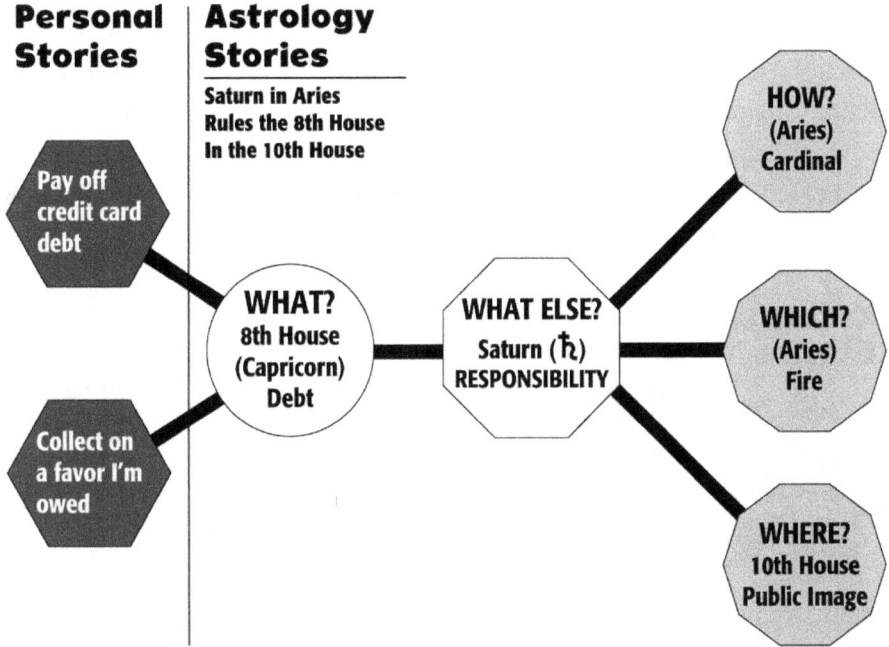

The connection between the **WHAT** of the house and the **WHAT ELSE** of the house ruler is quite important. For me, debt *is* responsibility. The connection between debt and responsibility might be objectively obvious, but it's not subjectively automatic. The reason that debt is responsibility for *me* is that Saturn, which symbolizes the **NEED** for responsibility, rules my Eighth House, which relates to stories about debt. Unless you also have Saturn as the ruler of your Eighth House, debt will be *something other than responsibility* for you, personally, in your stories.

If the Sun rules your Eighth House, debt is *integrity*. If the Moon rules your Eighth House, debt is *safety*. If Mercury rules your Eighth House, debt is *communication*. If Venus rules your Eighth House, debt is *validation*. If Mars rules your Eighth House, debt is *anger*. And if Jupiter rules your Eighth House, for you, debt is *growth*.

These identity statements that link the Character-level **Need** of the planet to the Plot-level **Goal** of the house are Theme-level astrology stories. They're quite advanced, and you don't need to understand them to be able to tell better astrology stories. They're relevant because you can't separate a house from the planet that rules it. We'll explore the **What Else** of the planet from the context of the **What** of the house.

In other words, to explore my Character-level story about responsibility, we begin with the Plot-level story about debt and then apply the **How**, **Which**, and **Where**.

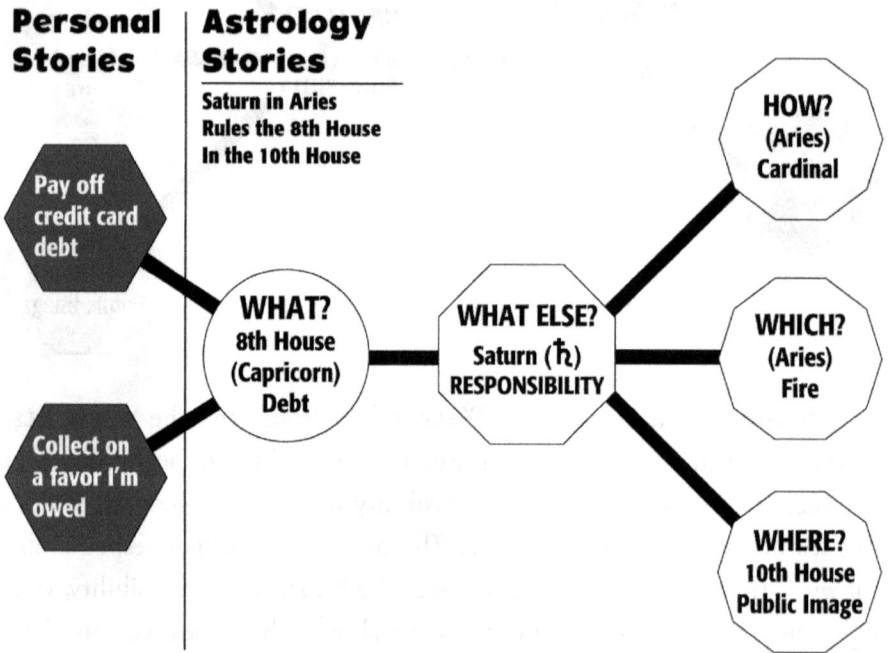

The Cardinal story tropes mean that I approach my debt as an *Archery Target* and also that I tend to cling to the past. Paying off my debts will address my **Need** for responsibility because when I no longer have credit card debt, I will no longer have the burden of that responsibility. And I would like to meet and discharge that responsibility all at once, in a single shot because I've been carrying it with me for far too long. The *On Fire* story trope makes both my debt and the burden of the responsibility for my debt urgent and immediate. And the Tenth House location means that when I pay off my debts, not only do I get to advance my reputation of handling my finances well, but I also get to advance my reputation of being responsible.

This gives me a clear understanding of how responsibility is an integral part of my stories about debt. But because the way that I approach stories about debt is also the way that I approach stories about responsibility, these options are now available to me in any story that involves responsibility.

I can make responsibility the **WHAT** and connect it directly to any Plot-level story that deals with the subject (or theme) of responsibility.

Now, let's expand the map by considering a second expression of Saturn. Another possible answer to the **WHAT ELSE** question of Saturn is authority.

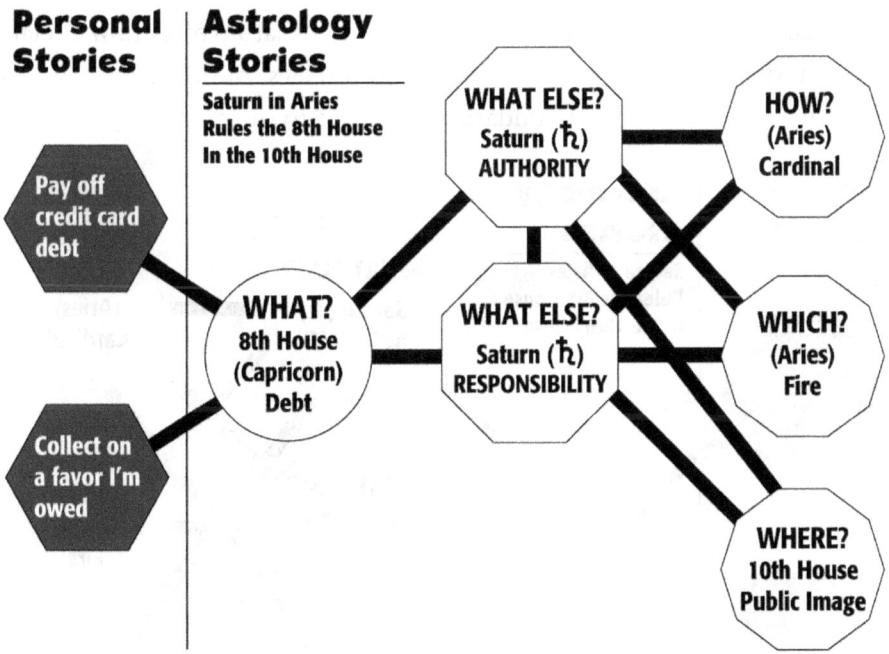

Notice how the **WHAT ELSE** of authority connects to everything: it connects to the **WHAT** of Eighth House debt, it connects to the **WHAT ELSE** of responsibility, and it also connects to the **HOW**, **WHICH**, and **WHERE**.

Let's explore these new connections one at a time.

First, this map indicates that for me, debt is authority. When I consider this idea, it tracks. I can easily see this theme in my stories about debt. I often give my power away to my debts and let my debts dictate my options and choices. And authority is clearly related to responsibility. One reason that I care about meeting my responsibilities is to win the approval of authority; and if I don't meet my responsibilities, I could be punished by authority.

The **How**, **Which**, and **Where** tropes that apply to debt and responsibility also apply to how I engage with authority. I want to limit and concentrate my interactions with authority and address them all at once, and I'm strongly influenced by past experiences with authority (Cardinal). I often find authority figures to be intense, dangerous, and unpredictable (Fire). And I encounter authority when I pursue my personal and professional advancement (Tenth House).

I can now use this map to explore any story that involves how I relate to authority. In keeping with The Rule of Three, let's consider a third **What Else** for Saturn, and add boundaries and limits to the map.

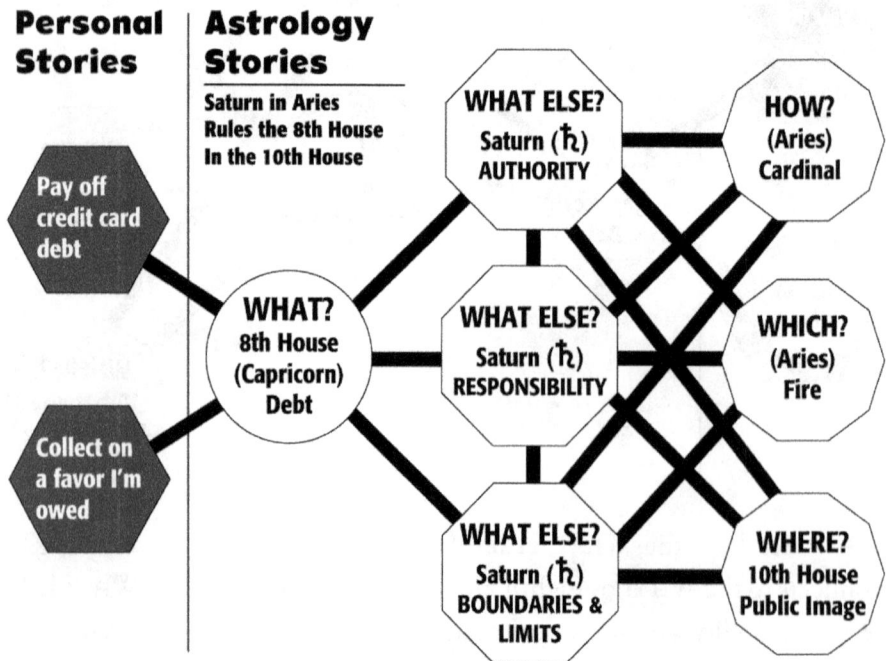

It's easy to wire up these new connections. The connection between debt and limitations is obvious. And I can easily recognize that I approach boundaries and limits the same way that I approach responsibility, authority, and debt because the same **How**, **Which**, and **Where** story tropes apply.

And remember, these connections apply not only to my Eighth House stories: they also apply to my Ninth House stories because Saturn rules both my Eighth House and my Ninth House.

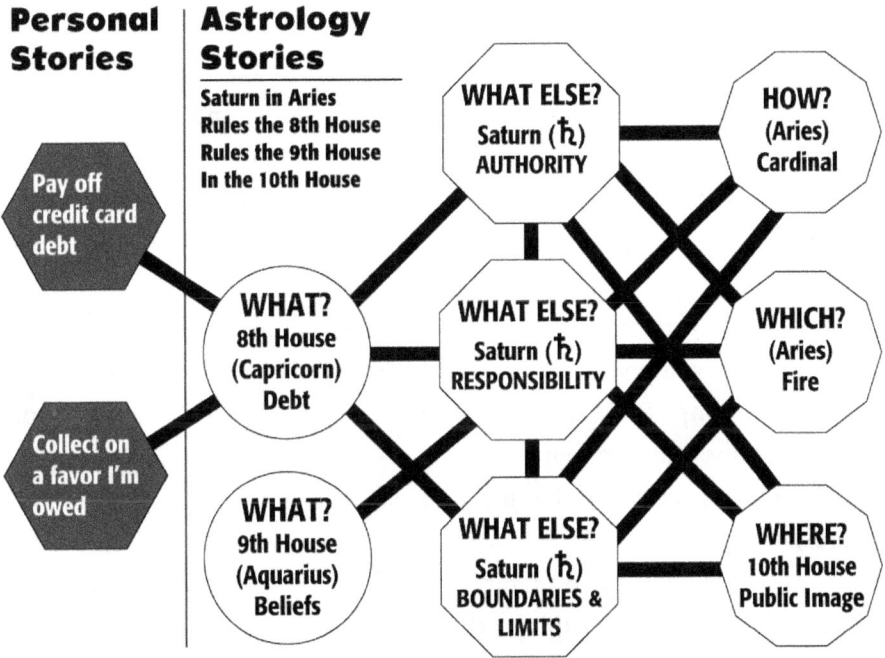

So this is a reasonably complete astrology map that explores all of the connections that involve Saturn and the houses Saturn rules in my chart.

This map is useful to me because I built it, and because I built it one connection at a time. I took the time to consider each individual connection and identify how that pattern shows up in a personal story. I found a light bulb moment for each connection, which makes it possible for me to see the different paths and options in this map.

The next time I find myself lost in an Eighth House story, or caught up in a story that features issues of responsibility, authority, or boundaries, I can use this map to figure out where I am and how to get to where I'd like to be. The map will remind me of options that I might have overlooked, and it will help me view the story from different perspectives. It's how astrology can provide clear, simple, precise, immediate, and practical answers to real-life questions.

One Final Reminder

Just because I've broken down this process and walked you through it step by step doesn't mean that you fully understand or appreciate it. This process is obvious to me because it connects to my stories and my chart. At each step of this process, I connected an astrology symbol and a story trope to my personal story, and that connection turned on a light bulb for me.

This is a sample of my map of my Eighth House neighborhood. Unless your Eighth House neighborhood has the same blueprint as mine, this map won't work for you.

The point of this chapter is to demonstrate how you will create your own maps. As you progress through this program, I will give you the tools, tropes, and templates you need to create your own maps and experience your own light bulb moments.

Until you experience this for yourself, you won't fully understand or appreciate it. Once you experience it for yourself, the sky's the limit. You'll be able to use astrology to map out The Story of Your Life, and you'll be one giant step closer to helping other people to do the same.

CHAPTER 6
Foundations of Happiness Stories

I'd like to begin this chapter with a story.

A young woman is walking down the street one night and sees an elderly man on his hands and knees under a streetlight. She asks him what's wrong, and he tells her he's looking for his lost car keys. She offers to help him look. After a few minutes of fruitless searching, the young woman is ready to give up.

"They don't seem to be here," she says. "Where did you last have them?"

The old man points down the street and says, "Back there, near my car."

"If you lost them back there, why are you looking for them here," she asks?

The old man replies, "Because the light is better."

It's an old joke, and you may have heard it before. But you may not realize that this old joke illustrates the secret of happiness.

The reason you spend your life looking for happiness and never finding it is that you're looking in the wrong place. You're looking for happiness in the outside world—in the Plot-level story—where the light is better.

When you approach happiness from the Plot-level story, happiness is a **GOAL**. To achieve a **GOAL**, you need to know three things. First, you need to know **WHAT** the **GOAL** is. You have to have a clear definition of the **GOAL** so you understand the requirements to achieve it and can identify when you have achieved it. Second, you need to know **WHERE** the **GOAL** is in relation to your current location. Third, you need a strategy that tells you **HOW** to achieve the **GOAL**.

Your current story about happiness isn't working too well for you. You don't have a good definition of **What** happiness is, and you're not entirely clear about **Where** it is, either. Until you address these issues, there's no value in upgrading the strategy of **How** you pursue happiness.

In this chapter, we will use the tools of the Human Game to upgrade your story about happiness. By the end of this chapter, you will have better answers to each of the key questions about happiness. You will know **What** happiness is. You will know **Where** happiness is. And you will understand your current approach to find happiness—and **How** you can improve it.

Your Current Story About Happiness

Up to this point in your life, you've experienced only moments of happiness. Most of the time, these moments of happiness immediately followed achieving a **Goal** or getting something you **Want**. This formed your current definition of happiness: **Happiness is the feeling you experience when you get what you Want.**

For this definition to be accurate, getting what you **Want** would always make you feel happy and not getting what you **Want** would never make you feel happy. Let's see if this is the case.

Sometimes getting what you **Want** makes you feel happy, but sometimes you get what you **Want** and you don't feel happy. Most of the time, when you don't get what you **Want**, you're not happy, but sometimes you don't get what you **Want** and you end up very happy about it.

Getting what you **Want** has some connection to feeling happy, but it's not the only requirement. Getting what you **Want** isn't a reliable way to create happiness.

Happiness is a feeling, so it lives inside you, not in the outside world. This is what's meant by the cliché, money can't buy happiness. The problem is that you don't know how to look for happiness inside you.

You spend most of your time focused on the outside world, and you're used to looking for happiness there. And sometimes, when you achieve a **Goal** in the outside world, you get what you **Want**, and some of the time, that makes you feel happy. Worldly success might not be the same thing as happiness, but it's certainly happiness-adjacent.

Your current strategy to find happiness is to pursue your external goals, hoping that eventually you'll acquire enough money and success to feel happy. The summary of your happiness story is people who think money can't buy happiness don't know where to shop.

This isn't a bad story—but it could be better. Money and happiness go very well together, but the Human Game makes it clear that happiness comes first. Let's consider happiness from the context of the Human Game.

The Human Game Story of Happiness

The Human Game easily addresses the question of **Where** happiness exists. Happiness is a feeling, so happiness—and your Happily Ever After—is a part of the Character-level story.

Act 1 of the Character-level story begins with something you **Want**. **Want** is a feeling—specifically, it's a feeling of lack. You go after what you **Want** in **Act 1**, but in **Act 2**, you discover what it is that you **Need**. In **Act 3**, you make a **Choice**: you can either focus on what you **Want** or you can give up what you **Want** and go after what you **Need**. At the end of **Act 3**, if you meet your **Need** and no longer feel any lack, which means you no longer **Want** anything—you feel happy.

This gives us a better definition of happiness.

Happiness is the feeling you experience when you are free from Want and free from Need.

Consider this for a moment. Happiness doesn't mean you feel *good*; happiness means you no longer feel *bad*. When you are happy, you don't have to do anything. You have unlimited options and you're free to choose any path that inspires you. When you build a foundation of happiness—your Happily Ever After—you can create Prosperity, experience Joy, and discover the Meaning and purpose of your life.

But happiness comes first.

You know that getting what you **WANT** isn't enough to create happiness. This suggests that the critical factor of happiness is getting what you **NEED**. What you *think* you **WANT** is the MacGuffin in the Plot-level story. What you actually **WANT** is to meet a **NEED** in the Character-level story. When that **NEED** is met, you no longer **WANT** anything, which creates the feeling of happiness.

When you get what you **WANT** and it makes you feel happy, getting what you **WANT** also meets a **NEED**. When you get what you **WANT** and you don't feel happy, getting what you **WANT** didn't meet a **NEED**.

If getting what you **WANT** takes too much effort—if it costs too much so it wasn't worth it—it doesn't make you happy. This suggests that getting what you **WANT** makes you happy when you make some kind of a profit. It also suggests that making a profit is how you meet a **NEED**.

This is easier to understand if you think of a **NEED** as a bank account. When you maintain the minimum balance in your Need Bank Account, you experience that **NEED** as being met, which makes you feel happy. When you get what you **WANT**, it makes a deposit in your Need Bank Account. If that raises the balance in your Need Bank Account above the minimum level, you experience a moment of happiness. To build a foundation of happiness and experience Happily Ever After, you simply maintain the minimum balance in your Need Bank Account.

WANT is a feeling, which means it's a part of the Character-level story. But when you **WANT** something, you look for it in the outside world. You believe when you achieve an external **GOAL**, it will fulfill an internal **WANT**. The external **GOAL** is a part of the Plot-level story. You believe that when you achieve an external **GOAL**, you will get what you **WANT**, which will make a deposit in your Need Bank Account, which will make you happy.

The problem is that to pursue an external **GOAL**, you have to spend some of the resources from your Need Bank Account. If you don't make a profit—if it costs more to achieve the **GOAL** than you gain when you achieve it—you won't be happy because you'll end up with a lower balance in your Need Bank Account.

Let's put together all of the pieces now and reveal your current strategy to create happiness.

To build a foundation of happiness and experience your Happily Ever After, you need to maintain a minimum balance in your Need Bank Account. You receive deposits in your Need Bank Account when you get what you **WANT**. To get what you **WANT** in the Character-level story you chose an external **GOAL** in the Plot-level story. But to pursue the **GOAL**, you have to spend resources from your Need Bank Account, which lowers the balance and puts your happiness at risk.

There's no guarantee that you will achieve the **GOAL**, and even if you do, there's no guarantee that getting what you **WANT** will mean you receive more resources than you spent and meet the minimum balance in your Need Bank Account.

In other words, your current strategy to build a foundation of happiness and acquire enough resources to maintain a minimum balance in your Need Bank Account is to gamble in the Happiness Casino.

Gambling in a casino isn't the best way to maintain your bank balance. The odds always favor the house. No matter how much you win in the short term, in the long term you'll end up losing.

But the Happiness Casino isn't an actual casino: it's a story about a casino. You're not playing with money, you're playing with happiness. And with a few minor edits to the story, we'll transform it from a game you can't win to a game you can't lose.

Gambling in a casino can be fun if the stakes are low: if winning is a bonus but losing doesn't cost you anything.

You can receive deposits in your Need Bank Account by playing the Plot-level game in the Happiness Casino, choosing an external **Goal** and getting what you **Want**—but that's not the only way you can meet your needs and experience happiness.

The Human Game can show you how to focus on the Character-level story and meet your needs directly. This lets you have fun gambling in the Happiness Casino, playing the Plot-level games. When you achieve your **Goal** and get what you **Want**, it makes you happy because it always increases the balance in your Need Bank Account. If you lose, it doesn't cost you anything: the balance in your Need Bank Account doesn't change and it doesn't limit your happiness. Either way, you have fun playing the game.

You now have a new story about happiness. You have a clear definition of what happiness is—that it means you're free from **Want** and free from **Need**, which gives you options to choose what you would like to do with The Story of Your Life. You understand the relationship between your external **Goal** and your internal feelings of happiness. And most importantly, you know that happiness is not the end of your story. Happily Ever After is happy beginning, not a happy ending—so you can start to build your foundation of happiness right now.

You have everything you need to embark on The Quest for Happiness. You're ready to assemble the story of the Happiness GPS and use astrology stories from your unique birth chart to beat the odds in the Happiness Casino so you can get what you **Want** and still be happy.

PART 2
THE QUEST FOR HAPPINESS

CHAPTER 7
The Story of Your Need Bank Accounts

Let's review your new story about happiness. Happiness is the feeling you experience when you are free from **Want** and free from **Need**. When you maintain a minimum balance in your Need Bank Account, you experience that **Need** as being met and this creates a moment of happiness. You can receive deposits in your Need Bank Account when you get what you **Want** by achieving a **Goal** in the external Plot-level story by gambling in the Happiness Casino. It's also possible to receive deposits in your Need Bank Account outside of the Happiness Casino, which is a more sustainable strategy to build a foundation of happiness.

To build a foundation of happiness and create your Happily Ever After, you need to maintain the minimum balance in your Need Bank Account, so this is the new **Goal**. To achieve this **Goal**, you need to know **What**, **Where**, and **How**. This chapter will focus on the **What**, because at the moment you don't have any idea **What** a **Need** is. We'll create a story that identifies different types of **Need** and different kinds of **Need**, and explains how each of these relates to happiness.

To create the story about Need Bank Accounts and happiness, we'll not only draw from astrology stories, we'll also draw from psychology stories.

The Astrology Story of Your Needs

Most of the time you don't know what you **Want**, let alone what you **Need**. What you think you **Want** is usually a **Goal**, something external that you hope to accomplish in the Plot-level story. The **Goal** itself is a MacGuffin. You don't care about the actual **Goal**; you care that you've placed a bet in the Happiness Casino, and if you achieve the **GOAL**, you will get what you **WANT**: resources that you can deposit in your Need Bank Account, which will make you happy. It's rare to be conscious of the actual **WANT** because that's a part of the Character-level story and you're used to focusing on the Plot-level story.

Because your external **GOAL** is tied to your internal **WANT**, if you can organize the **GOAL** in a meaningful way, it will also organize what you **WANT**. A **GOAL** always involves improving some part of your life, and your birth chart is a map of The Story of Your Life.

Think of your life as a city. The City of Your Life is divided into twelve neighborhoods—the twelve houses in the birth chart. Each neighborhood is zoned for a different type of activity. The Second House neighborhood contains all of your personal resources, your money, and your skills and talents. The Sixth House neighborhood is where you work. The Ninth House neighborhood contains experts and authorities to help you navigate the unknown.

Every **GOAL** you have belongs to one of these neighborhoods. The planet that rules the house of the **GOAL** is in charge of that **GOAL**, and the astrology stories of that planet can help you choose the best strategy to achieve the **GOAL**. The modality of the planet tells you **HOW** you approach the goal, the element of the planet tells you **WHICH** resources you require, and the house the planet occupies tells you **WHERE** you can find those resources.

While the houses in the birth chart relate to an external **GOAL**, the seven personal planets in the birth chart each represent an internal **NEED**. The Sun symbolizes your **NEED** for integrity, authenticity, and vitality. The Moon symbolizes your Safety Needs, and your **NEED** to express feelings and emotions. Mercury symbolizes your **NEED** for understanding, communication, and story. Venus symbolizes your Validation Needs, your **NEED** for approval, and your **NEED** to align with your values. Mars symbolizes your **NEED** to express your desire, your anger, and your ego. Jupiter symbolizes your **NEED** for growth, faith, and imagination. Saturn symbolizes your **NEED** for responsibility, authority, and boundaries.

This story creates a clear link between the external **GOAL** and the internal **NEED**. The **GOAL** and the **WANT** connect to a house in the natal chart, and the planet that rules that house reveals the underlying **NEED**. This can be useful in the Happiness Casino because addressing the **NEED** of the planet in charge of the **GOAL** improves your chance of success and makes it easier to get what you **WANT**. But we're not looking for winning strategies in the Happiness Casino (at least not yet). We're looking for a way to bypass the Happiness Casino and manage your Need Bank Accounts directly.

This story makes the Need Bank Accounts more practical. It identifies seven types of **NEED**, and provides an objective way to associate an external **GOAL** with an internal **NEED**. The problem with this story is that if we combine it with the story of happiness, to build a foundation of happiness and experience your Happily Ever After you would have to maintain the minimum balance in seven different Need Bank Accounts.

This would mean that The Quest for Happiness would involve seven tasks. That's not a bad story. But it would be a better story if it incorporated The Rule of Three.

What if you could build a foundation of happiness by managing the balance in only three Need Bank Accounts? Managing the balance in the remaining Need Bank Accounts could be how you create Prosperity, experience Joy, and discover the Meaning of your life.

We need a story that can organize the different Need Bank Accounts and identify which are the most essential to happiness. Astrology can't provide that story, but psychology can.

The Psychology Story of Your Needs

Our story begins in a time of economic strife, political uncertainty, record unemployment, and global unrest—and no, I'm not talking about 2011. This story begins in the 1920s, the *first* time Wall Street's unregulated behavior plunged America into a Great Depression. A psychologist by the name of **Abraham Maslow** was preparing to revolutionize the entire field of head shrinking (which, at the time, had been around for about 30 years). Up to this point, psychology assumed that people were basically screwed up. The main objectives of psychology were to (a) figure out exactly how people were screwed up, (b) figure out how to blame it all on the patient's mother, and (c) figure out how to get patients to pay for a full hour, but give them only 50 minutes of therapy.

Maslow approached things from the opposite direction. He wondered what would happen if instead of assuming people were fundamentally sick, we assumed people were fundamentally healthy. What motivates the behavior of healthy people? And more importantly, how do you get healthy people to pay for a full hour but give them only 50 minutes?

Maslow proposed that we are motivated by our unmet needs. He discovered that all needs are not created equal—some needs are more important than others. In fact, until we've met all of our "lower" needs, we won't be motivated to meet any of our "higher" needs. Maslow summed up his approach in a hierarchy of needs that's usually illustrated in a pyramid, as shown below.

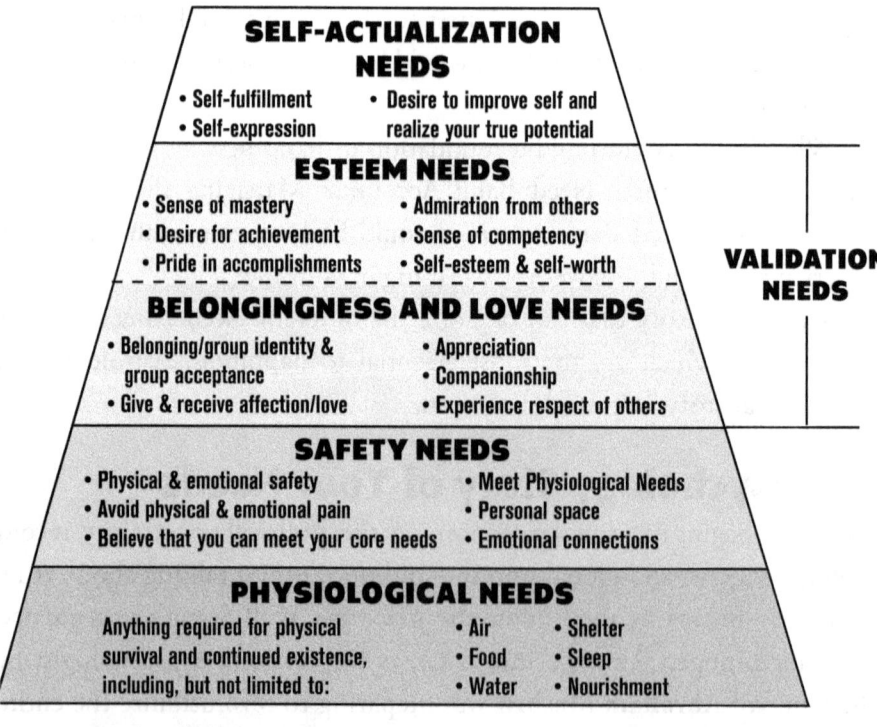

In my book, *The Relationship Handbook: How to Understand and Improve Every Relationship in Your Life*, I used Maslow's pyramid as the inspiration for the story of the Need Bank Accounts, which I then connected to the astrology stories.

Your **Physiological Needs** include everything you need to survive, such as air, food, water, sleep, and shelter. You will do anything to meet these needs, and I do mean anything. If these needs aren't being met, the body's instinctive, animal nature takes over. It's not pretty. Mars is the planet in charge of your Physiological Needs.

Your **Safety Needs** include everything you *think* you need to survive. In fact, you could survive without most of these things, although probably not without whining about it. To meet your Safety Needs, you have to believe that your Physiological Needs will be met in the future. Your Safety Needs motivate you to avoid physical and emotional pain. The Moon is the planet in charge of your Safety Needs.

Maslow's next two categories have to do with being loved and appreciated. **Belongingness and Love Needs** are about being loved and appreciated by other people, and **Esteem Needs** are about being loved and appreciated by yourself. Since both categories involve love and appreciation, I combined them to form a single category, **Validation Needs**. Venus is the planet in charge of your Validation Needs.

The highest needs in Maslow's pyramid are the **Self-Actualization Needs**. These are the things that you do to fulfill your potential as an individual. The Sun is in charge of your Self-Actualization Needs.

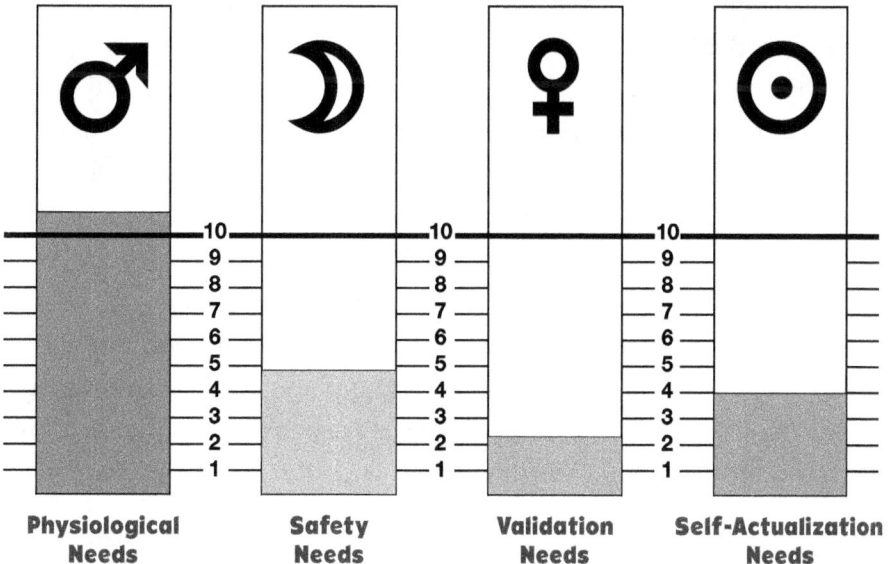

The Need Bank Accounts still exist in a hierarchy, and the lower needs take priority, but each Need Bank Account is independent of the others. If the balance in your Safety Need Account is below the minimum level, you can still receive deposits in your Validation Need Account. However, you won't notice those deposits until you've met your Safety Needs.

This story whittles down the number of Need Bank Accounts to a more manageable four, connects those needs to planets, and establishes a hierarchy that could clarify the relative value of each **Need**.

The Story of Your Need Bank Accounts

The psychology story gets us down from seven Need Bank Accounts to four, but we still need to eliminate one to arrive at the magic number of three. Physiological Needs are the most important needs because they relate to actual survival. But most of the time, your Physiological Needs are met. If you're reading this book, you're not fighting for your life or concerned with your day-to-day survival. Because you can take your Physiological Needs for granted, we can write them out of this story: they're not a part of The Quest for Happiness and we don't need them to build the Happiness GPS.

This leaves us with three Need Bank Accounts: Safety (Moon), Validation (Venus), and Self-Actualization (Sun). Let's connect these to the story of happiness and determine if meeting the minimum balance in these three Need Bank Accounts results in happiness.

When you maintain the minimum balance in your Safety Need Account and your Validation Need Account you get access to your Self-Actualization Account. However, you experience happiness before you reach the minimum balance in your Self-Actualization Need account. This means meeting your Self-Actualization Needs isn't a requirement to create happiness, so we have to take that Need Bank Account out of the story.

This leaves us with two Need Bank Accounts for the happiness story, which is less than ideal. So we'll add a Happiness Bank Account to the story to replace the Self-Actualization Need Account[1]. The planet in charge of your Happiness Bank Account is the planet that rules your First House

---

[1] The Identity Quest story, covered in Part 4, is all about meeting your Self-Actualization Needs.

because the First House contains your happiness. You will use the resources in your Happiness Bank Account to build a foundation of happiness.

The Quest for Happiness

Now, we can build the framework for the story of The Quest for Happiness. Your **Goal** is to build a foundation of happiness. To accomplish this, you must complete three tasks. First, you must acquire resources for your Safety Need Account. Second, you must acquire resources for your Validation Need Account. This gives you access to your Happiness Account, and your final task is to manage your Safety Needs and Validation Needs while gathering resources for your Happiness Account. To make these tasks easier, we'll create a story of the Happiness GPS that will use the map of your birth chart to help you locate and acquire the resources to complete each task.

Each task in The Quest for Happiness is its own story, and we'll build out those stories over the next few chapters. We'll begin with the first task and explore how to manage the balance in your Safety Need Account. We'll create a specific, practical story to define what Safety Needs are and how they relate to your happiness.

Then, we'll assemble the first set of astrology stories, exploring the modality, element, and house placement of the Moon to create the default safety instructions for the Happiness GPS. We'll repeat the process with your Validation Need Account and your Happiness Account to complete the story of The Quest for Happiness.

CHAPTER 8
The Story of Your Safety Needs

Welcome to the first task in The Quest for Happiness: maintain a minimum balance in your Safety Need Account. Your current strategy to acquire safety resources is to win them in the Happiness Casino, and in this chapter we'll take a closer look at the actual Plot-level game you play there. This game involves more skill than luck, so when you understand the game, you can win more than you lose. You'll also learn how to acquire safety resources outside of the Happiness Casino, which eliminates all of the risk and makes it fun to pursue your **GOAL** in the Plot-level game.

The ultimate **GOAL**, however, is to acquire safety resources, so we need a story that explains **WHAT** those are. We'll begin by exploring what Safety Needs are and how the Safety Need Account operates.

The Evolution of Safety Needs

Your top priority in life is to keep living. Every life form fights for survival. The most important needs in Maslow's hierarchy, the Physiological Needs, are things you can't survive without, such as air, food, water, shelter, and sleep. When your Physiological Needs are met, you will live a long and healthy life unless you're eaten by a predator (which satisfies *their* Physiological Needs for food and survival).

All animals come preprogrammed with an emergency response protocol that improves the odds of surviving an encounter with a predator. In human beings, it's the autonomic nervous system, and the response protocol is known as fight or flight.

When triggered, the fight-or-flight response heightens your senses, making you more aware of your surroundings so you can detect possible threats before they become actual threats. In a genuine emergency, your autonomic nervous system either shuts down or diminishes normal biological functions and directs all resources to give you the strength to overcome the threat (fight) or outrun the predator (flight).

The problem is that the fight-or-flight response is extremely expensive. It consumes resources that would otherwise meet your Physiological Needs. It's designed for emergencies only: if you survive the threat, your physical body needs time to recover.

Safety Needs help you optimize the fight-or-flight response by monitoring the potential threat level. Anything you've experienced before is not a threat: it didn't kill you before, so you don't expect it to kill you now. You can recognize known threats on sight and hit the panic button. Anything new or unfamiliar concerns you because it could represent a threat. You power up the fight-or-flight response to evaluate the new situation and remain on high alert until it passes or you can confirm that it is not a threat.

Let's connect this to the story of your Safety Need Account. Any time you encounter something new, unfamiliar, or unexpected, it represents a potential threat and makes a withdrawal from your Safety Need Account. When the balance in your Safety Need Account drops below a minimum level, it activates the fight-or-flight response, which sends you an alert by making you feel tense, stressed, worried, anxious, or fearful. Think of these feelings as alarms. When you notice an alarm, you are meant to investigate what triggered it. If you don't find a problem, you can reset the alarm. If there's an actual problem, you can fix it. In either case, you restore the balance in your Safety Need Account, deactivate the fight-or-flight response, and no longer feel worried or anxious.

This system exists to protect you from actual threats to your survival, which are rare in the modern world. Human beings have evolved to the point that they hope to thrive rather than merely survive, and Safety Needs have evolved to support this. Your Safety Need Account not only monitors potential threats to your survival, it also monitors potential threats to your happiness.

At this point, things get a bit complicated.

When you encounter something unfamiliar or unexpected that interferes with achieving a **Goal** or getting what you **Want**, it makes a withdrawal from your Safety Need Account to make you aware of a potential threat to your happiness. However, a drop in the balance of your Safety Need Account is an *actual* threat to your happiness. The fight-or-flight response kicks in and the alarms sound to alert you to the problem, but because these are the same alarms that sound when you're experiencing a physical threat, a threat to your happiness feels like a threat to your survival. This raises the stakes. It also raises your blood pressure, your stress, and your anxiety.

You assume that the threat is external and look for a solution in the Plot-level story. You head to the Happiness Casino, identify the **Goal**, and bet some of your remaining safety resources, hoping that if you achieve the **Goal**, you'll get what you **Want**, which is enough safety resources to meet your Safety Needs and reset the alarms.

This is how you end up spending so much of your life in the Happiness Casino, playing the Plot-level game in pursuit of safety resources. Let's take a closer look at the Plot-level game and learn how to win it.

Safety Bets and the Plot-Level Game

Think of the Plot-level game as a traditional board game with a timer (see illustration on next page. Each round you have the potential to move ahead a number of spaces toward the finish line. If you reach the finish line before time runs out, you will achieve the **Goal** and win the safety resource jackpot.

You begin the round by choosing a **Goal** you believe will advance you toward the finish line. You pursue that **Goal** until you encounter an **Obstacle**. You have a limited amount of time to choose how to respond to the **Obstacle**, and to make a choice, you have to wager some of your safety resources. You learn the outcome of the choice in the **Resolution**. If you **Win**, you advance in the game and receive additional safety resources. If you **Miss**, you stay where you are in the game and forfeit the resources you bet. If you **Lose**, you go backward in the game, forfeit your bet, and pay an additional penalty from your Safety Need Account.

Remember that your ultimate objective is to increase the balance in your Safety Need Account. Winning the game—reaching the finish line and claiming the safety resource jackpot—may not accomplish this because you have to wager safety resources each round. The jackpot prize may not be large enough to cover your losses.

On the other hand, if you take the time and consistently choose the best options, you can increase the balance in your Safety Need Account while you approach the finish line. Even if time runs out and you don't win the jackpot prize, you still achieved your ultimate objective. And incidentally, choosing the best option is also the fastest route to the finish line and the jackpot prize.

Choosing the best option is less like gambling in a casino and more like gambling in the stock market. The value of an option depends on the current conditions, and timing is important. Let's explore the story of the Options Market and how it relates to your Safety Need Account.

The Options Market

When you encounter an OBSTACLE in the Plot-level game, you visit the Options Market, review the Options Board, and choose the most attractive option. The Options Board includes all the information you need to evaluate and compare each option. This process happens so quickly that you usually don't notice it and you go through this process and analyze the different options automatically. This story will help you understand what you already do.

OPTION BOARD – MARKET RATES				
OPTION	BET COST	WIN	LOSE	WIN %
Option A	5	3	1 + Bet	90%
Option B	10	10	3 + Bet	75%
Option C	15	16	6 + Bet	70%
Option D	25	40	5 + Bet	85%
Option E	35	55	5 + Bet	90%
TIME LEFT TO CHOOSE: 6D 3H 24M				

The first consideration is the BET COST. This is the amount of safety resources you have to wager to choose that option. The BET COST reflects the subjective safety of the option. The more familiar an option is, the less expensive it is.

The next consideration is the WIN amount. This is the prize you will receive if your choice is successful. If the WIN amount is larger than the BET COST, this option has the potential to increase the balance in your Safety Need Account. If the WIN amount is smaller than the BET COST, you will have a net loss of safety even if you overcome the OBSTACLE and advance in the game.

The LOSE column shows you the worst case scenario where you go back a few spaces in the game, lose your bet and pay an additional penalty. If you

Lose, the balance in your Safety Need Account will decrease by the total of the penalty and the **Bet Cost**.

The **Win** % column shows you the odds of a **Win**: an outcome where you receive the prize and advance in the game.

The time left to choose is listed at the bottom of the Option Board. If you don't choose an option before the timer runs out, you will lose a turn.

The best option isn't always obvious. In the example above, Option A is objectively bad because even if you win, you'll still end up with a net loss of safety. Option E is objectively the best because it has a potential profit of 20 and a 90% chance of success, but it's also the most expensive and could result in the biggest loss of safety.

The **Bet Cost** is linked to the current balance in your Safety Need Account. When the balance in your Safety Need Account is low, the **Bet Cost** of the options goes up, but the **Win** amount stays the same. In the Option Board above, Option C, Option D, and Option E are attractive because a **Win** would raise the balance in your Safety Need Account. In the example below, the **Bet Costs** have gone up and the only option with a chance of a profit is Option D.

OPTION BOARD – MARKET RATES

OPTION	BET COST	WIN	LOSE	WIN %
Option A	5 → 8	3	1 + Bet	90%
Option B	10 → 14	10	3 + Bet	75%
Option C	15 → 19	16	6 + Bet	70%
Option D	25 → 35	40	5 + Bet	85%
Option E	35 → 55	55	5 + Bet	90%

TIME LEFT TO CHOOSE: 4 D 19 H 43 M

When the balance in your Safety Need Account is high, the **Bet Cost** of the options goes down, which makes all of the options more attractive. In the example below, you would break even with a **Win** with Option A, and a **Win** with every other option would show a profit.

OPTION BOARD – MARKET RATES

OPTION	BET COST	WIN	LOSE	WIN %
Option A	5 → 3	3	1 + Bet	90%
Option B	10 → 8	10	3 + Bet	75%
Option C	15 → 10	16	6 + Bet	70%
Option D	25 → 15	40	5 + Bet	85%
Option E	35 → 20	55	5 + Bet	90%

TIME LEFT TO CHOOSE: 3 D 15 H 8 M

The next step is to connect the story of the Options Market to your reality so you can activate it.

Activate the Story of the Options Market

You've experienced the changes in the Options Market many times before. Think of a time when you struggled to make a decision. You didn't like any of the options and couldn't find a solution. You decide to sleep on it and pick it up again in the morning. Sure enough, when you considered the story after a good night's sleep, you found a solution you liked.

What actually happened was that you encountered an **Obstacle** in the Plot-level game, visited the Options Market, and didn't see any attractive choices based on the current balance in your Safety Need Account. A good night's sleep added resources to your Safety Need Account, and when you returned to the Options Market, the **Bet Cost** of the options had gone down, and you were able to choose an option that enabled you to make a profit.

Look back on The Story of Your Life and find other examples of how you were able to make a choice and find a solution after stepping away from it for a time, and revise each of those stories to incorporate the story of the Options Market and your Safety Needs. When you recognize how you've experienced this story in the past, it becomes easier to recognize it in the present so you can take advantage of it.

The next time you have trouble making a decision or taking action, apply the story of the Options Market. The challenge is that you don't see an option that leads to a positive outcome, and a net loss of safety will make it harder for you to feel happy.

First, check the countdown clock and see how much time you have before you must either make a decision or lose your turn. If the countdown clock is running out and none of your choices are good, consider the option to let the clock run out without taking action.

If you don't have to make a decision right away, then don't make one. You can afford to wait and see if the Options Market moves in your favor. You can also manipulate the Options Market by adding resources to your Safety Need Account.

How to Acquire Safety Resources

You will acquire safety resources with an astrology story. Your birth chart is a map of The Story of Your Life, and the Moon symbolizes your Safety Needs. The modality of the Moon describes **How** you approach safety. The element of the Moon tells you **Which** language you speak to meet your Safety Needs. And the house the Moon occupies tells you **Where** you can find safety.

In the next chapter, I provide you with default astrology stories for the Happiness GPS that cover the Moon in each of the modalities, elements, and houses. These stories provide the turn-by-turn directions to acquire safety resources, which makes it easier to win when you play in the Happiness Casino. These stories were created using the astrology story tropes presented in Chapter 4.

CHAPTER 9

Safety Need Astrology Stories

Please take a moment and read this introduction before you jump right to the stories that apply to your Moon and take them for a test drive. You need a bit of context to get the most out of this.

These stories are specifically designed to be used within the story of the Options Market and the Happiness Casino. When you don't see an attractive option to overcome an **OBSTACLE**, you can use the modality, element, and/or house story of your Moon to acquire additional safety resources. This can move the Options Market and improve the chances of a positive outcome.

The first paragraph of each story establishes the context and describes how the story trope affects your approach to safety. The second paragraph is how you use the story trope to create a new story and acquire safety resources.

You have two objectives during this process. The first objective is to increase the balance in your Safety Need Account. The second objective is to understand that you created this experience by telling a story. For the best results, follow every instruction, especially the first, which is to state your intention to acquire safety resources.

Okay. Go play with your safety stories. I'll wait here for you.

With that out of your system, we can look at the bigger picture.

I'm providing these astrology stories as examples. By studying these examples, you will understand how I created the stories. You can then use my example stories as a starting point and expand or alter them. This will help you get comfortable creating astrology stories. And with practice, you'll be able to tell better astrology stories.

I created each of these stories by combining the **WHAT** of Safety Needs (the Moon) with a single astrology trope for each modality, element, and house occupied. The objective of these stories is to acquire safety resources, and I selected the tropes that I thought would best support that.

Take some time and read each story. This will help you to become familiar with the structure and the approach to the turn-by-turn Happiness GPS directions. We'll analyze the story structure and approach further in later chapters.

The Moon in the Modalities
Moon in a Cardinal Sign

With the Moon in a Cardinal Sign, you approach your safety **GOAL** as an archery target that you must hit with a single arrow. You spend time planning and preparing, but once you take your shot, there's nothing more you can do. If you hit the target, you take a giant leap forward, but if you miss the target you stay where you are and have to start over again. It's easier to hit the target and acquire safety resources if you move the target closer with a new story about your current situation.

Begin the story by stating your intention to acquire safety resources. Make a note of how you feel right now to be able to track your progress. Identify a target that you believe would meet all of your Safety Needs. Look for ways you can break that objective into a sequence of smaller targets. Treat each task or objective as its own target. When you complete the task and hit the target, you will receive some safety resources. This may not resolve the entire problem, but it will improve conditions. For larger, more complicated tasks, set time-based targets as well as task-based targets so you can acquire safety resources whether you complete a task or not. Take a few moments to explore these stories, adjust your strategies, and gather the safety resources. Notice how you feel now and compare it to how you felt at the start. End the story by acknowledging that you feel better now because you successfully acquired more safety resources.

Moon in a Fixed Sign

With the Moon in a Fixed Sign, meeting your safety **GOAL** is an ongoing process that requires planning, resources, and logistical support. You rely on your internal accounting department to coordinate everything and keep an eye on the big picture. You have multiple simultaneous projects that require safety resources, and your top priority is to keep the projects funded. Each project has a preapproved budget and expected income targets. You have operational accounts with the safety resources budgeted for each **GOAL**, and you also have a substantial reserve of safety resources you maintain to protect against future shortages. Rather than acquiring new safety resources for your current project, you can make existing resources available. You just need a story to get approval from your accounting department.

Begin the story by stating your intention to acquire safety resources. Make a note of how you feel right now to be able to track your progress. Consider the obstacle you face in your current story and review all available options. Focus on the options that promise the best return, but that you can't yet choose. These options cost more safety resources than you have budgeted, and this is why you're unable to commit. You need additional instructions and approval from your accounting department before you can make a choice. Consider each option and identify the potential risk and the potential reward, and also how much additional safety you would need to choose it. Check the countdown clock and become conscious of how long you have to make a choice. Finally, consider the consequences of not making a choice and taking no action at all. Once you've assembled this information, imagine putting it in an eMail and sending it to your accounting department. Trust that your accounting department will review everything and provide you with the answer, and there's nothing more you can do until then. Take a few moments to explore these stories and gather the safety resources. Notice how you feel now and compare it to how you felt at the start. End the story by acknowledging that you feel better now because you successfully acquired more safety resources.

Moon in a Mutable Sign

With the Moon in a Mutable Sign, you take a nonlinear approach to your safety **GOAL**. Rather than identifying a sequence of steps to arrive at the finish line, you break the **GOAL** into component tasks and organize them on a to-do list. When you have checked every item off the list, you will achieve the **GOAL**. The flexibility of this approach allows you to keep moving and avoid most obstacles and delays. But just because you're moving doesn't mean you're making progress. If you hope to acquire resources to meet your safety **GOAL**, you need to organize your to-do list through a new story.

Begin the story by stating your intention to acquire safety resources. Make a note of how you feel right now to be able to track your progress. Create your task list and identify all of the things you can do that will make deposits in your Safety Need Account. Review the list and flag the tasks that are the easiest and fastest to accomplish. Review the list again and identify the tasks that will generate the most safety resources; these tasks require the most effort and take the longest to complete. Completing the easy tasks keeps you motivated and gives you a sense of accomplishment, but the hard tasks are how you make progress. Choose a strategy where you spend a set amount of time working towards a more significant task, and then reward yourself by completing a few easy tasks. This way, you feel a sense of accomplishment *and* you make actual progress. You can also break the more significant tasks into time-based tasks. Each unit of time becomes a task you can check off the list. Take a few moments to explore these stories, adjust your strategies, and gather the safety resources. Notice how you feel now and compare it to how you felt at the start. End the story by acknowledging that you feel better now because you successfully acquired more safety resources.

The Moon in the Elements
Moon in a Fire Sign
With the Moon in a Fire Sign, safety requires passion, intensity, and urgency. You experience safety by taking action and expending energy. For you, safety is a verb, not a noun; it must be expressed to be experienced. You can acquire Fire resources to meet your Safety Needs by expending some energy to heat things up through a new story.

Begin the story by stating your intention to acquire safety resources by engaging with the element of Fire. Make a note of how you feel right now to be able to track your progress. Moving your physical body is a great way to start; anything that gets your heart pumping will warm you up. Find something about your current story that excites you or ignites your passion. Look for a personal connection that creates an emotional investment in the outcome, but be careful not to raise the stakes too high. If all else fails, you can always tap into the energy of your anger. Ideally, find your anger or frustration by exploring an unrelated story. This makes it easier to use the energy of anger to power your current story without setting it on fire. Take a few moments to explore these stories and gather the safety resources. Notice how you feel now and compare it to how you felt at the start. End the story by acknowledging that you feel better now because you successfully acquired more safety resources.

Moon in an Earth Sign
With the Moon in an Earth Sign, you expect to find safety in the physical and material realm. Safety is practical and almost tangible. It's easiest for you to experience safety when you can associate it with something you can touch in the physical world. You can acquire Earth resources to meet your Safety Needs by interacting with the material world through a new story.

Begin the story by stating your intention to acquire safety resources by engaging with the element of Earth. Make a note of how you feel right now to be able to track your progress. Take a moment and become aware of your physical body; feel the weight of it and notice how your feet are on solid ground. When you are present in your physical body, explore the physical world around you. Time spent on a mindless physical activity, such as folding laundry or cleaning out a closet can reconnect you to the world of form and help you to advance in your current story. To find Earth resources in your current story, look for the parts that are constant and stable. You can't change these things, but you can build on them. Take a few moments to explore these stories and gather the safety resources. Notice how you feel now and compare it to how you felt at the start. End the story by acknowledging that you feel better now because you successfully acquired more safety resources.

Moon in an Air Sign

With the Moon in an Air Sign, you expect to find safety in the mental realm of the intellect. Safety is an abstract concept; it's a story, made up of words, so words are enough to meet your Safety Needs. You can acquire Air resources to meet your Safety Needs by rising high above the story to get a bird's eye view through a new story.

Begin the story by stating your intention to acquire safety resources by engaging with the element of Air. Make a note of how you feel right now to be able to track your progress. Shift your attention away from your feelings and your subjective experience of the story and focus on the rational, objective qualities. Tell your current story from the point of view of an observer, not from the point of view of your character. Focus on the facts not on what they mean. See the entire game board and consider the long-term strategy. Sacrifice is sometimes required: you may need to lose a battle to win the war. For now, listen to your head, not to your heart. Revise your current story to reflect the new perspective and the updated strategy. Take a few moments to explore the new story and gather the safety resources. Notice how you feel now and compare it to how you felt at the start. End the story by acknowledging that you feel better now because you successfully acquired more safety resources.

Moon in a Water Sign
With the Moon in a Water Sign, safety is a feeling; you look for it in the internal, personal, subjective realm of your emotions and your unconscious. Words create the bridge between your external story and your internal feelings, but words can never describe the feeling of safety. Even so, to acquire Water resources to meet your Safety Needs, you must find words to differentiate your feelings through a new story.

Begin the story by stating your intention to acquire safety resources by engaging with the element of Water. Make a note of how you feel right now to be able to track your progress. To acquire Water resources, you will need to dive into those feelings and analyze them. When feelings from different stories get tangled up, it muddies the waters making it harder to navigate the stories. Tune into a specific feeling, identify it by name, and then follow it back to its story. Repeat this process with another feeling until you've untangled the feelings and the waters are clear. When you understand what you are feeling and why, you can identify which story needs your attention. Take a few moments to explore these stories and gather the safety resources. Notice how you feel now and compare it to how you felt at the start. End the story by acknowledging that you feel better now because you successfully acquired more safety resources.

The Moon in the Houses
Moon in the First House
With the Moon in your First House, you find safety in your health, happiness, and physical appearance. When you take care of your physical body with movement and exercise, make supportive choices around nutrition and rest, or even take a few moments for personal grooming so you look your best, you generate safety resources. You also generate safety resources when you're engaged in activities that you enjoy and that contribute to your happiness. You can find safety in your current story by connecting it to the First House through a new story.

Begin the story by stating your intention to acquire safety resources from the First House. Make a note of how you feel right now to be able to track your progress. Look for the happiness in your current story: find something about it that gives you pleasure or satisfaction, even if it's a minor detail. Pay attention to your physical body and appreciate how your strength, vitality, and overall health are supporting you. Give some thought to your physical appearance. It may not be possible to feel your most attractive in the current circumstances, but you can at least feel more attractive. Take a few moments to explore these stories and gather the safety resources. Notice how you feel now and compare it to how you felt at the start. End the story by acknowledging that you feel better now because you successfully acquired more safety resources.

Moon in the Second House

With the Moon in your Second House, you find safety in your money, resources, skills, and talents. When you engage with your money and resources, whether by earning money, saving money, managing money, or spending money, you generate safety resources. You also generate safety resources when you're developing skills or using your talents. You can find safety in your current story by connecting it to the Second House through a new story.

Begin the story by stating your intention to acquire safety resources from the Second House. Make a note of how you feel right now to be able to track your progress. Look for all of the ways that money and resources relate to your current story. Consider the impact this story might have on your bottom line. Explore how you could create a profit or at least limit your expenses. Identify the different skills required to achieve your current **Goal** and evaluate how well you're using them. Consider if this story is an opportunity for you to show off your talent or if it's an opportunity to train and develop new skills. Take a few moments to explore these stories and gather the safety resources. Notice how you feel now and compare it to how you felt at the start. End the story by acknowledging that you feel better now because you successfully acquired more safety resources.

Moon in the Third House

With the Moon in your Third House, you find safety in your comfort zone and your habits and routines. The more familiar you are with your environment and the objectives in your current story, the more confident and comfortable you are, and this generates safety resources. You also generate safety resources when you can automate your life, using habits and routines so that you can direct your attention to more interesting or important things. You can find safety in your current story by connecting it to the Third House through a new story.

Begin the story by stating your intention to acquire safety resources from the Third House. Make a note of how you feel right now to be able to track your progress. Review your current story and focus on familiar patterns and consistent elements. Focus on what is old and comfortable rather than what is new and different. Become aware of everything in the story that is operating smoothly and doesn't require your attention. You can feel confident about these elements of the story, and you can draw on them for support. Take a few moments to explore these stories and gather the safety resources. Notice how you feel now and compare it to how you felt at the start. End the story by acknowledging that you feel better now because you successfully acquired more safety resources.

Moon in the Fourth House

With the Moon in your Fourth House, you find safety in your foundation, your sanctuary, and your privacy. When you take care of your foundation, the parts of your life that take priority and make the rest of your life possible, you generate safety resources. You also generate safety resources when you retreat to your personal sanctuary so you can enjoy your privacy and recharge your batteries. You can find safety in your current story by connecting it to the Fourth House through a new story.

Begin the story by stating your intention to acquire safety resources from the Fourth House. Make a note of how you feel right now to be able to track your progress. Consider how the current story relates to your personal foundation. If a successful outcome could strengthen your foundation, you have even more to gain. If the story has no connection to your foundation, it can't disrupt it; you can rely on your foundation for support as you navigate this story. Look for an opportunity to create a moment of privacy so that you can center yourself. If you can't be alone, you can still connect to your thoughts and feelings and appreciate how private they are. Take a few moments to explore these stories and gather the safety resources. Notice how you feel now and compare it to how you felt at the start. End the story by acknowledging that you feel better now because you successfully acquired more safety resources.

Moon in the Fifth House

With the Moon in your Fifth House, you find safety in your creativity, recreation, and risk. When you express your creativity, which includes everything from artistic expression to solving a problem, you generate safety resources. You also generate safety resources when you are having fun, playing games, experiencing pleasure, and taking risks. You can find safety in your current story by connecting it to the Fifth House through a new story.

Begin the story by stating your intention to acquire safety resources from the Fifth House. Make a note of how you feel right now to be able to track your progress. Consider how much fun you're having in your current story. If you're not having fun, the stakes are too high. Adjust the stakes of the story, lower your expectations, and remember that the outcome of the story will not affect your happiness. Find a game you can play within the story to amuse yourself. Think outside the box and look for creative and unusual ways to overcome the challenges. Then consider the risk and the reward (including the entertainment value) and ask how lucky you feel. Take a few moments to explore these stories and gather the safety resources. Notice how you feel now and compare it to how you felt at the start. End the story by acknowledging that you feel better now because you successfully acquired more safety resources.

Moon in the Sixth House

With the Moon in your Sixth House, you find safety in your work and your service. When you spend time working, whether at your job or meeting some other responsibility, you can't expect to be rewarded or appreciated for your effort—but you can expect to generate safety resources. You also generate safety resources when you perform selfless service, offering your time and energy in support of others. You can find safety in your current story by connecting it to the Sixth House through a new story.

Begin the story by stating your intention to acquire safety resources from the Sixth House. Make a note of how you feel right now to be able to track your progress. Identify your job in the current story, and what you're expected to do. Pay close attention to the parts of the story that require the most effort; often they're the parts of the story you resist the most. If you have to do these things, you can at least do them well so that you feel satisfied with your contribution. Consider how you can be of service and how your hard work could make someone else's story a little easier. Remember that your work has value, and it can be its own reward. Take a few moments to explore these stories and gather the safety resources. Notice how you feel now and compare it to how you felt at the start. End the story by acknowledging that you feel better now because you successfully acquired more safety resources.

Moon in the Seventh House

With the Moon in your Seventh House, you find safety in your relationships with other people. When you interact with individuals who play supporting roles in your story, you generate safety resources. You also generate safety resources when you relate to the general public—non-speaking background characters in your story—and when you become involved in stories about people you don't know personally such as celebrities or politicians. You can find safety in your current story by connecting it to the Seventh House through a new story.

Begin the story by stating your intention to acquire safety resources from the Seventh House. Make a note of how you feel right now to be able to track your progress. Shift your focus to the other people involved with your current story, and explore what functions they perform. Look for your partners, the characters who can help you achieve your **GOAL**. If you have an adversary in the story, someone who is making it harder to achieve your **GOAL**, consider how to give them what they **WANT** so you can get what you **WANT**. If you need more support, enlist the help of a new character to help you resolve the issue and advance in the story. Take a few moments to explore these stories and gather the safety resources. Notice how you feel now and compare it to how you felt at the start. End the story by acknowledging that you feel better now because you successfully acquired more safety resources.

Moon in the Eighth House

With the Moon in your Eighth House, you find safety in your debts, obligations, and shared resources. When you engage with debts and obligations by accepting support from others, repaying that support, and obeying the Law of Circulation, you generate safety resources. You also generate safety resources when you combine your resources with others to create more opportunity for all. You can find safety in your current story by connecting to the Eighth House through a new story.

Begin the story by stating your intention to acquire safety resources from the Eighth House. Make a note of how you feel right now to be able to track your progress. Review your current story and make note of what you owe and which obligations you hope to meet. Consider each debt and remember the support you received that created the debt. Look for ways that you can take advantage of your support network to help you advance in your current story. Ask for help and support from people you have helped in the past, and give them the opportunity to repay their debt to you. Take a few moments to explore these stories and gather the safety resources. Notice how you feel now and compare it to how you felt at the start. End the story by acknowledging that you feel better now because you successfully acquired more safety resources.

Moon in the Ninth House

With the Moon in your Ninth House, you find safety in your danger zone and your encounters with experts and authorities. When you leave your comfort zone behind and enter the danger zone, everything is distant, foreign, and unfamiliar. You return with new experiences, a greater understanding of your story, and safety resources. You also generate safety resources when you seek out experts and authorities to help you understand the unknown. You can find safety in your current story by connecting to the Ninth House through a new story.

Begin the story by stating your intention to acquire safety resources from the Ninth House. Make a note of how you feel right now to be able to track your progress. Review your current story and let everything that is familiar fade into the background so you can identify whatever is unfamiliar. This is your opportunity to expand your understanding and experience something new. Seek out the advice of experts or authorities to learn more about it. Other people's experiences can help you see the potential of the unknown and give you some idea of what to expect. When you feel prepared, lean into the unfamiliar and experience it directly. Take a few moments to explore these stories and gather the safety resources. Notice how you feel now and compare it to how you felt at the start. End the story by acknowledging that you feel better now because you successfully acquired more safety resources.

Moon in the Tenth House

With the Moon in your Tenth House, you find safety in your reputation, your advancement, and your public image. When you work for advancement in your personal, social, or professional life, and hope to create a reputation for success, you generate safety resources. You also generate safety resources when you engage with your public image through your social media presence. You can find safety in your current story by connecting to the Tenth House through a new story.

Begin the story by stating your intention to acquire safety resources from the Tenth House. Make a note of how you feel right now to be able to track your progress. Consider your current story and identify how you can use it to raise your profile, improve your reputation, and increase your success. Identify what this story will add to your resume thanks to your individual contribution. Pay attention to how your behavior might look to other people. You aren't the author of the story of your reputation. Your reputation is based on how your character behaves in someone else's story. Project the qualities you would like the world to notice, even if they don't reflect your inner experience. Take a few moments to explore these stories and gather the safety resources. Notice how you feel now and compare it to how you felt at the start. End the story by acknowledging that you feel better now because you successfully acquired more safety resources.

Moon in the Eleventh House

With the Moon in your Eleventh House, you find safety in your ambitions, aspirations, and acquisitions. When you engage with your ambitions, whether you create the story of your dream or work to make it a reality, you generate safety resources. You also generate safety resources when you set out to acquire the things you believe will make you happy. You can find safety in your current story by connecting it to the Eleventh House through a new story.

Begin the story by stating your intention to acquire safety resources from the Eleventh House. Make a note of how you feel right now to be able to track your progress. Consider the **GOAL** of your current story and review what you hope to accomplish. Now find a connection between this **GOAL** and your bigger dreams of happiness. Remind yourself of your bigger purpose and decide how this current story serves that **GOAL**. If you can see how achieving your current objectives will help you acquire something you believe will make you happy, the current story will become more important. If you realize the current story has no connection to your happiness, look for the fastest way to resolve the story so you can change course and pursue happiness. Take a few moments to explore these stories and gather the safety resources. Notice how you feel now and compare it to how you felt at the start. End the story by acknowledging that you feel better now because you successfully acquired more safety resources.

Moon in the Twelfth House

With the Moon in your Twelfth House, you find safety in adversity and in your blind spot. Adversity takes many forms, but it always creates an **OBSTACLE** you must overcome to achieve your **GOAL** and advance in your story. When you experience adversity you have the opportunity to discover hidden strength, and to generate safety resources. Because your safety resources occupy your blind spot, they're easy to overlook. You can find safety in your current story by connecting it to the Twelfth House through a new story.

Begin the story by stating your intention to acquire safety resources from the Twelfth House. Make a note of how you feel right now to be able to track your progress. Review your current story and look for the **OBSTACLE** and the challenges you faced. Take a thorough inventory of everything that limits you or makes it harder for you to get what you **WANT**. Now consider that however much adversity you faced, you survived it. Explore how you overcame the **OBSTACLE**, and notice what you learned from the experience. You paid a price with these challenges: find the gift you received in exchange. Overcoming adversity has made you aware of your strength, your courage, and your resilience. These gifts are yours and you can draw on them at any time. Take a few moments to explore these stories and gather the safety resources. Notice how you feel now and compare it to how you felt at the start. End the story by acknowledging that you feel better now because you successfully acquired more safety resources.

CHAPTER 10
The Story of Your Validation Needs

In its purest, uncut form, validation is Love. Even when diluted and packaged for distribution as approval, appreciation, or gratitude, the Love shines through. When you receive a deposit in your Validation Need Account, the feeling of Love creates a moment of Joy. Joy is far beyond Happiness. Happiness only means you no longer feel bad; Joy feels better than anything you've ever experienced. The experience is fleeting, but once you've had a taste of it, you will do anything to experience it again. You might as well face it: you're addicted to Love.

In many ways, the Human Game is a Love story. Love is often a dominant theme in The Story of Your Life. As you advance through the Human Game, your understanding of Love evolves. It begins as something that exists outside of you, which you must attain from other people. You compete for validation resources in the Happiness Casino but you value these resources only because you can convert them to safety resources. When your Safety Needs are met, you begin to experience the wonderful feelings of Love and realize that Love is essential to your happiness. When you discover that Love is everywhere, including within you, you learn to meet your Validation Needs and build a foundation of happiness without relying on other people's approval.

As you build on the foundation of happiness, you realize that Love is infinite, and the more you express it, the more you experience it. You play with gratitude and appreciation and the story of the Law of Attraction to develop The City of Your Life and create Prosperity. You understand that Love is eternal and beyond form. You turn your attention away from the

Plot-level story and seek the Truth of the Theme-level story, where you find the purest expression of Love and experience Joy.

Your experience of Love depends on your experience of safety.

When your Safety Needs are not met—when the balance in your Safety Need Account is below the minimum level—you are driven by the need to survive. Your experience of reality embodies the Lie of Duality. Resources are limited, and you must compete for them. When you win, someone else loses; and when you lose, someone else wins.

When your Safety Needs are met—when the balance in your Safety Need Account is above the minimum level—you aspire to thrive. Your experience of reality extends toward the Truth of Unity. Resources are infinite, and the world grows less competitive and more cooperative. Winning and losing are still options, but the best option is when everybody wins.

Think of your Safety Need Account as a reality light switch. Until you build a stable foundation of safety, the lights will flicker on and off. Your experience of validation can change from moment to moment. If you think your Validation Needs aren't being met, the first thing to do is to check the lights. You can't see the balance in your Validation Need Account in the dark.

Validation resources fall into two categories: **external approval** and **internal esteem**. You can win external approval in the Happiness Casino when other people make deposits in your Validation Need Account with an expression of approval, appreciation, or love. You can't rely on external approval, however. To maintain a minimum balance in your Validation Need Account, you need internal esteem. You can't find internal esteem in the Happiness Casino: you have to build it yourself out of external approval. Because you start with external approval, we'll begin the story of your Validation Needs in the Happiness Casino.

Approval Expectations in the Happiness Casino

When the balance in your Safety Need Account is below the minimum level, you view validation resources only in terms of safety. In the currency of happiness, safety resources are silver and validation resources are gold. Deposits in your Validation Need Account are converted to safety resources before you can experience any Joy. This continues until you restore the minimum balance in your Safety Need Account.

While playing the Plot-level games in the Happiness Casino, you may receive random deposits in your Validation Need Account when other people express gratitude, appreciation, or approval of you. If you're low on safety, one of these random validation deposits can turn things around, improve your options, and increase your chance of success. But why wait for that validation? Why not borrow against it, and pay back the loan when it arrives? When you're low on safety resources, you can use your Validation Resource Credit Card to buy better options now and pay for them later.

This can be an excellent strategy so long as you are able to pay off the debt promptly by restoring the minimum balance in your Safety Need Account (and remember, you can do this outside of the Happiness Casino). If you don't pay off the safety debt, your Expectations of Approval will make it impossible to meet your Validation Needs or experience happiness.

One reason that you aren't happy when you get what you **Want** is that you spent more safety resources than you received, so it cost too much. But if what you receive doesn't meet your expectations, you also won't be happy with the outcome. This is especially relevant with validation resources.

No matter how much validation you receive, if it's less than you expect, you will not be happy with the outcome. No matter how little validation you receive, if it's more than you expect, you will be happy with the outcome. This is worth remembering. You can't control how much validation you receive from other people, but you can control how much you expect.

The first problem with using the Validation Resource Credit Card is that the bigger the safety debt is, the higher your Expectations of Approval are. You expect more validation so you can pay off the debt, but you're less likely to receive enough to meet the expectation and be happy with the outcome.

This brings us to the second problem. When an expectation is not met, it makes a withdrawal from your Safety Need Account. You feel less safe, which means you need even more validation to cover the debt, which increases your Expectations of Approval, making them even harder to meet.

The third problem is that when other people fail to meet your Expectations of Approval, it can make you angry and resentful toward them. This makes other people even less inclined to express love and appreciation for you.

The only way to break this cycle is to manage your Safety Needs. First, use the Happiness GPS and the astrology stories related to your Moon to add resources to your Safety Need Account. This will lower the stakes of the story and make it easier to address your Expectations of Approval.

Once you're feeling safe, take a few moments to become conscious of your Expectations of Approval. Identify an individual you feel owes you validation resources, and question that story. Exactly how much approval, appreciation, and validation do you expect to receive from this person? What would they have to do to meet your expectations? You may be surprised at how unrealistic your unconscious expectations are. If possible, drop your expectations entirely. The truth is that you don't need approval from this person. If that's too difficult, adjust your expectations so that they're at least reasonable.

The higher the balance in your Safety Need Account, the easier it is to manage your Expectations of Approval because you no longer require validation resources to survive. You pursue validation resources because they feel good and can give you a taste of Joy. You can win validation resources in the Happiness Casino when you play validation games.

Validation Games in the Happiness Casino

When you play validation games in the Happiness Casino, you use both safety resources and validation resources. The objective is to have someone deposit validation resources in your Validation Need Account by expressing approval, appreciation, or love for you. The easiest way to achieve this is to express approval, appreciation or love for that person. When you make a deposit in someone else's Validation Need Account, they are far more likely to make a deposit in yours.

When the balance in your Safety Need Account is low, you're less willing to spend validation resources by expressing appreciation for other people. There's no guarantee you will get an immediate return on your investment, and you might receive less validation than you give. When you're in survival mode, you worry that expressing appreciation could lower the balance in your Validation Need Account.

When the balance in your Safety Need Account is high enough, you begin to understand how different validation resources are from safety resources. To meet your Safety Needs, you must experience safety. To meet your Validation Needs, you must both *experience* love and *express* love. When you spend safety resources, they leave your Safety Need Account and the balance goes down. When you spend validation resources, they stay in your Validation Need Account, and the balance goes up. Let's explore why.

The balance in your Validation Need Account reflects the amount of active validation resources available to you. To experience love and appreciation, you need to express love and appreciation. You must keep the energy of validation circulating. If you let validation resources sit in your Validation Need Account for too long, they grow dormant, which lowers the balance in your Validation Need Account. When someone expresses love or appreciation of you, their active validation resources activate your dormant validation resources. You experience this as a deposit in your Validation Need Account because the balance in your account goes up, although no actual resources changed hands.

In theory, validation games are easy to win. You can prepare for the games by expressing love and appreciation for anything in your current story: this activates your validation resources and raises the balance in your Validation Need Account. To play the game, you choose a partner and attempt to make a deposit in their Validation Need Account by expressing approval, appreciation, or love. If you succeed and activate some of their validation resources, it immediately activates more of your validation resources, raising the balance in your Validation Need Account. It also increases the chance that your partner will attempt to make a deposit in your Validation Need Account at some point in the future.

In practice, validation games require a lot of skill. Fluctuations in your Safety Needs can interfere with your experience of validation, and your unconscious Expectations of Approval make it harder to feel the love.

To get better at making successful deposits in other people's Validation Need Accounts, you will need to become familiar with the four different Validation Languages. The element of Venus in the birth chart determines **WHICH** language you speak for validation. You express validation in this language and you expect to experience validation in this language. If someone speaks a different language than you, you may not receive the full value of the validation they're sending. The best way to make a deposit in someone else's Validation Need Account is to speak their language.

Validation games can take you only so far. You can't manage the balance in your Validation Need Account if you rely on external approval. You need the ability to activate your own validation resources. This requires internal esteem.

The Story of Internal Esteem

Internal esteem gives you the ability to validate yourself and have that experience be as meaningful and as satisfying as if the approval came from someone else. Internal esteem isn't meant to replace external approval. It supplements external approval, which makes it easier to maintain a minimum balance in your Validation Need Account. When you activate your internal esteem resources, you attract more external approval resources. But most importantly, the amount of internal esteem you have determines how much external approval you can receive from other people. In other words, other people can love you only as much as you love yourself.

You build internal esteem from external approval. When you consistently receive external approval for something, you increasingly believe that you deserve it. You are worthy of praise, appreciation, and love as long as it's directed at this quality. This gives you permission to appreciate yourself for that quality: it gives you worth and value. When you know your worth, you no longer need other people to validate it, and you no longer expect other people to validate it. Others will still validate it from time to time, and because you have no expectations, you get the full benefit of the external approval, which further activates your internal esteem.

The key is to start with something small and specific. Don't get caught up in your bigger, lifelong stories about self-worth, self-esteem, and whatever love your parents failed to provide. Focus on what you can do right now to experience more validation and advance toward happiness. Find at least one aspect of yourself that you know has value. Make a point of appreciating yourself for that quality and noticing how this raises the balance in your Validation Need Account. Once you know you can love yourself for one quality, repeat the process with another. The modality, element, and house of Venus in your birth chart can help you identify these qualities and activate your validation resources.

How to Activate Validation Resources

You will activate your validation resources with an astrology story. Your birth chart is a map of The Story of Your Life. Venus symbolizes your Validation Needs. The modality of Venus describes **How** you approach validation. The element of Venus tells you **Which** validation language you speak. And the house Venus occupies tells you **Where** you can find validation.

In the next chapter, I provide you with default astrology stories for the Happiness GPS that cover Venus in each of the modalities, elements, and houses. These stories provide the turn-by-turn directions to activate validation resources and raise the balance in your Validation Need Account. These stories were created using the astrology story tropes presented in Chapter 4.

CHAPTER 11
Validation Need Astrology Stories

At first glance, the Venus/Validation Need stories look quite similar to the Moon/Safety Need stories. They follow the same format: the first paragraph establishes the context and explores how the story trope affects your approach to validation, and the second paragraph guides you to use the story trope to experience validation. The Venus stories even use the same astrology story tropes as the Moon stories. But this is where the similarities end.

The objective of the Moon stories is to acquire safety resources. This is a straightforward process: all you need to meet your Safety Needs is enough safety resources. The modality (**How**), element (**Which**), and house occupied (**Where**) represent three different and complementary ways to acquire safety resources.

Meeting your Validation Needs is more complicated. You don't have to acquire validation resources, but you do have to activate them. Lowering your Expectations of Approval is the most effective way to be happy with the approval you experience. The modality addresses **How** you can lower your Expectations of Approval. The element addresses **Which** validation language you speak so you can activate your validation resources. The house occupied tells you **Where** you will find the things you can easily love and appreciate, both in general and about yourself, so you can use these qualities to build internal esteem.

As with the Moon/Safety Need stories, follow the instructions precisely so you are conscious that you are creating a story, and that story is what changes your experience of reality by raising the balance in your Validation Need Account.

After you've explored your own Venus stories, take some time to compare and contrast these stories with the related Moon story. The modality stories have the most significant changes, and the house occupied stories have the fewest. And yet, because the subject of the story is different, the stories are different.

Venus in the Modalities
Venus in a Cardinal Sign

With Venus in a Cardinal Sign, you approach your validation **GOAL** as an archery target that you must hit with a single arrow. You spend time planning and preparing, but once you take your shot, you're done. If you hit the target, you take a giant leap forward, but if you miss the target you stay where you are and have to start over again. It's easier to hit the target and activate your validation resources if you move the target closer by telling a new story.

Begin the story by stating your intention to activate your validation resources. Make a note of how you feel right now to be able to track your progress. Identify a target—a **GOAL** that you believe would meet all of your Validation Needs when you achieve it. Look for ways you can break that **GOAL** into a sequence of smaller targets. Treat each task or objective as its own target. When you complete the task and hit the target, take a moment to validate yourself and appreciate what you've accomplished. For larger, more complicated tasks, set time-based targets as well as task-based targets so you can activate your validation resources whether you complete a task or not. Take a few moments to explore these stories, adjust your Expectations of Approval, and gather the validation resources. Notice how you feel now and compare it to how you felt at the start. End the story by acknowledging that you feel better now because you successfully activated your validation resources.

Venus in a Fixed Sign

With Venus in a Fixed Sign, meeting your validation **GOAL** is an ongoing process that requires planning, resources, and logistical support. You rely on your internal accounting department to coordinate everything and keep an eye on the big picture. You have multiple simultaneous projects that can activate validation resources, and each project has expected validation targets. If you repeatedly fail to receive the expected amount of approval from a specific project, you can call the accounting department for support. The accounting department will adjust the expectations for that project, and cover the shortfall with surplus validation from other projects. This maintains a consistent balance in your Validation Need Account. You just need a story to let the accounting department know they need to resolve the issue.

Begin the story by stating your intention to activate your validation resources. Make a note of how you feel right now to be able to track your progress. Review the recent history of your current story, and compare the validation you received with the validation you expected. Consider how much validation you believe you are owed to this point, and define what would need to happen to repay that debt. Make a note of how possible this is, how likely it is, and how reasonable it is. Look for any opportunities to generate your own validation resources rather than expect them from someone else. Now imagine sending all of this information to the accounting department in an email. You've now done everything you can do, so take a moment to validate yourself for taking care of this issue. While you're waiting for a response from the accounting department, check in on other projects and enjoy the validation they generate. Notice how you feel now and compare it to how you felt at the start. End the story by acknowledging that you feel better now because you successfully activated your validation resources.

Venus in a Mutable Sign

With Venus in a Mutable Sign, you take a nonlinear approach to your validation **GOAL**. Rather than identifying a sequence of steps to arrive at the finish line, you break the **GOAL** into component tasks and organize them on a to-do list. Each time you check an item off the list, you feel a sense of accomplishment that activates some of your validation resources. When you have checked every item off the list, you will achieve the GOAL and claim the associated validation resources. The flexibility of this approach allows you to keep moving and avoid most obstacles and delays. But just because you're moving doesn't mean you're making progress. If you hope to activate your validation resources, you need to organize your to-do list through a new story.

Begin the story by stating your intention to activate your validation resources. Make a note of how you feel right now to be able to track your progress. Create your task list and identify all you can do that will make deposits in your Validation Need Account. Review the list and flag the tasks that are the easiest and fastest to accomplish. Review the list again and identify the tasks that will generate the most validation resources; these tasks require the most effort and take the longest to complete. Completing the easy tasks keeps you motivated and gives you a sense of accomplishment, but the hard tasks are how you make progress and create a more substantial experience of validation. Choose a strategy to spend a set amount of time working toward a more significant task, and then reward yourself by completing a few easy tasks. This way, you feel a sense of accomplishment *and* you make actual progress. You can also break the more significant tasks into time-based tasks. Each unit of time becomes a task you can check off the list. Take a few moments to explore these stories, adjust your Expectations of Approval, and gather the validation resources. Notice how you feel now and compare it to how you felt at the start. End the story by acknowledging that you feel better now because you successfully activated your validation resources.

Venus in the Elements
Venus in a Fire Sign

With Venus in a Fire Sign, validation requires passion, intensity, and urgency. You experience validation by taking action and expending energy. For you, validation is a verb, not a noun; it must be expressed to be experienced. You can acquire Fire resources to meet your Validation Needs by expending some energy to heat things up through a new story.

Begin the story by stating your intention to activate your validation resources by engaging with the element of Fire. Make a note of how you feel right now to be able to track your progress. Moving your physical body is a great way to start; anything that gets your heart pumping will warm you up. Find something about your current story that excites you or ignites your passion. Look for a personal connection that creates an emotional investment in the outcome, but be careful not to raise the stakes too high. If all else fails, you can always tap into the energy of your anger. Ideally, find your anger or frustration by exploring an unrelated story. This makes it easier to use the energy of anger to power your current story without setting it on fire. Now take that passionate energy and use it to express love and appreciation for something. Speak—or even shout—about things that you value, and things you are grateful for. Notice how you feel now and compare it to how you felt at the start. End the story by acknowledging that you feel better now because you successfully activated your validation resources.

Venus in an Earth Sign

With Venus in an Earth Sign, you expect to find validation in the physical and material realm. Validation is practical and almost tangible. It's easiest for you to experience validation when you can associate it with something you can touch in the physical world. You can acquire Earth resources to meet your Validation Needs by interacting with the material world through a new story.

Begin the story by stating your intention to activate your validation resources by engaging with the element of Earth. Make a note of how you feel right now to be able to track your progress. Take a moment and become aware of your physical body; feel the weight of it and notice how your feet are on solid ground. When you are present in your physical body, explore the physical world around you, enjoying the sensations and expressing gratitude for it. Think about the tangible expressions of love and esteem in your life: gifts others have given you that made you feel validated. If you're able to put your hands on one of these objects, do it. The object is tangible evidence that you are loved. As you reflect on the object, the story behind it, and why that story matters to you, you will activate your validation resources. Notice how you feel now and compare it to how you felt at the start. End the story by acknowledging that you feel better now because you successfully activated your validation resources.

Venus in an Air Sign

With Venus in an Air Sign, you expect to find validation in the mental realm of the intellect. Validation is an abstract concept; it's a story, made up of words, so words are enough to meet your Validation Needs. You can acquire Air resources and activate your Validation Needs by rising high above the story to get a bird's eye view through a new story.

Begin the story by stating your intention to activate your validation resources by engaging with the element of Air. Make a note of how you feel right now to be able to track your progress. Shift your attention away from your feelings and your subjective experience of the story and focus on the rational, objective qualities. Tell your current story from the point of view of an observer, not from the point of view of your character. Focus on the facts, not on what they mean. Now that you have some perspective on the story, look for parts of the story that you can appreciate. Find the beauty in the story and describe it. Rather than lamenting how the story is not what you expected, celebrate the perfection of the story for what it is. Take a few moments to explore the new story and activate the validation resources. Notice how you feel now and compare it to how you felt at the start. End the story by acknowledging that you feel better now because you successfully activated your validation resources.

Venus in a Water Sign

With Venus in a Water Sign, validation is a feeling; you look for it in the internal, personal, subjective realm of your emotions and your unconscious. Words create the bridge between your external story and your internal feelings, but words can never describe the feeling of validation. Even so, to acquire Water resources to meet your Validation Needs, you must find words to differentiate your feelings through a new story.

Begin the story by stating your intention to activate your validation resources by engaging with the element of Water. Make a note of how you feel right now to be able to track your progress. To acquire Water resources, you will need to dive into those feelings and analyze them. When feelings from different stories get tangled up, it muddies the waters and makes it harder to navigate the stories. Tune into a specific feeling, identify it by name, and then follow it back to its story. Repeat this process with another feeling until you've untangled the feelings and the waters are clear. When you understand what you're feeling and why, you can locate a feeling of gratitude and use it to activate your validation resources. Surrender to the feeling of gratitude and let yourself flow with the current. It will lead you to the source of Love that connects to every story. Notice how you feel now and compare it to how you felt at the start. End the story by acknowledging that you feel better now because you successfully activated your validation resources.

Venus in the Houses
Venus in the First House

With Venus in your First House, you find validation in your health, happiness, and physical appearance. When you take care of your physical body with movement and exercise, make supportive choices around nutrition and rest, or even take a few moments for personal grooming so you look your best, you activate validation resources. You also activate validation resources when you're engaged in activities that you enjoy and that contribute to your happiness. You can find validation in your current story by connecting it to the First House through a new story.

Begin the story by stating your intention to activate validation resources in the First House. Make a note of how you feel right now to be able to track your progress. Look for the happiness in your current story: find something about it that gives you pleasure or satisfaction, even if it's a minor detail. Pay attention to your physical body and appreciate how your strength, vitality, and overall health are supporting you. Give some thought to your physical appearance. It may not be possible to feel your most attractive in the current circumstances, but you can at least feel more attractive. Take a few moments to appreciate these stories, express gratitude for them, and activate the validation resources. Notice how you feel now and compare it to how you felt at the start. End the story by acknowledging that you feel better now because you successfully activated your validation resources.

Venus in the Second House

With Venus in your Second House, you find validation in your money, resources, skills, and talents. When you engage with your money and resources, whether by earning money, saving money, managing money, or spending money, you activate validation resources. You also activate validation resources when you're developing skills or using your talents. You can find validation in your current story by connecting it to the Second House through a new story.

Begin the story by stating your intention to activate validation resources in the Second House. Make a note of how you feel right now to be able to track your progress. Look for all of the ways that money and resources relate to your current story. Consider the impact this story might have on your bottom line. Explore how you could create a profit or at least limit your expenses. Identify the different skills required to achieve your current GOAL and validate yourself for how well you're using them. Consider if this story is an opportunity for you to show off your talent or if it's an opportunity to train and develop new skills. Take a few moments to appreciate these stories, express gratitude for them, and activate the validation resources. Notice how you feel now and compare it to how you felt at the start. End the story by acknowledging that you feel better now because you successfully activated your validation resources.

Venus in the Third House

With Venus in your Third House, you find validation in your comfort zone and your habits and routines. The more familiar you are with your environment and the objectives in your current story, the more confident and comfortable you are, and this activates your validation resources. You also activate validation resources when you can automate your life, using habits and routines to direct your attention to more interesting or important things. You can find validation in your current story by connecting it to the Third House through a new story.

Begin the story by stating your intention to activate validation resources in the Third House. Make a note of how you feel right now to be able to track your progress. Review your current story and focus on familiar patterns and consistent elements. Focus on what is old and comfortable rather than what is new and different. Become aware of everything in the story that is operating smoothly and doesn't require your attention. You can feel confident about these elements of the story, and you can draw on them for support. Take a few moments to appreciate these stories, express gratitude for them, and activate the validation resources. Notice how you feel now and compare it to how you felt at the start. End the story by acknowledging that you feel better now because you successfully activated your validation resources.

Venus in the Fourth House

With Venus in your Fourth House, you find validation in your foundation, your sanctuary, and your privacy. When you take care of your foundation—the parts of your life that take priority and make the rest of your life possible—you activate validation resources. You also activate validation resources when you retreat to your personal sanctuary to enjoy your privacy and recharge your batteries. You can find validation in your current story by connecting it to the Fourth House through a new story.

Begin the story by stating your intention to activate validation resources in the Fourth House. Make a note of how you feel right now to be able to track your progress. Consider how the current story relates to your personal foundation. If a successful outcome could strengthen your foundation, you have even more to gain. If the story has no connection to your foundation, it can't disrupt it; you can rely on your foundation for support as you navigate this story. Look for an opportunity to create a moment of privacy so that you can center yourself. If you can't be alone, you can still connect to your thoughts and feelings and appreciate how private they are. Take a few moments to appreciate these stories, express gratitude for them, and activate the validation resources. Notice how you feel now and compare it to how you felt at the start. End the story by acknowledging that you feel better now because you successfully activated your validation resources.

Venus in the Fifth House

With Venus in your Fifth House, you find validation in your creativity, recreation, and risk. When you express your creativity, which includes everything from artistic expression to solving a problem, you activate validation resources. You also activate validation resources when you are having fun, playing games, experiencing pleasure, and taking risks. You can find validation in your current story by connecting it to the Fifth House through a new story.

Begin the story by stating your intention to activate validation resources in the Fifth House. Make a note of how you feel right now to be able to track your progress. Consider how much fun you're having in your current story. If you're not having fun, the stakes are too high. Adjust the stakes of the story, lower your expectations, and remember that the outcome of the story will not affect your happiness. Find a game you can play within the story to amuse yourself. Think outside the box and look for creative and unusual ways to overcome the challenges and validate yourself for these innovative ideas. Then consider the risk and the reward (including the entertainment value) and ask how lucky you feel. Take a few moments to appreciate these stories, express gratitude for them, and activate the validation resources. Notice how you feel now and compare it to how you felt at the start. End the story by acknowledging that you feel better now because you successfully activated your validation resources.

Venus in the Sixth House

With Venus in your Sixth House, you find validation in your work and your service. When you spend time working, whether at your job or meeting some other responsibility, you can't expect to be rewarded or appreciated for your effort—but you can expect to activate validation resources. You also activate validation resources when you perform selfless service by offering your time and energy in support of others. You can find validation in your current story by connecting it to the Sixth House through a new story.

Begin the story by stating your intention to activate validation resources in the Sixth House. Make a note of how you feel right now to be able to track your progress. Identify your job in the current story and what you're expected to do. Pay close attention to the parts of the story that require the most effort; often they're the parts of the story you resist the most. If you have to do these things, you can at least do them well and feel satisfied with your contribution. Consider how you can be of service and how your hard work could make someone else's story a little easier. Remember that your work has value and it can be its own reward. Take a few moments to appreciate these stories, express gratitude for them, and activate the validation resources. Notice how you feel now and compare it to how you felt at the start. End the story by acknowledging that you feel better now because you successfully activated your validation resources.

Venus in the Seventh House

With Venus in your Seventh House, you find validation in your relationships with other people. When you interact with individuals who play supporting roles in your story, you activate validation resources. You also activate validation resources when you relate to the general public—nonspeaking background characters in your story—and when you become involved in stories about people you don't know personally, such as celebrities or politicians. You can find validation in your current story by connecting it to the Seventh House through a new story.

Begin the story by stating your intention to activate validation resources in the Seventh House. Make a note of how you feel right now to be able to track your progress. Shift your focus to the other people involved with your current story and explore what functions they perform. Look for your partners: the characters who can help you achieve your GOAL. If you have an adversary in the story, someone who is making it harder to achieve your

GOAL, consider how to give them what they **WANT** so you can get what you **WANT**. If you need more support, enlist the help of a new character to help you resolve the issue and advance in the story. Take a few moments to appreciate these stories about other people, express gratitude for how well other people fulfill their functions in your story, and activate the validation resources. Notice how you feel now and compare it to how you felt at the start. End the story by acknowledging that you feel better now because you successfully activated your validation resources.

Venus in the Eighth House

With Venus in your Eighth House, you find validation in your debts, obligations, and shared resources. When you engage with debts and obligations by accepting support from others, repaying that support, and obeying the Law of Circulation, you activate validation resources. You also activate validation resources when you combine your resources with others to create more opportunity for all. You can find validation in your current story by connecting to the Eighth House through a new story.

Begin the story by stating your intention to activate validation resources in the Eighth House. Make a note of how you feel right now to be able to track your progress. Review your current story and make note of what you owe and which obligations you hope to meet. Consider each debt and remember the support you received that created the debt. Take a few moments to appreciate that support and express gratitude for it. Look for ways that you can take advantage of your support network to help you advance in your current story. Ask for help and support from people you have helped in the past, and give them the opportunity to repay their debt to you. Take a few moments to appreciate these stories, express gratitude for them, and activate the validation resources. Notice how you feel now and compare it to how you felt at the start. End the story by acknowledging that you feel better now because you successfully activated your validation resources.

Venus in the Ninth House

With Venus in your Ninth House, you find validation in your danger zone and your encounters with experts and authorities. When you leave your comfort zone behind and enter the danger zone, everything is distant, foreign, and unfamiliar. You return with new experiences, a greater understanding of your story, and validation resources. You also activate validation resources when you seek out experts and authorities to help you understand the unknown. You can find validation in your current story by connecting to the Ninth House through a new story.

Begin the story by stating your intention to activate validation resources in the Ninth House. Make a note of how you feel right now to be able to track your progress. Review your current story and let everything that is familiar fade into the background so you can identify whatever is unfamiliar. This is your opportunity to expand your understanding and experience something new. Seek out the advice of experts or authorities to learn more about it, and take a moment to express gratitude for their help. Other people's experiences can help you see the potential of the unknown and give you some idea of what to expect. When you feel prepared, lean into the unfamiliar and experience it directly. Take a few moments to appreciate these stories, express gratitude for them, and activate the validation resources. Notice how you feel now and compare it to how you felt at the start. End the story by acknowledging that you feel better now because you successfully activated your validation resources.

Venus in the Tenth House

With Venus in your Tenth House, you find validation in your reputation, your advancement, and your public image. When you work for advancement in your personal, social, or professional life and hope to create a reputation for success, you activate validation resources. You also activate validation resources when you engage with your public image through your social media presence. You can find validation in your current story by connecting to the Tenth House through a new story.

Begin the story by stating your intention to activate validation resources in the Tenth House. Make a note of how you feel right now to be able to track your progress. Consider your current story and identify how you can use it to raise your profile, improve your reputation, and increase your success. Identify what this story will add to your resume thanks to your individual contribution. Pay attention to how your behavior might look to other people. You are not the author of the story of your reputation. Your reputation is based on how your character behaves in someone else's story. Project the qualities you would like the world to notice, even if they don't reflect your inner experience. Take a few moments to appreciate these stories, express gratitude for them, and activate the validation resources. Notice how you feel now and compare it to how you felt at the start. End the story by acknowledging that you feel better now because you successfully activated your validation resources.

Venus in the Eleventh House

With Venus in your Eleventh House, you find validation in your ambitions, aspirations, and acquisitions. When you engage with your ambitions, whether you create the story of your dream or work to make it a reality, you activate validation resources. You also activate validation resources when you set out to acquire the things you believe will make you happy. You can find validation in your current story by connecting it to the Eleventh House through a new story.

Begin the story by stating your intention to activate validation resources in the Eleventh House. Make a note of how you feel right now to be able to track your progress. Consider the GOAL of your current story and review what you hope to accomplish. Now find a connection between this GOAL and your bigger dreams of happiness. Remind yourself of your bigger purpose and decide how this current story serves that GOAL. If you can see how achieving your current objectives will help you acquire something you need to be happy, the current story will become more important. If you realize the current story has no connection to your happiness, look for the fastest way to resolve the story so you can change course and pursue happiness. Take a few moments to appreciate these stories, express gratitude for them, and activate the validation resources. Notice how you feel now and compare it to how you felt at the start. End the story by acknowledging that you feel better now because you successfully activated your validation resources.

Venus in the Twelfth House

With Venus in your Twelfth House, you find validation in adversity and in your blind spot. Adversity takes many forms, but it always creates an **OBSTACLE** you must overcome to achieve your **GOAL** and advance in your story. When you experience adversity you have the opportunity to discover hidden strength and to activate validation resources. Because your validation resources occupy your blind spot, they're easy to overlook. You can find validation in your current story by connecting it to the Twelfth House through a new story.

Begin the story by stating your intention to activate validation resources in the Twelfth House. Make a note of how you feel right now to be able to track your progress. Review your current story and look for the **OBSTACLE** and the challenges you faced. Take a thorough inventory of everything that limits you or makes it harder for you to get what you **WANT**. Now consider that however much adversity you faced, you survived it. Explore how you overcame the **OBSTACLE**, and notice what you learned from the experience. Overcoming adversity has made you aware of your strength, your courage, and your resilience. Take a few moments and validate yourself for what you have accomplished so far. You paid a price with these challenges; find the gift you received in exchange. These gifts are yours and you can draw on them at any time. Take a few moments to appreciate these stories, express gratitude for them, and activate the validation resources. Notice how you feel now and compare it to how you felt at the start. End the story by acknowledging that you feel better now because you successfully activated your validation resources.

CHAPTER 12
The Story of Your Happiness Account

You have reached the final task in The Quest for Happiness. Having completed the first two tasks, you can now maintain a minimum balance in both your Safety Need Account and your Validation Need Account. These give you access to your Happiness Account, for which you can acquire and store the happiness resources you will use to build your foundation of happiness. Once again, you will use the Happiness GPS to locate these resources, based on the modality, element, and house of your happiness.

Sort of.

Up to this point, the first step in creating the story was to define the subject of the story. Safety resources were easy to define; the experience of safety is built into your biology. Validation resources were a bit more complicated because the nature of validation resources depends on the balance in your Safety Need Account. Still, we were able to define validation resources because you've had enough experiences of different kinds of love to understand the distinctions.

Here's the problem. The nature of happiness resources depends on the balance in your Validation Need Account. You've never experienced happiness on its own before, independent of validation. We can't define happiness resources in a meaningful or practical way because that story doesn't yet connect to a personal story.

We can create a story that describes **How** you pursue happiness resources, **Which** kind of happiness resources you prefer, and **Where** you can find happiness resources. But without a clear understanding of **What** happiness resources are, the story won't be nearly as practical as the stories about safety resources and validation resources.

The purpose of the story of your Happiness Account is to complete **Act 3** of The Quest for Happiness. The story shows you how you can arrive at your ultimate destination of happiness, and it encourages you to work through the two tasks and meet your Safety Needs in **Act 1** and your Validation Needs in **Act 2**, which, incidentally, improves every part of your life. You'll be able to use the story of your happiness resources to help advance the stories of your safety and validation resources. But when you're ready to build your foundation of happiness, you'll realize that the story of happiness resources and your Happiness Account is an allegory.

When you are meeting your safety needs and your validation needs, you discover that the "Happiness Account" is actually your Self-Actualization Need Account. To actualize yourself, experience happiness, and fulfill your potential, you first need to know precisely who you are. This is the story of The Identity Quest, which we'll explore in Part 4.

For now, let's turn to astrology to build the story of happiness resources.

What is Happiness?

As you learned in Chapter 5, every astrology story begins with a personal planet at the center. The planet is the subject of the story—the **What**—and the element, modality, and house placement of the planet tell you **How**, **Which**, and **Where**. To build an astrology story about happiness, we first need to find the planet that symbolizes happiness.

The personal planets in the birth chart symbolize different categories of **Need**. The Moon symbolizes Safety Needs, and Venus, which represents all expressions of Love, symbolizes Validation Needs. Happiness is not a **Need**; happiness is what you experience when you are free from **Need** (and free from **Want**). No single planet symbolizes happiness for everyone. The feeling of happiness is subjective and personal. Happiness is found in the First House.

The planet that rules the sign on the cusp of the First House is known as the Chart Ruler. The Chart Ruler is the planet that symbolizes your happiness. This is how we can make the First House, happiness, the **What** of the story. The modality of the sign of the Chart Ruler tells you **How** you approach happiness goals, the element of the sign of the Chart Ruler tells you **Which** language you speak for happiness, and the house occupied by the Chart Ruler tells you **Where** you can find happiness. This is enough information to complete the story of The Quest for Happiness. The story of your happiness resources will help you to advance toward happiness by meeting your Safety Needs and your Validation Needs.

Everything so far has been practical because every story so far has had a direct connection to the Plot-level story. As you engage with these stories and experience how it feels to meet your Safety and Validation Needs, you become more aware of the Character-level story, and it becomes possible to explore the stories of your happiness resources in a more meaningful way.

What we haven't addressed yet is the Chart Ruler: the specific planet and the associated Need that comprise the **What Else** of your happiness. The story of the Chart Ruler and your happiness is a part of the Theme-level story. It's powerful and important, but it doesn't have a direct connection to the Plot-level story, so it's not useful at the moment.

I'm going to give you a taste of these Theme-level stories that explore what happiness really is. These stories are worth contemplating, but don't expect them to make sense to you yet. The main reason I've included them is so you can experience the difference between a Plot-level story and a Theme-level story.

What Else Is Happiness?

When a planet rules a house, that planet *is* that house. There's no relationship *between* the Chart Ruler and your happiness. For you, the essential nature of happiness is meeting the **Need** of the Chart Ruler. The titles of these stories can be expressed as identity statements. For example, if Saturn is the ruler of your First House, the identity statement would be "Your happiness is your responsibility; your responsibility is your happiness." Every possible interpretation of this is relevant and true for you. This also applies to the other expressions of the Chart Ruler. If Saturn is your Chart

Ruler, happiness is responsibility, happiness is authority, and happiness is boundaries.

Theme-level stories are vast, and they move very slowly. They're the hour hand of the story clock. They rarely affect the Plot-level story, but a little insight from the Theme-level story can help you advance the Plot-level story. You don't need to engage with or understand the Theme-level story to experience happiness.

That all being said, here's a peek into the true nature of happiness.

If you have **Aries** or **Scorpio** on the Ascendant, **Mars** is your Chart Ruler. This means that your happiness is desire. Happiness isn't about getting what you W*ANT*, it's about the wanting itself. You can't imagine happiness without a G*OAL* to inspire you and a prize to acquire.

If you have **Taurus** or **Libra** on the Ascendant, **Venus** is your Chart Ruler. This means that your happiness is validation. The story of your Validation Needs is entangled with the story of your happiness. You can't imagine happiness without the feeling of love, and you must discover the Truth of Love to experience happiness.

If you have **Gemini** or **Virgo** on the Ascendant, **Mercury** is your Chart Ruler. This means that your happiness is understanding and communication. We understand and communicate through story, so in fact you need story to be happy. The better the story, the happier you are. You can't imagine happiness without a story, so it's essential that you remember that Happily Ever After is the end of a chapter, not the end of The Story of Your Life.

If you have **Cancer** on the Ascendant, the **Moon** is your Chart Ruler. This means that your happiness is safety. The story of your Safety Needs is entangled with the story of your happiness. Initially, this makes it easier to meet your Safety Needs, but then you must be willing to move beyond safety. Happiness is not the ultimate prize in the Human Game. Even so, you can't imagine happiness without absolute safety.

If you have **Leo** on the Ascendant, the **Sun** is your Chart Ruler. This means that your happiness is integrity. You need authenticity, truth, and transparency to experience happiness. You must shine bright enough to banish every shadow. Any trace of deception or dishonesty prevents you from feeling happy.

If you have **Sagittarius** or **Pisces** on the Ascendant, **Jupiter** is your Chart Ruler. This means that your happiness is growth. You need to expand in every direction and every dimension to experience happiness. Happiness is the experience of Unity, where you know your infinite potential. You can't imagine feeling happy if you are limited or restricted.

If you have **Capricorn** or **Aquarius** on the Ascendant, **Saturn** is your Chart Ruler. This means that your happiness is responsibility. For you, happiness needs boundaries, limits, and structure. You have a role to play in the universal story, and you experience happiness when you fulfill your responsibilities. You can't imagine happiness without rules and boundaries; you need to know where the lines are so you can stay within them to feel happy.

How to Acquire Happiness Resources

Even though the story of happiness resources doesn't have the same practical value as the stories of safety and validation resources, it's still worth exploring. You can get quite a lot out of it if you manage your expectations.

In the next chapter, I provide you with default astrology stories for the Happiness GPS that cover the Chart Ruler in each of the modalities, elements, and houses. These stories provide the turn-by-turn directions to help you acquire happiness resources and increase the balance in your Happiness Account. These stories were created using the astrology story tropes presented in Chapter 4.

CHAPTER 13
Happiness Resource Astrology Stories

This is the third set of astrology stories created for the Happiness GPS story. These most closely resemble the Moon/Safety Need stories because the objective is to generate or acquire happiness resources. These stories are far less practical than the Moon or Venus stories, and it's useful for you to experience that and to understand why.

The Moon and Venus stories are practical because they have a direct connection to your personal story. You understand exactly what safety and validation resources are. You know how they fit in your story, you know how they relate to your happiness, and you know how they make you feel. The happiness resource stories are not as practical because you don't yet fully understand what happiness resources are.

One of the reasons I've included these stories is so you can learn from them. You now have three sets of stories built from the same astrology story tropes, intended to secure deposits in different Need Bank Accounts. You can compare and contrast these stories and fully appreciate how the Moon and Venus stories are better stories than the happiness resource stories.

The happiness resource stories aren't *bad* stories, but they could be *better*. We'll explore how to make these astrology stories better in later chapters.

Chart Ruler in the Modalities
Chart Ruler in a Cardinal Sign

If your Chart Ruler is in a Cardinal Sign, you approach your happiness GOAL as an archery target that you must hit with a single arrow. You spend time planning and preparing, but once you take your shot, you can do no more. If you hit the target, you take a giant leap forward, but if you miss the target you stay where you are and have to start over again. It's easier to hit the target and acquire happiness resources if you move the target closer with a new story about your current situation.

Begin the story by stating your intention to acquire happiness resources. Make a note of how you feel right now to be able to track your progress. Identify a target that you believe would make you feel happy. Look for ways you can break that **GOAL** into a sequence of smaller targets. Treat each task or objective as its own target. When you complete the task and hit the target, you will receive some happiness resources. This may not resolve the entire problem, but it will improve conditions. For larger, more complicated tasks, set time-based targets as well as task-based targets so you can acquire happiness resources whether you complete a task or not. Take a few moments to explore these stories, adjust your strategies, and gather the happiness resources. Notice how you feel now and compare it to how you felt at the start. End the story by acknowledging that you feel better now because you successfully acquired more happiness resources.

Chart Ruler in a Fixed Sign

If your Chart Ruler is in a Fixed Sign, meeting your happiness **GOAL** is an ongoing process that requires planning, resources, and logistical support. You rely on your internal accounting department to coordinate everything and keep an eye on the big picture. You have multiple simultaneous projects that can generate happiness resources, and each project has expected happiness targets. If you repeatedly fail to receive the expected amount of happiness from a specific project, you can call the accounting department for support. The accounting department will adjust the expectations for that project, and cover the shortfall with surplus happiness resources from other projects. This insures that you always have sufficient happiness resources available. You just need a story to let the accounting department know they need to resolve the issue.

Begin the story by stating your intention to acquire happiness resources. Make a note of how you feel right now to be able to track your progress. Consider the **OBSTACLE** you face in your current story and review all available options. Focus on the options that promise the best return, but that you can't yet choose. These options cost more happiness resources than you have budgeted, which is why you're unwilling to commit. You need additional instructions and approval from your accounting department before you can make a choice. Consider each option and identify the potential risk and the potential reward, and also how much additional happiness you would need to choose it. Check the countdown clock and be conscious of how long you have to make a choice. Finally, consider the consequences of not making a choice and taking no action at all. Once you've assembled this information, imagine putting it in an email and sending it to your accounting department. Trust that your accounting department will review everything and provide you with the answer, and you can do nothing more until then. While you're waiting for a response from the accounting department, check in on other projects and enjoy the happiness they generate. Notice how you feel now and compare it to how you felt at the start. End the story by acknowledging that you feel better now because you successfully acquired more happiness resources.

Chart Ruler in a Mutable Sign

If your Chart Ruler is in a Mutable Sign, you take a nonlinear approach to your happiness GOAL. Rather than identifying a sequence of steps to arrive at the finish line, you break the GOAL into component tasks and organize them on a to-do list. When you have checked every item off the list, you will achieve the GOAL. The flexibility of this approach allows you to keep moving and avoid most obstacles and delays. But just because you're moving doesn't mean you're making progress. If you hope to acquire resources to meet your happiness GOAL, you need to organize your to-do list with a new story.

Begin the story by stating your intention to acquire happiness resources. Make a note of how you feel right now to be able to track your progress. Create your task list and identify all of the things you can do that will make deposits in your Happiness Account. Review the list and flag the tasks that are the easiest and fastest to accomplish. Review the list again and identify the tasks that will generate the most happiness resources; these tasks require the most effort and take the longest to complete. Completing the easy tasks keeps you motivated and gives you a sense of accomplishment, but the hard tasks are how you make progress. Choose a strategy where you spend a set amount of time working toward a more significant task and then reward yourself by completing a few easy tasks. This way, you feel a sense of accomplishment *and* you make actual progress. You can also break the more significant tasks into time-based tasks. Each completed unit of time becomes a task you can check off the list. Take a few moments to explore these stories, adjust your strategies, and gather the happiness resources. Notice how you feel now and compare it to how you felt at the start. End the story by acknowledging that you feel better now because you successfully acquired more happiness resources.

Chart Ruler in the Elements
Chart Ruler in a Fire Sign

If your Chart Ruler is in a Fire Sign, happiness requires passion, intensity, and urgency. You experience happiness by taking action and expending energy. For you, happiness is a verb, not a noun; it must be expressed to be experienced. You can acquire Fire resources to meet your happiness GOAL by expending some energy to heat things up with a new story.

Begin the story by stating your intention to acquire happiness resources by engaging with the element of Fire. Make a note of how you feel right now to be able to track your progress. Moving your physical body is a great way to start; anything that gets your heart pumping will warm you up. Find something about your current story that excites you or ignites your passion. Look for a personal connection that creates an emotional investment in the outcome, but be careful not to raise the stakes too high. If all else fails, you can always tap into the energy of your anger. Ideally, find your anger or frustration by exploring an unrelated story. This makes it easier to use the energy of anger to power your current story without setting it on fire. Take a few moments to explore these stories and gather the happiness resources. Notice how you feel now and compare it to how you felt at the start. End the story by acknowledging that you feel better now because you successfully acquired more happiness resources.

Chart Ruler in an Earth Sign

If your Chart Ruler is in an Earth Sign, you expect to find happiness in the physical and material realm. Happiness is practical and almost tangible. It's easiest for you to experience happiness when you can associate it with something you can touch in the physical world. You can acquire Earth resources to meet your happiness GOAL by interacting with the material world with a new story.

Begin the story by stating your intention to acquire happiness resources by engaging with the element of Earth. Make a note of how you feel right now to be able to track your progress. Take a moment and become aware of your physical body; feel the weight of it and notice how your feet are on solid ground. When you are present in your physical body, explore the physical world around you. Time spent on a mindless physical activity, such as folding laundry or cleaning out a closet, can reconnect you to the world of form and help you to advance in your current story. To find Earth resources in your current story, look for the parts that are constant and stable. You can't change these things, but you can build on them. Take a few moments to explore these stories and gather the happiness resources. Notice how you feel now and compare it to how you felt at the start. End the story by acknowledging that you feel better now because you successfully acquired more happiness resources.

Chart Ruler in an Air Sign

If your Chart Ruler is in an Air Sign, you expect to find happiness in the mental realm of the intellect. Happiness is an abstract concept; it's a story made up of words, so words are enough to generate happiness resources. You can acquire Air resources to meet your happiness GOAL by rising high above the story to get a bird's eye view with a new story.

Begin the story by stating your intention to acquire happiness resources by engaging with the element of Air. Make a note of how you feel right now to be able to track your progress. Shift your attention away from your feelings and your subjective experience of the story and focus on the rational, objective qualities. Tell your current story from the point of view of an observer, not from the point of view of your character. Focus on the facts, not on what they mean. See the entire game board and consider the long-term strategy. Sacrifice is sometimes required: you may need to lose a battle to win the war. For now, listen to your head, not to your heart. Revise your current story to reflect the new perspective and the updated strategy. Take a few moments to explore the new story and gather the happiness resources. Notice how you feel now and compare it to how you felt at the start. End the story by acknowledging that you feel better now because you successfully acquired more happiness resources.

Chart Ruler in a Water Sign

If your Chart Ruler is in a Water Sign, happiness is a feeling; you look for it in the internal, personal, subjective realm of your emotions and your unconscious. Words create the bridge between your external story and your internal feelings, but words can never describe the feeling of happiness. Even so, to acquire Water resources to meet your happiness **GOAL**, you must find words to differentiate your feelings with a new story.

Begin the story by stating your intention to acquire happiness resources by engaging with the element of Water. Make a note of how you feel right now to be able to track your progress. To acquire Water resources, you will need to dive into those feelings and analyze them. When feelings from different stories get tangled, it muddies the waters making it harder to navigate the stories. Tune into a specific feeling, identify it by name, and then follow it back to its story. Repeat this process with another feeling until you've untangled the feelings and the waters are clear. When you understand what you are feeling and why, you can identify which story needs your attention. Take a few moments to explore these stories and gather the happiness resources. Notice how you feel now and compare it to how you felt at the start. End the story by acknowledging that you feel better now because you successfully acquired more happiness resources.

Chart Ruler in the Houses
Chart Ruler in the First House

If your Chart Ruler is in your First House, you find happiness in your health, happiness, and physical appearance. When you take care of your physical body with movement and exercise, make supportive choices around nutrition and rest, or even take a few moments for personal grooming to look your best, you generate happiness resources. You also generate happiness resources when you're engaged in activities that you enjoy and that contribute to your happiness. You can find happiness in your current story by connecting it to the First House with a new story.

Begin the story by stating your intention to acquire happiness resources from the First House. Make a note of how you feel right now to be able to track your progress. Look for the happiness in your current story: find something about it that gives you pleasure or satisfaction, even if it's a minor detail. Pay attention to your physical body and appreciate how your strength, vitality, and overall health are supporting you. Give some thought to your physical appearance. It may not be possible to feel your most attractive in the current circumstances, but you can at least feel more attractive. Take a few moments to explore these stories and gather the happiness resources. Notice how you feel now and compare it to how you felt at the start. End the story by acknowledging that you feel better now because you successfully acquired more happiness resources.

Chart Ruler in the Second House

If your Chart Ruler is in your Second House, you find happiness in your money, resources, skills, and talents. When you engage with your money and resources, whether by earning money, saving money, managing money, or spending money, you generate happiness resources. You also generate happiness resources when you're developing skills or using your talents. You can find happiness in your current story by connecting it to the Second House with a new story.

Begin the story by stating your intention to acquire happiness resources from the Second House. Make a note of how you feel right now to be able to track your progress. Look for all the ways that money and resources relate to your current story. Consider the impact this story might have on your bottom line. Explore how you could create a profit or at least limit your expenses. Identify the different skills required to achieve your current **Goal** and evaluate how well you're using them. Consider if this story is an opportunity for you to show off your talent or if it's an opportunity to train and develop new skills. Take a few moments to explore these stories and gather the happiness resources. Notice how you feel now and compare it to how you felt at the start. End the story by acknowledging that you feel better now because you successfully acquired more happiness resources.

Chart Ruler in the Third House

If your Chart Ruler is in your Third House, you find happiness in your comfort zone, and your habits and routines. The more familiar you are with your environment and the objectives in your current story, the more confident and comfortable you are, and this generates happiness resources. You also generate happiness resources when you can automate your life by using habits and routines to direct your attention to more interesting or important things. You can find happiness in your current story by connecting it to the Third House with a new story.

Begin the story by stating your intention to acquire happiness resources from the Third House. Make a note of how you feel right now to be able to track your progress. Review your current story and focus on familiar patterns and consistent elements. Focus on the old and comfortable rather than the new and different. Become aware of everything in the story that is operating smoothly and doesn't require your attention. You can feel confident about these elements of the story, and you can draw on them for support. Take a few moments to explore these stories and gather the happiness resources. Notice how you feel now and compare it to how you felt at the start. End the story by acknowledging that you feel better now because you successfully acquired more happiness resources.

Chart Ruler in the Fourth House

If your Chart Ruler is in your Fourth House, you find happiness in your foundation, your sanctuary, and your privacy. When you take care of your foundation—the parts of your life that take priority and make the rest of your life possible—you generate happiness resources. You also generate happiness resources when you retreat to your personal sanctuary so you can enjoy your privacy and recharge your batteries. You can find happiness in your current story by connecting it to the Fourth House with a new story.

Begin the story by stating your intention to acquire happiness resources from the Fourth House. Make a note of how you feel right now to be able to track your progress. Consider how the current story relates to your personal foundation. If a successful outcome could strengthen your foundation, you have even more to gain. If the story has no connection to your foundation, it can't disrupt your foundation; you can rely on your foundation for support as you navigate this story. Look for an opportunity to create a moment of privacy to center yourself. If you can't be alone, you can still connect to your thoughts and feelings and appreciate how private they are. Take a few moments to explore these stories and gather the happiness resources. Notice how you feel now and compare it to how you felt at the start. End the story by acknowledging that you feel better now because you successfully acquired more happiness resources.

Chart Ruler in the Fifth House

If your Chart Ruler is in your Fifth House, you find happiness in your creativity, recreation, and risk. When you express your creativity, which includes everything from artistic expression to solving a problem, you generate happiness resources. You also generate happiness resources when you are having fun, playing games, experiencing pleasure, and taking risks. You can find happiness in your current story by connecting it to the Fifth House with a new story.

Begin the story by stating your intention to acquire happiness resources from the Fifth House. Make a note of how you feel right now to be able to track your progress. Consider how much fun you're having in your current story. If you're not having fun, the stakes are too high. Adjust the stakes of the story, lower your expectations, and remember that the outcome of the story will not affect your happiness. Find a game you can play within the story to amuse yourself. Look for creative and unusual ways to overcome the challenges. Then consider the risk and the reward (including the entertainment value) and ask how lucky you feel. Take a few moments to explore these stories and gather the happiness resources. Notice how you feel now and compare it to how you felt at the start. End the story by acknowledging that you feel better now because you successfully acquired more happiness resources.

Chart Ruler in the Sixth House

If your Chart Ruler is in your Sixth House, you find happiness in your work and your service. When you spend time working, whether at your job or meeting some other responsibility, you can't expect to be rewarded or appreciated for your effort—but you can expect to generate happiness resources. You also generate happiness resources when you perform selfless service and offer your time and energy in support of others. You can find happiness in your current story by connecting it to the Sixth House with a new story.

Begin the story by stating your intention to acquire happiness resources from the Sixth House. Make a note of how you feel right now to be able to track your progress. Identify your job in the current story, and what you're expected to do. Pay close attention to the parts of the story that require the most effort; often they're the parts of the story you resist the most. If you have to do these things, you can at least do them well, so that you feel satisfied with your contribution. Consider how you can be of service and how your hard work could make someone else's story a little easier. Remember that your work has value and it can be its own reward. Take a few moments to explore these stories and gather the happiness resources. Notice how you feel now and compare it to how you felt at the start. End the story by acknowledging that you feel better now because you successfully acquired more happiness resources.

Chart Ruler in the Seventh House

If your Chart Ruler is in your Seventh House, you find happiness in your relationships with other people. When you interact with individuals who play supporting roles in your story, you generate happiness resources. You also generate happiness resources when you relate to the general public—nonspeaking background characters in your story—and when you become involved in stories about people you don't know, personally such as celebrities or politicians. You can find happiness in your current story by connecting it to the Seventh House with a new story.

Begin the story by stating your intention to acquire happiness resources from the Seventh House. Make a note of how you feel right now to be able to track your progress. Shift your focus to the other people involved with your current story, and explore what functions they perform. Look for your partners, the characters who can help you achieve your **GOAL**. If you have an adversary in the story, someone who is making it harder to achieve your **GOAL**, consider how to give them what they **WANT** so you can get what you **WANT**. If you need more support, enlist the help of a new character to help you resolve the issue and advance in the story. Take a few moments to explore these stories and gather the happiness resources. Notice how you feel now and compare it to how you felt at the start. End the story by acknowledging that you feel better now because you successfully acquired more happiness resources.

Chart Ruler in the Eighth House

If your Chart Ruler is in your Eighth House, you find happiness in your debts, obligations, and shared resources. When you engage with debts and obligations by accepting support from others, repaying that support, and obeying the Law of Circulation, you generate happiness resources. You also generate happiness resources when you combine your resources with others' to create more opportunity for all. You can find happiness in your current story by connecting to the Eighth House with a new story.

Begin the story by stating your intention to acquire happiness resources from the Eighth House. Make a note of how you feel right now to be able to track your progress. Review your current story and make note of what you owe and which obligations you hope to meet. Consider each debt and remember the support you received that created the debt. Look for ways to take advantage of your support network to help you advance in your current story. Ask for help and support from people you have helped in the past, and give them the opportunity to repay their debt to you. Take a few moments to explore these stories and gather the happiness resources. Notice how you feel now and compare it to how you felt at the start. End the story by acknowledging that you feel better now because you successfully acquired more happiness resources.

Chart Ruler in the Ninth House

If your Chart Ruler is in your Ninth House, you find happiness in your danger zone and your encounters with experts and authorities. When you leave your comfort zone behind and enter the danger zone, everything is distant, foreign, and unfamiliar. You return with new experiences, a greater understanding of your story, and happiness resources. You also generate happiness resources when you seek out experts and authorities to help you understand the unknown. You can find happiness in your current story by connecting to the Ninth House with a new story.

Begin the story by stating your intention to acquire happiness resources from the Ninth House. Make a note of how you feel right now to be able to track your progress. Review your current story and let everything familiar fade into the background so you can identify whatever is unfamiliar. This is your opportunity to expand your understanding and experience something new. Seek out the advice of experts or authorities to learn more about it. Other people's experiences can help you see the potential of the unknown and give you some idea of what to expect. When you feel prepared, lean into the unfamiliar and experience it directly. Take a few moments to explore these stories and gather the happiness resources. Notice how you feel now and compare it to how you felt at the start. End the story by acknowledging that you feel better now because you successfully acquired more happiness resources.

Chart Ruler in the Tenth House

If your Chart Ruler is in your Tenth House, you find happiness in your reputation, your advancement, and your public image. When you work for advancement in your personal, social, or professional life and hope to create a reputation for success, you generate happiness resources. You also generate happiness resources when you engage with your public image through your social media presence. You can find happiness in your current story by connecting to the Tenth House with a new story.

Begin the story by stating your intention to acquire happiness resources from the Tenth House. Make a note of how you feel right now to be able to track your progress. Consider your current story and identify how you can use it to raise your profile, improve your reputation, and increase your success. Identify what this story will add to your resume thanks to your individual contribution. Pay attention to how your behavior might look to other people. You aren't the author of the story of your reputation. Your reputation is based on how your character behaves in someone else's story. Project the qualities you would like the world to notice, even if they don't reflect your inner experience. Take a few moments to explore these stories and gather the happiness resources. Notice how you feel now and compare it to how you felt at the start. End the story by acknowledging that you feel better now because you successfully acquired more happiness resources.

Chart Ruler in the Eleventh House

If your Chart Ruler is in your Eleventh House, you find happiness in your ambitions, aspirations, and acquisitions. When you engage with your ambitions, whether you create the story of your dream or work to make it a reality, you generate happiness resources. You also generate happiness resources when you set out to acquire the things you believe will make you happy. You can find happiness in your current story by connecting it to the Eleventh House with a new story.

Begin the story by stating your intention to acquire happiness resources from the Eleventh House. Make a note of how you feel right now to be able to track your progress. Consider the **GOAL** of your current story and review what you hope to accomplish. Now find a connection between this **GOAL** and your bigger dreams of happiness. Remind yourself that you have a bigger purpose and decide how this current story serves that **Goal**. If you can see how achieving your current objectives will help you acquire something you believe will make you happy, the current story will become more important. If you realize the current story has no connection to your happiness, look for the fastest way to resolve the story so you can change course and pursue happiness. Take a moment to explore these stories and gather the happiness resources. Notice how you feel now and compare it to how you felt at the start. End the story by acknowledging that you feel better now because you successfully acquired more happiness resources.

Chart Ruler in the Twelfth House

If your Chart Ruler is in your Twelfth House, you find happiness in adversity and in your blind spot. Adversity takes many forms, but it always creates an **Obstacle** you must overcome to achieve your **Goal** and advance in your story. When you experience adversity, you have the opportunity to discover hidden strength and to generate happiness resources. Because your happiness resources occupy your blind spot, they're easy to overlook. You can find happiness in your current story by connecting it to the Twelfth House with a new story.

Begin the story by stating your intention to acquire happiness resources from the Twelfth House. Make a note of how you feel right now to be able to track your progress. Review your current story and look for the **Obstacle** and the challenges you faced. Take a thorough inventory of everything that limits you or makes it harder for you to get what you **Want**. Now consider that however much adversity you faced, you survived it. Explore how you overcame the **Obstacle**, and notice what you learned from the experience. You paid a price with these challenges; find the gift you received in exchange. Overcoming adversity has made you aware of your strength, your courage, and your resilience. These gifts are yours and you can draw on them at any time. Take a few moments to explore these stories and gather the happiness resources. Notice how you feel now and compare it to how you felt at the start. End the story by acknowledging that you feel better now because you successfully acquired more happiness resources.

# PART 3
OBSTACLES

CHAPTER 14
Obstacle Stories

Until you step into a story and experience it, the story is an abstract idea. It's a plan of action, but not yet the action itself. When you take the time to explore the story, you can prepare yourself and even anticipate how to overcome expected challenges. A good story can turn an adequate plan into the best plan. Then you can lay out that best plan and study it until you're ready to follow it. It's your best-laid plan: what could possibly go wrong?

Thanks to The Rules of Story, the answer is anything. If everything goes exactly as planned, it's a good story, but if something unexpected forces you to adjust the plan and follow a new path, it's a *better* story, and the only Law of the Human Game is The Best Story Wins. Something going wrong is built in to the very shape of story: ACT 2 of the Plot-level of every story is the OBSTACLE.

The point of an OBSTACLE is to overcome it. You don't need to understand what it is or how it got there. You only need to find a way to move past it so you can advance toward your GOAL. Your current GOAL is to build a foundation of happiness. You encounter an OBSTACLE as you play the Plot-level game in the Happiness Casino. The next few chapters explore how to get better at overcoming the ACT 2 OBSTACLE.

When you encounter an OBSTACLE in the Plot-level game, you visit the Options Market to choose how to respond to that OBSTACLE. You can adjust the cost of the options by increasing the balance of your Safety Need Account, but you can't add new options to the mix when you're actively engaged with an OBSTACLE. After you've encountered an OBSTACLE, you may choose to explore the story of the OBSTACLE and come up with new options that will be available the next time you encounter it. This requires strategy.

Remember that your current **GOAL** is a foundation of happiness. Time spent exploring an **OBSTACLE** story is time not spent advancing toward happiness. Not every **OBSTACLE** story is worth exploring. An **OBSTACLE** that you expect to encounter again that you can't easily overcome with your current options is worth a second look. Time spent exploring this kind of **OBSTACLE** story is a good investment that can help you reach your happiness **GOAL** more quickly. But to take advantage of new **OBSTACLE** strategies, you need to be able to navigate between the different levels of story.

If you think of a story as a clock, the current time indicates where you are in the story. Your primary focus is on the Plot-level story. An **OBSTACLE** blocks you from advancing for a period of time. If you can overcome the **OBSTACLE**, you can continue to advance. Otherwise, you have to wait for the hands of the clock to arrive at the designated time when the **OBSTACLE** becomes irrelevant.

The hands of the clock are a story about time, not time itself. When you engage with the **OBSTACLE** from the Plot-level story, you advance the second hand of the clock. If you engage with the Character-level story, you advance the minute hand of the clock. This is like running the Plot-level story at 60x speed. When you return to the Plot-level story, the time delay of the **OBSTACLE** will have expired and the **OBSTACLE** will no longer be a problem. You haven't sped up actual time, but you've jumped ahead in the timeline of the Plot-level story.

You've spent your life engaged with the Plot-level story, and that's what you know best. The Quest for Happiness story is written from the perspective of the Plot-level story, but it's designed to help you experience the Character-level story. When you follow the Happiness GPS instructions and meet your Safety and Validation Needs, you engage directly with the Character-level story and become more familiar with it. You need this skill to take advantage of the **OBSTACLE** stories.

Until you have a personal experience of the difference between the Plot-level story and the Character-level story, the **OBSTACLE** stories will be abstract and theoretical. They will feel different from the stories about Safety and Validation Needs because you won't be able to connect them to your personal experience. The story will make sense, but you won't be able to inhabit it the way you can inhabit the stories about your Safety and Validation Needs.

The astrology related to **Obstacle** stories will only complicate things more. Your first instinct will be to bridge the gap by leaning into the astrology. Astrology stories of planetary aspects are seductive, but they won't give you any useful answers. Astrology stories are Theme-level stories and they won't help you navigate your Plot-level stories. You can bridge the gap only by becoming familiar with the Character-level story, and the best way to do that is to continue to use the Happiness GPS to build a foundation of happiness.

Moving forward with **Obstacle** stories will be easier when you have some clear and reasonable expectations.

First and foremost, you don't need to understand **Obstacle** stories to build a foundation of happiness. The Happiness GPS stories that allow you to manage your Safety and Validation Needs are Character-level strategies to bypass a Plot-level **Obstacle**. You can take advantage of these stories without understanding exactly how and why they work.

Second, exploring the theory of the **Obstacle** story gives you a deeper understanding of the Human Game and helps you to advance in The Quest for Happiness. As you build your foundation of happiness, you will find places where the theoretical **Obstacle** story connects to your current reality. This is how the theory becomes practical. Expect that your understanding will develop over time.

Third, you can benefit from the **Obstacle** story without understanding the whole story. As you work through the next few chapters, you will gather pieces of a bigger puzzle. Assembling all of the pieces into a bigger picture will take time, but each individual piece of the puzzle has value. Sometimes a random piece of the puzzle is all you need to move past an **Obstacle**.

Internal Obstacles vs. External Obstacles

We'll begin by defining two types of **Obstacle**: internal and external. An internal **Obstacle** comes from within the story itself, and The Rule of Conservation means that everything required to overcome the **Obstacle** already exists in the story. Consider the story tropes for the modalities as an example. The first paragraph describes **How** you approach the **Goal**. The second paragraph describes the internal **Obstacle**, which is a direct consequence of the approach you take to the **Goal**. The third paragraph provides the strategy to overcome the internal **Obstacle**, which is based on the original approach to the **Goal**. For example, in the Cardinal *Archery Target* story trope, the **Goal** is to hit the target with a single arrow; the **Obstacle** is that the target may be too far to hit; the **Resolution** is to move the target closer so you can hit it with a single arrow.

An external **Obstacle** is the intersection of two stories. Your current story is the Titanic, and the **Obstacle** story is the iceberg. You're moving across the surface of the water, the Plot-level story, in pursuit of your **Goal**. You see the iceberg in your way, and you have to adjust your plan to overcome the **Obstacle**. This may be more difficult than you expect, because you see only the tip of the iceberg: the part of the iceberg story that intersects with Plot-level story of the Titanic. The iceberg story is bigger than that—it extends through the Character-level story all the way down to the Theme-level story.

Your immediate priority is to avoid the iceberg and minimize the damage, but the iceberg is not going away. The more you understand about the iceberg story, the more options you will have to respond to it the next time you encounter it. Aspects in the natal chart can help you understand both the Character-level and the Theme-level story of the external **Obstacle**.

Aspects and Obstacles

An aspect shows a relationship between a pair of planets. It means that the stories associated with each planet are inclined to intersect in a particular way. You can use this Theme-level framework to construct a Character-level story that identifies the **Need** that is the subject of the **Obstacle** story. Finally, you can link this to the Plot-level challenges and look for more effective strategies, so you will have additional options the next time you encounter a Plot-level challenge related to this **Obstacle** story.

An aspect in your birth chart is always operational in the Theme-level story, but it does not always interfere with the Plot-level story. An aspect-based **OBSTACLE** story is not inevitable, not always a problem, and not always noticeable.

In every possible sense, aspect stories are optional. You don't need to engage with aspect stories to build a foundation of happiness, or to experience the bigger prizes in the Human Game of Prosperity, Joy, or Meaning. Exploring aspect stories will not directly advance you on The Quest for Happiness. But once you've mastered the basics of The Quest for Happiness, aspect stories can give you additional options to win more in the Happiness Casino.

We will be taking a limited and specific approach to aspect stories and consider only six aspects, ignoring the rest for the time being. I'll demonstrate how to assemble aspect stories using story tropes for the aspects, and story tropes for the "iceberg" planet. Then we'll be ready to explore how the outer planets can influence The Story of Your Life.

This measured and cautious approach to aspect stories is designed to protect you from a bigger problem caused by exploring aspects and **OBSTACLE** stories.

Obstacle Stories Create Prophecies

Prophecies are unavoidable. *As the Prophecy Foretold* is the salt of the story trope spice rack. When you explore astrology stories, you expect to find prophecies, and the moment you find a prophecy, it becomes a part of your story. Most of the time, this isn't a problem, because the stories affected by the prophecy are big and broad and they don't interfere with your active E-Class stories. From this point forward, this is no longer the case.

You have activated the stories of your Safety Needs, your Validation Needs, and your happiness. When you explore aspects to your Moon or Venus, you expose yourself to a prophecy that directly affects your active stories. This can create a new **OBSTACLE** that makes it more difficult to meet your needs and experience happiness. If you're careful about how you explore the aspects, you can limit the scope of the prophecy and understand how to beat it. But if you wander around the birth chart, you may create new prophecy stories before you have the skills to beat them.

This causes another delay on the path to happiness. While you beat the prophecy, you're developing new skills, but you're not building a foundation of happiness. These skills will be useful when you move beyond Happiness in the Human Game, but they're not required to get to Happiness.

Remember that an aspect to a planet represents a *potential* external **Obstacle**. It doesn't mean that you will encounter that **Obstacle** every time you engage with a story related to that planet. The point of an **Obstacle** is to overcome it, and you can overcome the **Obstacle** at the Plot-level story without connecting it to the Theme-level story of the aspect in your birth chart.

CHAPTER 15
Astrology Aspect and Planet Story Tropes

This chapter contains almost everything you need to know about aspect-based **Obstacle** stories. We'll begin with the mechanics of aspects: what they are, and how to identify them in the chart. Then we'll consider the three components of aspect-based **Obstacle** stories: **How**, **Where**, and **What Else**. The aspect itself addresses **How** the **Obstacle** of the secondary story might disrupt the primary Plot-level story. The house occupied by the aspecting planet tells you **Where** the disruption comes from; this makes it easier to determine if an **Obstacle** is related to a particular aspect. Finally, the **Need** associated with the planet making the aspect tells you **What Else** the **Obstacle** is about.

This chapter provides you with the story tropes and the instructions to create aspect-based **Obstacle** stories, but for several very good reasons, it does not include examples of these stories, which would be long, complicated, difficult to follow, and of little practical value. Aspect stories have a staggering number of configurations. I couldn't illustrate all of them, and any examples I provided would become your default templates. It's best that you assemble your own aspect stories without any examples to guide you. Aspect stories are optional. When you're comfortable assembling an aspect story on your own, you'll also have the skills to make use of it.

Everything in this chapter specifically applies to aspects between the seven personal planets. I'll address outer planet aspect stories in the next chapter.

Aspects Defined

In the language of astrology, an aspect describes any connection between two planets. In this program, we'll consider angular aspects in longitude: aspects based on the relative positions of two planets in the zodiac. The "major" aspects generally refer to the aspects included in the *Tetrabiblos*, written by **Claudius Ptolemy** in the 2nd century. These aspects are based on the relationship between the signs, and are sometimes referred to as "whole-sign" aspects. The minor aspects were introduced in the 17th century by **Johannes Kepler**, based on geometry, harmonics, and the "music of the spheres." Divide the 360° of the chart by a whole number (the harmonic) to determine the angle of the aspect.

The six whole sign aspects I've selected for this program address the most useful and significant **OBSTACLE** stories that may affect The Quest for Happiness. The illustration on the next page shows the relationship between the planets and the glyph for each aspect.

The **conjunction** is a 1st harmonic aspect (0°). It occurs when two planets occupy the same degree in the same sign.

The **opposition** is a 2nd harmonic aspect (180°). Planets that oppose each other are six signs apart. Both planets have the same modality and different elements in the same polarity (Fire/Air or Earth/Water).

The **trine** is a 3rd harmonic aspect (120°). Planets that trine each other are four signs apart. Both planets have the same element, but different modalities.

The **square** is a 4th harmonic aspect (90°). Planets that square each other are three signs apart. Both planets have the same modality, but different elements in different polarities. One planet will be in a masculine element (Fire or Air) and the other in a feminine element (Earth or Water).

The **sextile** is a 6th harmonic aspect (60°). Planets that sextile each other are two signs apart. The planets have different modalities and different elements, but the same polarity (Fire/Air or Earth/Water).

The **quincunx** is a 12th harmonic aspect (150°)[1]. Planets that quincunx each other are five signs apart. The planets have different modalities, elements, and polarities, so they have nothing at all in common.

---

[1] The 12th harmonic includes both the semi-sextile (30°) and the quincunx (150°). The semi-sextile does not create any conflict between stories, so it's not worth considering.

Astrology Aspect and Planet Story Tropes

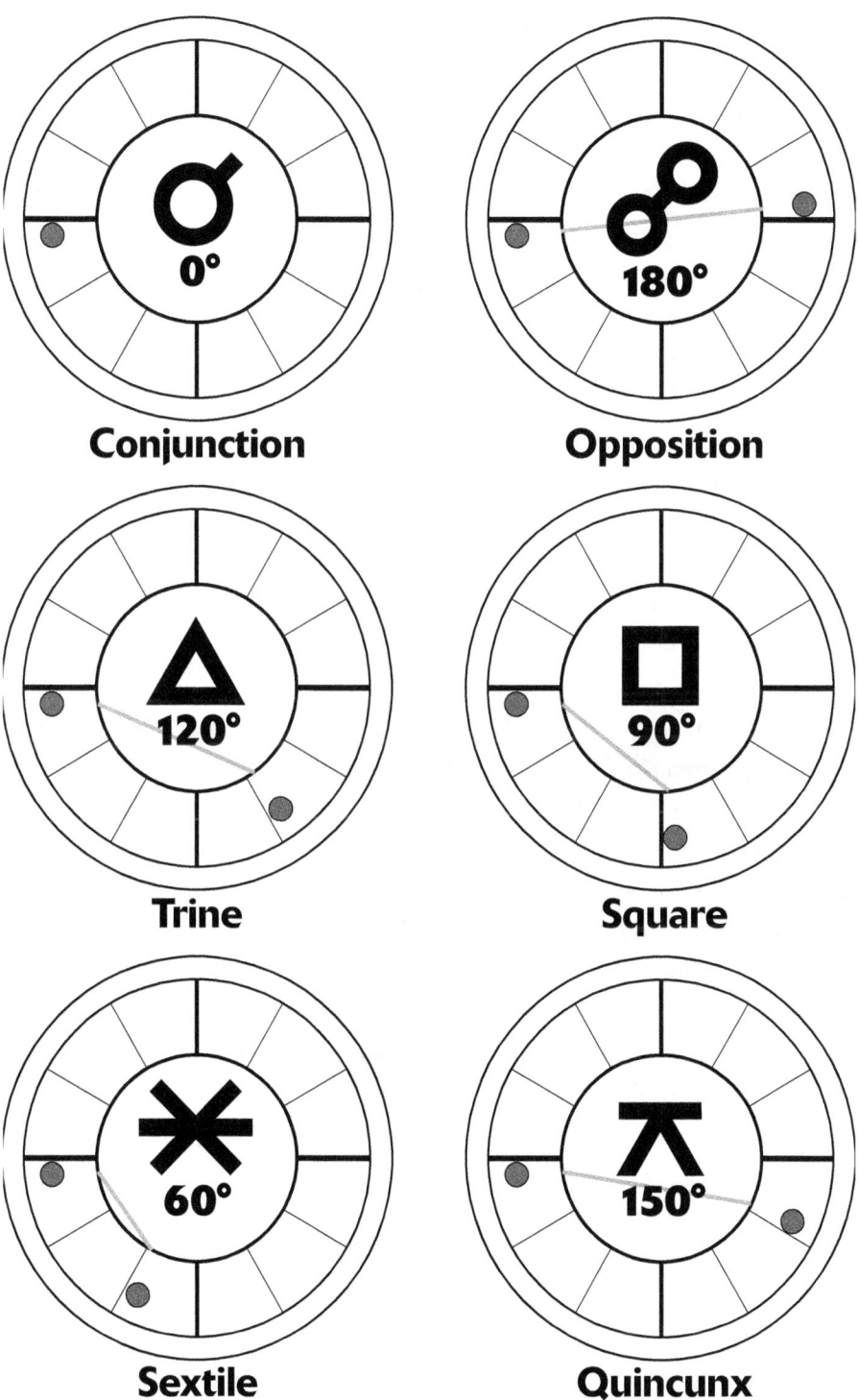

Aspect Orbs and Signs

Working with aspects can be complicated because you're likely to come up against the *Swiss Watch* astrology story trope. The math of astrology allows for precise calculations. As the planets move toward each other, the aspect **applies**; it **perfects** at the moment when the planets form the exact angle; the aspect **separates** as the planets move apart. This level of precision must translate to the interpretations in some way. The *Swiss Watch* story trope encourages astrologers to look for definitive rules and boundaries to know if an aspect is valid or not. This focuses on the astrology but not on the astrology story.

From the Human Game perspective, aspect stories are no different from any other stories. If the story connects to your existing stories and improves them, the story becomes a part of your reality whether or not you can link the story to the birth chart. Aspect stories are optional. You don't need them to navigate The Story of Your Life. And astrology stories matter only when they connect to your personal stories.

Aspects do not have objective rules, but without some kind of structure, the astrology story of aspects falls apart. After many years of struggle trying to reconcile these two stories, I settled on a set of guidelines that I use when evaluating aspects in the context of the natal chart.

When astrologers talk about the "orb" of an aspect, they mean the number of degrees on either side of the exact angle. For example, an exact square is a 90° angle; a 4° orb would mean that two planets would be square if they are between 86° and 94° apart (90° plus or minus 4°). Precise orbs are more important when considering minor aspects (which are entirely based on harmonics) than with major or whole-sign aspects. With regard to orbs, I rarely consider aspects with orbs greater than 5°, and I expect aspects with smaller orbs to be more useful.

I rarely consider out-of-sign aspects, no matter how small the orb. Technically, a planet at 0° Aries is square a planet at 29° Gemini: they're 89° apart, which is a 1° orb. They may be square by angle, but they're sextile by sign. For me, the challenge of a square is because the two planets have the same modality but different elements, so the square story trope wouldn't apply. This has no objective truth: it's just a story. It's been my story for many years, and I have no reason to change it. However, it doesn't need to be your story.

Aspect Story Tropes: How

The traditional approach to aspects classifies aspects as either "hard" or "soft." The "hard" aspects are "bad" because they're "challenging," while the "soft" aspects are "good" because they're "easy." These classifications are not useful in this context. For our purposes every aspect is an OBSTACLE. An OBSTACLE is something unexpected that affects how you pursue a GOAL. An OBSTACLE is not automatically a challenge, nor does it necessarily involve conflict. It requires only that you choose an option from the Options Market to respond to it.

When considering aspects and OBSTACLE stories, remember The Rule of Compensation: every gift has a price, and every price has a gift. Make sure you understand both when you take on an aspect story. You may notice only one or the other when you experience the aspect's influence in a Plot-level story.

The aspect story tropes refer to the primary story and the secondary story. The primary story is your current priority: it's the WHAT the OBSTACLE story disrupts. The aspect story trope describes HOW the secondary story disrupts the primary story. This can provide useful insight and strategies to overcome the OBSTACLE without considering the specific details of the secondary story. Test the new strategies from the aspect story trope before adding to the aspect story. Remember, the point is to find a better option to overcome the OBSTACLE, not to explore the OBSTACLE story.

Because your main objective is to build a foundation of happiness, consider only aspects to the Moon or Venus. Each aspect to the Moon represents a potential OBSTACLE when meeting your Safety Needs, and each aspect to Venus represents a potential OBSTACLE when meeting your Validation Needs. When you encounter a particularly challenging OBSTACLE while pursuing either safety or validation, you can consider if the experience of the OBSTACLE fits the pattern of an aspect to your Moon or Venus. Not every OBSTACLE will reflect an aspect! Explore the aspect story only if the connection is obvious and you need additional choices in the Options Market the next time you encounter the OBSTACLE.

Conjunction: Merging Realities

When two planets are conjunct each other, the primary story and the secondary story become entangled. Advancing the primary story also advances the secondary story, but an **OBSTACLE** in the secondary story becomes an **OBSTACLE** in the primary story. This is often difficult to recognize from the Plot-level story because the **OBSTACLE** may not appear to be external. Instead, you may experience the **OBSTACLE** as internal resistance: an extra burden that slows your progress in the primary story with no obvious reason. The entanglement is between the Character-level stories, and the extra burden is that you expect the **GOAL** of the primary story to meet the **NEED** of both the primary story planet and the secondary story planet.

The price and the gift of the conjunction are equally entangled. When you hope to meet the **NEED** of the primary planet, the price is that you must also consider the **NEED** of the secondary planet, which makes it more challenging to achieve the Plot-level **GOAL**. The gift is that you can advance the Character-level story of two planets for the price of one.

The strategy with a conjunction is to realize that the secondary story of the secondary **NEED** is secondary: it's not as important as the primary story of the primary **NEED**. It's not necessary to make the same size deposit in each Need Bank Account. It's necessary only that you avoid making withdrawals from the secondary Need Bank Account while you pursue deposits in the primary Need Bank Account. Because a conjunction can be resolved only in the Character-level story, the actual planets involved in the conjunction matter, and you will need to consider the **WHAT ELSE** of the planet story trope as well as the **HOW** of the aspect story trope. But because the two planets involved occupy the same house, the **WHERE** component of the aspect story is irrelevant.

Opposition: Mirror Image

When two planets are in opposition to each other, the primary story and the secondary story mirror each other and reflect opposite points of view. You will often experience this in the Plot-level story as an adversarial relationship with another individual. In fact, that individual may appear to be the **Obstacle** standing between you and your **Goal**. Whether this plays out as a friendly competition or all-out war depends on how high the stakes are for you. The problem with war is that even if you win, you lose. The other person in this story is a mirror image of you. You are literally fighting yourself.

The price of an opposition story is that it will always end with some kind of compromise. You will never get everything you **Want**, and the more you get what you **Want**, the less happy you are about it because the cost is always too high. The gift of an opposition story is that you have the opportunity to move beyond the Lie of Duality which requires a winner and a loser and discover a solution where everybody wins.

The strategy with an opposition is to negotiate from the Character-level story, not from the Plot-level story. What matters to you is that you meet the **Need** of the primary planet, and you can do this without achieving your Plot-level **Goal** and getting everything that you **Want**. In the Plot-level story, find the common ground between you and your adversary. What each of you **Want** is in conflict, but what each of you **Need** is not. When you address the **Need** rather than the **Want** you can find a strategy where everybody wins.

Trine: Grease the Wheels

When two planets are trine each other, the secondary story clears the path so the primary story can advance at maximum speed. Trines have a reputation in astrology as being the most "favorable" of all of the aspects because they have the least friction and the smoothest experience. A trine can feel like you're getting the VIP treatment. You skip the lines, you travel in comfort, and you hardly have to lift a finger to get whatever it is that you **Want**. A trine greases the wheels, which is wonderful until you need to hit the brakes.

The gift of a trine story is that it's easy and effortless. Once you set it in motion, it keeps moving forward and you don't have to think about it. A trine story gives you everything you **Want** almost as soon as you ask. That gift comes with a hefty price. Getting what you **Want** isn't enough to make you happy. And if you always get what you **Want**, you have no reason to discover what you **Need**, which will make you happy. A trine offers an escape, and that can be welcome and necessary, but you can't always take the easy way out. If you don't struggle, you won't grow.

The strategy with a trine is to challenge yourself and test your limits. A trine represents greater potential than you know, but it requires discipline and dedication to realize that potential. A trine has the potential to make it easier to advance in other, unrelated stories. When you learn the lessons of the trine and understand how it clears the path, you can use that skill in any situation.

Square: Collision Course

When two planets are square each other, the primary story and the secondary story are heading for the same intersection. They both think they have the right of way and that the other side has a stop sign, and if nothing changes, they will collide. The stories are perpendicular to each other, so they don't see each other coming, and the collision comes out of left field. Even if the stories don't collide, when they reach the intersection they will need to change course and choose a different path to move forward.

The price of a square story is frustration and inconvenience. You have to adjust your strategy, change your route, or even abandon the original **Goal** if it becomes clear that getting what you **Want** has no chance of meeting a **Need** or making you happy. The gift of a square is that it forces you to leave your comfort zone and experience something new. It may prevent you from getting what you **Want**, but it won't prevent you from being happy. You may not appreciate it at the time, but whatever detour a square story forces you to take is protecting you from something far worse.

A square story generates anger, because that's what you experience when you don't get what you **Want**. The strategy is to use the energy of that anger in a constructive way. The energy of anger can help you to overcome resistance to leaving your comfort zone or taking a risk. You can use the energy of anger to clear a new path or to choose a new **Goal**. When you master a square story, you can use the energy generated by the friction between the two planets to power virtually anything in your life.

Sextile: May I Help You?

When two planets are sextile each other the secondary story can help you to advance the primary story, but only if you seek out that help. The **OBSTACLE** of a sextile story rarely disrupts the Plot-level story, which makes it easy to overlook. The **OBSTACLE** of a sextile story is a missed opportunity.

The gift of a sextile story is reliable help and support. You don't have to do everything yourself to achieve your **GOAL**, get what you **WANT**, or meet your **NEED**. Help is available for the asking, and that help comes without cost or penalty. You can handle it all yourself, but it will take longer, require more effort, and won't earn you bonus points. The price of a sextile is that you must ask for help. Much of the time, this price is too high, so it's rarely an attractive option.

The strategy with a sextile story is to lower the price and lower the risk to make asking for help a more attractive option. The help you receive from a sextile story is mutually beneficial. It's a fair exchange, which is why it doesn't create a debt or obligation. You have something to offer from within the primary story that will help advance the secondary story. You can exchange this for help from the secondary story that will help advance the primary story. The house occupied by the secondary story planet tells you **WHERE** you can find the help, and the **NEED** of the planet (the **WHAT ELSE**) tells you what kind of help is available. Keep in mind that you don't always need the help to come from another person. The help comes from another *story*. You can help yourself once you make that connection.

Quincunx: Irreconcilable Differences

When two planets are quincunx each other, two fundamentally incompatible and unrelated stories have become entangled and must be separated. Initially, a quincunx story may look like an opposition story, and another person is taking the adversarial position. Unlike an opposition story, you have no common ground. Whether you address the stories from the Plot-level story or the Character-level story, compromise is not possible. For one story to advance, the other will have to retreat.

The price of a quincunx story is the frustration that comes from extended conflict and irreconcilable differences. The gift is that you don't have to reconcile the irreconcilable. The two stories don't belong together and collided only by chance. Once you separate the two stories, they can continue with no ill effects.

The only way to separate the two stories in a quincunx story is to run them on different story levels. If one story operates at the Plot-level and the other operates at the Character-level, they can move past each other without any interference. But if both stories operate at the same level, neither story can advance.

House Occupied: Where

The house occupied by the aspecting planet tells you **Where** the secondary story is based. This is useful information when considering your strategy to overcome the **Obstacle** because it helps you to anticipate **Where** you are likely to encounter this particular **Obstacle**. When you pursue a **Goal** related to the primary story, you can monitor stories related to the house of the aspecting planet so that you can anticipate and even avoid a collision. In theory, this is a promising strategy. In practice, it doesn't always live up to that promise.

The secondary story will always belong to the house occupied by the planet, but the connection to that house won't always be obvious. Some houses are easier to spot than others. For example, an **Obstacle** related to a secondary story coming from the Second House will almost always involve money. An **Obstacle** related to the Seventh House involves another individual. An **Obstacle** related to the Sixth House usually involves your job, but it could also just involve hard work that you would rather not have to do. But connecting an **Obstacle** to the Third House (for example) is more challenging. The **Obstacle** might relate to your habits and routines—your unconscious, automatic behaviors may be the source of the **Obstacle** in the primary story. But the **Obstacle** might just be local and familiar; something subjectively safe and part of your comfort zone.

Although the **Where** of the aspect won't always help you avoid the aspect, it can help you find more effective strategies to overcome the **Obstacle**.

Sometimes, all you need is to separate the primary story and the secondary story. When the two stories intersect, the house of the secondary story contributes to the **Obstacle** you experience in the primary story. You can edit the primary story and remove the elements related to the house of the secondary story. (This is the opposite of what you do with the Happiness GPS stories when you move a story to a new house so you can gather resources there.) You identify the qualities of the secondary house and set them aside. For example, if the secondary story comes from the Second House, eliminate all concerns about money from your story until you can overcome the current **Obstacle**.

Planet Story Tropes: What Else

When you consider only the **How** and the **Where** of an aspect story, you stay close to the primary story: you never leave the Titanic. When you begin to consider the **What Else** of the planet of the secondary story, you start to consider the perspective of the iceberg.

Up to this point, it's been possible to address aspect-based **Obstacle** stories almost entirely from the Plot-level story. The **What Else** of the aspecting planet comes from the Theme-level story, and you will engage with it from the Character-level story in the form of a **Need**. The challenge is that each planet represents more than one **Need**. You must choose which **Need** seems to be the subject of the secondary story, and then consider your current story about that **Need** and what you believe is required to meet it. Often you can overcome the **Obstacle** in the primary story by meeting the **Need** of the secondary story.

The Sun: Integrity, Authenticity, and Vitality

The Sun symbolizes your **Need** for **integrity**, **authenticity**, and **vitality**. Integrity literally means being whole, unbroken, complete, and undivided; it's a personal quality of fairness that involves doing the right thing in a reliable way. We'll explore integrity in more detail in Part 4 in The Identity Quest. Authenticity is the quality of being genuine, real, legitimate, and true; it's the **Need** to express your essence and to be honest and truthful.

Vitality relates to physical energy, health, and overall well-being; it's your **Need** to express your life force.

The Moon: Safety, Feelings, and Emotions
The Moon symbolizes your **Safety Needs**, and your **Need** to experience your **feelings** and your **emotions**. You now have an extensive, practical story that defines your Safety Needs. Feelings are how human beings experience vibrations of consciousness; they are not the effect of anything, and ideally you use them to navigate away from the Lie of Duality and toward the Truth of Unity. Emotions are feelings with stories attached to them so that they appear to be the effect of circumstances rather than the cause of them.

Mercury: Understanding, Communication, and Story
Mercury symbolizes your **Need** for **understanding**, **communication**, and **story**. Understanding is your **Need** to orient your perceptions and experiences into your current reality; it reflects your **Need** to know how you relate to your reality. Communication is the **Need** to seek confirmation of your subjective reality from other people. Story is how you create your reality, and in particular, it's the content of your reality.

Venus: Validation, Approval, and Values
Venus symbolizes your **Validation Needs**, your **Need** for **approval**, and your **Need** to align with your **values**. You now have extensive, practical stories that describe both your Validation Needs and your **Need** for—and expectations of—approval. Values represent the things you care about personally; your values guide you to experiences of love and appreciation.

Mars: Desire, Anger, and Ego
Mars symbolizes your **Need** to express your **desire**, your **anger**, and your **ego**. Desire is an essential part of **Act 1** of every story; it's how you select a **Goal**, and it's what gives you the energy to take action and pursue the goal. Anger is a valuable and misunderstood resource; the energy of

anger makes it possible for you to overcome the OBSTACLE in ACT 2 and to break through your limitations. Your ego is your "little s" self; it's the character you play in The Story of Your Life. We'll explore this expression of Mars in Part 4 in The Identity Quest.

Jupiter: Growth, Faith, and Imagination

Jupiter symbolizes your NEED for **growth**, **faith**, and **imagination**. Growth is an essential function of life; it's the NEED to fulfill your potential in every dimension. Faith is how you align with the Truth of Unity, even when it's not reflected in your current reality. Imagination expands the context of your story and makes it possible for you to create your reality.

Saturn: Responsibility, Authority, and Boundaries

Saturn symbolizes your NEED for **responsibility**, **authority**, and **boundaries**. Responsibility includes your experience of duties and obligations, and your expectations of reward and punishment. Authority stories operate on multiple dimensions, including your "inner parent" (the voice of your internalized authority figure), external authority figures, and how you exercise authority in your story. Boundaries include all form, structure, and limitations, whether they are physical, mental, emotional, or spiritual.

The View from the Iceberg

The Plot-level story of the Titanic describes an objective event: the Titanic colliding with an iceberg. The Character-level story and the Theme-level story are what make this event interesting, and those depend on the point of view of the story. The story from the point of view of the Titanic is quite different from the story from the point of view of the iceberg.

The biggest challenge with aspects between the personal planets is that the aspect operates in both directions. Each story is affected by the interaction in some way. It's natural to want to explore both points of view, but it's rarely useful to do so. Most of the time, the OBSTACLE story is a Titanic versus iceberg situation: it's a much bigger deal for the Titanic than for the iceberg. Whatever planet is the subject of your primary story is the Titanic; the aspecting planet in charge of the secondary story is the iceberg.

When considering aspect stories, it's not practical to be fair and balanced. You have to pick a side and stick to it. You must always tell the story from the perspective of the Titanic. However, when considering an aspect between two personal planets, whichever planet relates to the active (primary) story is the Titanic. This means you will eventually explore both directions of the aspect. Sometimes planet A will be the Titanic and planet B will be the iceberg, and other times, the roles will be reversed. It all depends on which Plot-level story encounters the **Obstacle**.

CHAPTER 16
Outer Planet Aspect Stories and The Quest for Happiness

The personal planets are also known as the inner planets. They exist within your story and operate on all three levels of story. The astrology symbol of the planet belongs to the Theme-level story. Each planet represents a category of **Need** in the Character-level story. And meeting the **Need** of a planet can express in the Plot-level story as a **Goal** or as an **Obstacle**.

The outer planets, **Uranus (⛢)**, **Neptune (♆)**, and **Pluto (♇)**, are *outer*. They are not a part of your personal story, and they exist outside of your reality. They operate exclusively in the Theme-level story. When an outer planet creates an **Obstacle** in a story, it confronts you with a Theme-level awareness that your reality is based on a **Lie**. This comes as quite a shock.

You encounter the **Obstacle** in your Plot-level story, but in this case you see the entire iceberg, not just the tip. You feel overwhelmed by the magnitude of the **Obstacle** story, and you ask the wrong question. Instead of asking **How** to overcome the **Obstacle**, you ask **Why** this is happening. The story you create to answer that question embraces the **Lie** and creates a future Theme-level **Obstacle** that you will need to overcome by wielding a nugget of **Truth**.

Remember, the only possible answer to "Why" is "Because." Everything that follows "Because" is a story, and nothing about this story will be true. The story you create tells you that you will never overcome this **Obstacle**, and by extension, you will never get what you **Want**, meet that **Need**, or be truly happy. This is a heavy price to pay. The gift you receive in exchange is that it's not your fault. You get to blame someone or something else for your suffering. You experienced some trauma in your past, and that G-Class Ghost story haunts you in the present. It limits you and gives you an excuse to avoid situations that could cause you more pain or suffering. If you don't touch the hot stove, you won't get burned.

Addressing the Theme-level story, confronting the **Lie** with the **Truth**, and resolving the trauma of your character's Ghost stories are important parts of The Story of Your Life. However, they're bigger story arcs, and they don't help you to build a foundation of happiness. You don't yet have the tools or the skills needed to navigate these stories. The challenge is that these stories are big and powerful and have so much more meaning than your day-to-day, Plot-level, event-based E-Class stories. When you encounter one of these Theme-level stories, it commands your attention—but when you step into the story, you can't control it. Instead of moving the Titanic, you try to move the iceberg.

An outer planet **Obstacle** is no different from any other **Obstacle**. You don't need to eliminate the iceberg, you need only to steer the Titanic and overcome the **Obstacle**. With an outer planet **Obstacle**, sometimes you have the additional first step of leaving the iceberg and returning to the Titanic. This can be more challenging than you expect.

Steering the Titanic to avoid the iceberg addresses the symptom, not the disease. Because the outer planet **Obstacle** comes from the Theme-level story, you see the entire iceberg and you know that at some point, you will need to confront it, address the underlying cause, and eliminate it once and for all. But you're not ready to deal with the iceberg yet, and you don't have to eliminate it to achieve your current **Goal**. Think of this as foreshadowing. You're laying the groundwork for a future story while you focus on your current quest.

Your current quest, of course, is The Quest for Happiness. If an outer planet makes an aspect to the Moon or Venus it can create an **Obstacle** that affects your happiness because it interferes with either your Safety Needs or your Validation Needs. The story tropes for these aspects are brief and limited because it's not useful to assemble a detailed outer planet **OBSTACLE** story. You need enough detail only to recognize when you're trying to steer the iceberg.

It's worth repeating the guidelines about aspects from the previous chapter. An **OBSTACLE** is not automatically a challenge, nor does it necessarily involve conflict. It requires only that you choose an option from the Options Market to respond to it. An aspect won't always create an **OBSTACLE**, and the point is to find a better option to overcome the **OBSTACLE**, not to explore the **OBSTACLE** story. Finally, even with outer planet **OBSTACLE** stories, The Rule of Compensation applies: every gift has a price, and every price has a gift.

Uranus (⛢): Disruption, Rejection, Unreliability

Uranus creates random, unexpected disruptions to your experience of reality. Uranus is a flash of lightning that momentarily reveals the bigger **TRUTH** outside of the bubble of your reality. It creates a crack in the foundation of your story, and makes it more difficult to believe the **LIE**. Uranus aspects create a theme of experiences of rejection, abandonment, and unreliability. This theme is most obvious in stories that involve relationships with other individuals.

Safe Doesn't Feel Safe (Moon–Uranus)

A primary requirement to feel safe is to know what to expect. Every time an expectation is not met, it lowers the balance in your Safety Need Account. When Uranus aspects the Moon, it disrupts your expectations of safety itself. You don't expect your Safety Needs to be met reliably or continuously. Over time, this uncertainty becomes familiar, and the lack of safety—the expectation that you can never let your guard down—becomes your definition of safety. So when you experience objective safety for any length of time, it will set off your alarms because it's unfamiliar and subjectively unsafe. Safe doesn't feel safe to you.

The details and experience of this story depend on the specific aspect between the Moon and Uranus.

With the **Moon conjunct Uranus**, you don't trust yourself: your unreliability creates your lack of safety. With the **Moon opposite**

Uranus, you don't trust anyone *but* yourself, because other people are unreliable.

With the **Moon trine Uranus**, the disruptions are so constant and consistent that you've learned to adapt. You are the person everyone needs with them in a crisis because you feel the safest in a crisis. The price of this gift is that you may not know how to function *without* a crisis. The **Moon sextile Uranus** is available to help you in a crisis, but it stays dormant until then.

With the **Moon square Uranus**, the disruptions come from other stories and external events, but the cause-and-effect relationship is clear. You can limit the safety challenges to specific stories and select contexts, and even use the disruptions to your advantage. But with the **Moon quincunx Uranus**, you will never make sense of the disruptions. No consistent pattern exists, nor anywhere to place the blame. You can't find a cause-and-effect relationship, so you never know when a disruption will hit. This can create the experience of learned helplessness where you no longer feel safe enough to choose any option in the Options Market, and instead let the clock run out.

All that's required to address any of these stories is that you upgrade your safety story. First, you need to address the immediate lack of safety. Then, you need to address your definition of safety.

Shift your attention away from the bigger, Theme-level stories of disruption, rejection, abandonment, and unreliability, and focus on your current E-Class story: the GOAL you are pursuing in the Happiness Casino. You feel overwhelmed because you have no viable options in the Options Market because the balance in your Safety Need Account is so low. Use your Happiness GPS stories and acquire safety resources so you are safe enough right now to choose the best option to overcome your immediate OBSTACLE.

When you have restored the balance in your Safety Need Account, take a few moments and notice how that feels. Recognize that you created this experience by acquiring more safety resources, and you can do that whenever you like. Even if something disrupts your expectations and interferes with your Safety Needs, you can recover from it immediately. As you become comfortable with this experience, your definition of safety will shift, and over time, when something is objectively safe, it will feel subjectively safe.

Brief Encounters (Venus–Uranus)

Uranus in aspect to Venus disrupts your Validation Needs. This affects your Expectations of Approval and can create an **Obstacle** in stories that involve relationships with other individuals. Expectations of disruption, rejection, abandonment, and unreliability mean you don't expect other people to make consistent deposits in your Validation Need Account. Love and appreciation never last, so you need to protect yourself. It's less painful if you expect your experiences of approval to be brief.

The details and experience of this story depend on the aspect between Venus and Uranus.

With **Venus conjunct Uranus**, you may not have much experience of being rejected or abandoned by other people, but that's because you reject and abandon yourself first. It's difficult for anyone to make a deposit in your Validation Need Account, and you limit how much approval you can feel so that it will hurt less when it's taken away. With **Venus opposite Uranus**, you expect nothing but rejection and abandonment from other people. No matter how careful you are about trusting another person, the minute you make yourself vulnerable to them so they can meet your Validation Needs, they will break the connection—and your heart.

Venus trine Uranus encourages you to reject conventional ideas of love and embrace the unconventional. Your encounters are brief because you don't attach to any one person as your primary source of validation. Especially when it comes to romantic and sexual relationships, your true nature may be at odds with the social norms and standards that surround you. You may think you have to choose between social acceptance and a personal experience of love. **Venus sextile Uranus** offers the opportunity to explore the broader truth of love, but the door stays closed until you choose to open it.

With **Venus square Uranus**, an unexpected conflict always shows up that could spell the end of the relationship. Often the problem will come from the area of life associated with the house of Uranus, and any **Goal** related to that part of your life will interfere with your ability to experience love and appreciation. It may require hard work and adjustment, but it's always possible to navigate this **Obstacle** because the cause-and-effect relationship is clear. With **Venus quincunx Uranus**, you will never make sense of the disruptions. No consistent pattern exists, nor anywhere to place the blame. You can't find a cause-and-effect relationship, so you never know when a disruption will hit. This can create a pattern of learned helplessness, in which you don't see the point of pursuing your Validation Needs and simply abandon your GOAL the moment you encounter an unexpected OBSTACLE.

The strategy to address any of these patterns is to develop a reserve of internal esteem. When you know you can validate yourself, you can more easily navigate disruptions in the external approval you receive from others.

Neptune (♆): Dissolve, Deceive, Escape

Neptune dissolves the boundaries and structures of your reality. The Lie of Duality becomes thin and transparent, which makes it harder to believe. This can be disorienting and make it more difficult to navigate in the world of form because you can't quite decide what's real. Neptune reveals the infinite creative possibilities of the Universe and gives temporary access to higher vibrations of consciousness. These glimpses of the bigger Truth of Unity are inspiring, but they can also become addictive. Neptune offers a temporary escape from the suffering of your current reality by giving you a taste of what awaits you at the end of your story. However, when you return to your reality you are even more aware of the LIE and the suffering it's causing you. The only way out is through. Neptune can remind you of why you're on the journey, but it doesn't offer a shortcut.

Space Invaders (Moon–Neptune)

The most noticeable effect of Moon–Neptune aspects is a lack of boundaries. Concepts such as division, separation, personal space, and privacy are ultimately rooted in the Lie of Duality, but they're essential tools to navigate the Plot-level story and engage with other individuals. If you're the one invading other people's space, it may create some discord and resentment in your one-to-one relationships. But if you're primarily on the receiving end and are unable to define and defend your own boundaries, this story can be uncomfortable for your character. A lack of boundaries is objectively unsafe, but the experience may become familiar, which makes it subjectively safe. Most Moon–Neptune aspects will also involve the *Safe Doesn't Feel Safe* story trope. When you encounter a situation with healthy, appropriate, objectively safe boundaries, it may feel threatening to you.

The details and experience of this story depend on the specific aspect between the Moon and Neptune.

With the **Moon conjunct Neptune**, you have no concept of boundaries. You feel so connected to everyone and everything that it's difficult to know where you end and someone or something else begins. This experience is active at all times and in every story. With the **Moon opposite Neptune**, your lack of boundaries is limited to one-to-one relationships. You unconsciously try to merge with your partner and you may lose a sense of your individual identity, especially in romantic relationships.

The **Moon trine Neptune** can be quite challenging. Trines remove all obstacles and are constantly active, and this can create the experience of continuous boundary violations. It's common to experience this as emotional sensitivity. You might have such a high level of empathy that you always feel what other people are feeling. The bigger challenge is that this aspect offers an easy Neptune-related escape to avoid any pain or discomfort. This is a short-term solution, but when you escape, you don't confront the OBSTACLE, learn your lessons, or advance your story. **Moon sextile Neptune** offers the opportunity for an escape when needed, but doesn't present the escape as the default option.

With the **Moon square Neptune**, you are acutely conscious of the boundary violations. You have a history of experiences during which other people violate your boundaries and you feel unable to protect or defend yourself. With the **Moon quincunx Neptune**, you are unaware of the boundary violations, which makes this the most challenging OBSTACLE of the set. When the boundary violations reach a critical mass, they often trigger some kind of health crisis—allergies, illness, or worse. The health crisis forces you to isolate yourself, which effectively removes you from at least some of the boundary violations.

Moon–Neptune aspects draw your attention to the Theme-level story where they give you a glimpse of the Truth of Unity. You become one with the iceberg and see no reason why the Titanic needs to keep its distance. Even though you know that boundaries and separation are an expression of the Lie of Duality, you must shift your focus back to the Plot-level story, return to the Titanic, and pay attention to where the boundaries are supposed to be. Pretend that the boundaries exist and choose to contain yourself within those boundaries so you can move past the **Obstacle** in your Plot-level story.

Rose-Colored Glasses (Venus–Neptune)

Venus–Neptune aspects affect your expectations of approval, especially in the context of romantic relationships. Neptune gives you a glimpse of the infinite possibilities of Love, but this ideal is often far removed from your current reality. You expect other people to live up to your fantasies, and when they fall short, you feel disillusioned, disappointed, and invalidated. But soon, Neptune draws you back into the fantasy and you begin the cycle again. Whether you experience this **Obstacle** as a challenge or a gift depends on the nature of the aspect.

With **Venus conjunct Neptune**, you know exactly what love looks like and how to experience it. You go through life guided by this approach, expressing love and appreciation and expecting it in return. What you can't understand is why other people don't always agree with you or appreciate your efforts. You speak only your validation language and find it almost impossible to express or experience love in any other form. You can easily meet your Validation Needs as long as you find partners who speak the same validation language as you. **Venus opposite Neptune** means you see only the idealized version of other individuals. You see their highest potential and expect that's how they will behave. When their current reality fails to live up to that standard, you feel betrayed and disillusioned. This can be especially challenging in romantic relationships.

Because **Venus trine Neptune** is always active without interruption, you may never take off your rose-colored glasses. You practically live in a Disney movie. So far, woodland creatures haven't appeared to fold your laundry and crowds of strangers haven't spontaneously burst into a musical number, but you wouldn't be a bit surprised if they did. Your boundless, limitless optimism and unshakable faith in the best of everyone may not make sense to others—and it doesn't protect you from unpleasant experiences, either. But you recover quickly and escape back to your ideal story where pretending to be happy creates a reality where you are happy. **Venus sextile Neptune** offers the opportunity to visit this magical world, but you'll have to find the hidden door.

With **Venus square Neptune**, you may have a history of disappointment and betrayal in your relationships, especially your romantic relationships. The root of this pattern is that you refuse to accept the reality of your partner and instead base your Expectations of Approval on your idealized version. In romantic partnerships, you may expect the perfect relationship without being willing to put in the hard work required to create that relationship. You can't expect your partner to do all the work and make all of the adjustments; you will have to adjust your goals and expectations as well. **Venus quincunx Neptune** can create a host of challenges in romantic relationships because you may be holding out for the perfect partner. Your Expectations of Approval are not only unreasonable, they're also not connected to your personal values. Often, the challenge is that you have adopted external ideals of beauty and bought into the LIE that love is conditional.

The gift of Venus–Neptune aspects is a greater appreciation of the TRUTH of love. Neptune dissolves the illusion of separation, and, as a result, you expect love to be unconditional. This makes it easier for you to express love and appreciation freely and with reckless abandon, which is an essential part of meeting your Validation Needs. All you need to address the OBSTACLE is to adjust your Expectations of Approval. Other people won't always be able to respond in kind, and while you build your foundation of happiness this may be discouraging. Once you can manage your Expectations of Approval, your rose-colored glasses and belief in unconditional love will propel you to Prosperity and beyond.

Pluto (♇): Power, Control, Manipulation

Pluto destroys your reality. It's slow, methodical, ruthless, and unstoppable, and it eliminates every trace of the Lie of Duality leaving behind the Truth of Unity. Your entire sense of self is an expression of the Lie of Duality. Your reality exists because you believe that you are separate from the rest of creation: the Universe is divided into "me" and "not me." The character you play in The Story of Your Life will not survive the effects of Pluto. When Pluto is involved, the stakes are literally life and death, and this creates themes of power, control, and manipulation as you fight for your very existence at every level of your story. Spoiler alert: your character dies at the end of your story and there's nothing you can do to stop it. Pluto will destroy your reality, but the TRUTH of your eternal, multi-dimensional authentic "Big S" Self will remain.

Pluto aspects are inherently threatening. Even if the aspect affects only Venus and your Validation Needs, it still creates underlying challenges to meeting your Safety Needs. The *Safe Doesn't Feel Safe* story trope may be present with both Moon–Pluto and Venus–Pluto aspects, in addition to any other story tropes.

Invisible Hand (Moon–Pluto)

With Moon–Pluto aspects, you attempt to control feelings and emotions—both yours and those of other people. You may be particularly sensitive to the destructive power of anger. You understand the power dynamic in every situation, and you instinctively look for ways to turn it to your advantage. It's preferable to make use of the *Invisible Hand* to manipulate or control in ways that don't immediately lead back to you.

The details and experience of this story depend on the specific aspect between the Moon and Pluto.

With the **Moon conjunct Pluto**, you believe you must control and contain yourself. You are acutely aware of the raw power of your feelings and emotions. You fear that if you ever lost control of your anger, not even the cockroaches would survive the planetwide devastation. With the **Moon opposite Pluto**, you project that power and those fears onto other individuals. You feel the need to protect yourself from other people's need to control you. You are afraid that if you ever let down your guard, the other person's feelings would consume you.

With the **Moon trine Pluto**, you have learned to embrace the energy of death, transformation, and transmutation. You appreciate that whatever

Pluto destroys is an expression of the Lie of Duality, and that however uncomfortable you may feel while it's being obliterated, when it's over, you will experience greater freedom and be one step closer to the Truth of Unity. Often the price paid for this gift involves a G-Class Ghost story of deep and unrelenting trauma. You may choose to explore that story and resolve it after you complete The Quest for Happiness, but not before. The **Moon sextile Pluto** offers the opportunity to tap deep reserves of power when required, but until then, it lies dormant and rarely causes problems.

The **Moon square Pluto** creates the greatest sensitivity to being controlled or manipulated by others. This fear of being manipulated or controlled can create the need to control every situation to protect yourself, which, ironically, causes you to control and manipulate other people. This aspect can create a significant drain on your Safety Need Account and is always accompanied by the *Safe Doesn't Feel Safe* story trope. With the **Moon quincunx Pluto**, you may believe that you lack the power to protect yourself or survive. You can never protect yourself from vast, external forces, and this means you rarely, if ever, feel safe. With this aspect, you must learn to take control of your story and focus on the things that exist within the bubble of your reality, rather than the forces that exist outside of it.

With every Moon–Pluto aspect, you associate power with control. You don't need to explore the Theme-level difference between the two to navigate these obstacles. Your first reaction to these aspects is to control the iceberg, which is impossible. You can control the Titanic, however. Shift your attention to your choices, your options, and your intentions and don't worry about the outside world.

My Way or the Highway (Venus–Pluto)

Venus–Pluto aspects can cause you to control everything about the deposits you receive in your Validation Need Account. Often, you place so many conditions on love that it becomes virtually impossible to experience it. A popular expression of this involves being blessed with an abundance of physical beauty, money, celebrity, or power. This makes you extremely attractive to other people, but it also means you don't know if they love you for who you are, or if they love you only because of some external quality. Most people spend their lives pursuing of the attention and external approval of other people, but you may spend your life avoiding it. It's possible to have too much of a good thing.

The details and experience of this story depend on the specific aspect between Venus and Pluto.

With **Venus conjunct Pluto**, other people find you powerfully charismatic. Something about you commands their attention and their approval. You may reach the point at which you ignore or reject expressions of love and appreciation that include this quality. You want other people to love and appreciate you, but not for that. With **Venus opposite Pluto**, you may find yourself in relationship with other individuals who refuse to receive your deposits in their Validation Need Account because they don't believe you appreciate them in the right way.

Venus trine Pluto is its own challenge. Often, Venus trine Pluto creates exceptional physical beauty and powerful sex appeal. Everybody wants you, and no one understands why this can be so difficult for you. Your entire life, you have been subject to unwanted attention. Either you learn how to use your beauty to manipulate and control others, or you find some way to hide your sex appeal to ward off unwanted advances, such as by gaining weight. **Venus sextile Pluto** offers the best of both worlds. You have the opportunity to tap into the power of your beauty and attract the attention of others when you need it, and you can turn it off when you don't.

With **Venus square Pluto**, you may also struggle with why other people find you attractive. You long to be loved for your authentic self, and you fear that other people appreciate only your external appearance: your beauty, your wealth, or both. However, you have the opportunity to build on this and use it to your advantage. You can capture the attention of the world with your most obvious qualities, and then keep that attention by demonstrating that you're more than just a pretty face or a blank check. **Venus quincunx Pluto** is challenging because it often makes you believe that you must change who you are and compromise something essential about yourself to experience love. Often, but not always, this story involves the difference between your internalized perceptions of what society accepts as beautiful or valuable, and your own authentic standards of beauty.

A common theme of Venus–Pluto aspects is the **Lie** that love is conditional. This is not true, but it's real for you, and overcoming the **Obstacle** means you must work within your current reality. It's real for you that love is conditional, but you get to define the conditions. When you add to your story and incorporate a set of conditions for love that you can easily meet, when you meet those conditions you can demand to feel loved and appreciated.

PART 4
THE IDENTITY QUEST

CHAPTER 17
Overview of The Identity Quest

When we left the story of The Quest for Happiness, you had just realized that the "Happiness Bank Account" is actually the Self-Actualization Need Bank Account. This makes the bigger happiness story better because now it's more consistent with the **Need**-based stories and the definition that happiness is the feeling you experience when you are free from **Want** and free from **Need**. When you began The Quest for Happiness, you could barely imagine the experience of happiness, let alone anything beyond it. Now that happiness is within reach, the realization that happiness is not the end of the journey is encouraging.

You gain access to your Self-Actualization Need Account when you maintain the minimum balance in your Safety Need Account and your Validation Need Account. As you add resources to your Self-Actualization Need Account, you build a foundation of happiness. When you meet your Self-Actualization Needs, you fulfill your potential as an individual. This process is how you create Prosperity, experience Joy, and find the Meaning of your life. It's about being the best you that you can be. You have to answer only one question before you can get started:

Who are you?

You may think you know the answer to this question, but you don't. Until you build a foundation of happiness, this question isn't relevant. Your life is defined by what you **Want** and **Need**, and that's all you've ever known. When you build a foundation of happiness and are free from **Want** and **Need**, only the question matters. You are now free to create anything you like in the next chapter of The Story of Your Life, which may be the scariest thing you've ever had to face.

The Human Game can help with that.

The Story of Your Life can be seen as your character's journey of self-discovery. Before you built a foundation of happiness, you weren't conscious of this. Your story so far is filled with clues and insights, gifts and lessons. When you stand on a foundation of happiness, you can review your story and look for what you missed. You can learn about yourself at the Plot-level story by identifying who other people think you are. You can learn about yourself at the Character-level story by exploring who you think you are. And at the Theme-level story, you can discover who you truly are. Your identity is a combination of these three components: **Human Seeming**, **Human Doing**, and **Human Being**.

The Human Seeming component is based on how you appear to other people. This is your avatar: it's how you show up as a character in other people's stories, and it encompasses both your physical appearance and your external personality. Astrology usually refers to this as your Rising Sign or your Ascendant, but it's actually the planet that rules your First House—the Chart Ruler.

The Human Doing component is your ego. This is the character you play in The Story of Your Life. Mars symbolizes your "little s" self, which embodies and expresses both desire and anger.

The Human Being component is your authentic "Big S" Self. This is who you truly are: an eternal, multidimensional being. This is the actor inhabiting the character you play in The Story of Your Life. The Sun symbolizes your eternal, authentic "Big S" Self.

All three components contribute to your identity, and you must understand each of them to know yourself well enough to actualize your Self and meet your Self-Actualization Needs. That being said, one component of your identity is far more important than the others. This is the self you need to actualize, embody, and express fully to find the meaning and purpose of your life. The other two components of identity support it and help you to define it, but ultimately they take a back seat to it. It's not always obvious, and it's not always easy, but the point of The Story of Your Life is to embody your ego, express your "little s" self, and fulfill the potential of Mars.

Bet you didn't see that coming.

Whose Life Is It Anyway?

The Story of Your Life is the story of the life of the character you play during this iteration of the Human Game. We have quite a bit to unpack in that statement. Let's consider it from the perspective of the Sun, your authentic "Big S" Self.

The truth is that you are an eternal, multidimensional being. You are currently playing the Human Game and having a human experience. The Human Game takes place in the world of form. You operate freely in three dimensions and you are limited by a linear and sequential perception of time. The objective of the Human Game is to move your bubble of reality away from the Lie of Duality and toward the Truth of Unity. This process unfolds over many lifetimes. Each lifetime is the story of a different character. The choices you make in one lifetime translate into karmic conditions that present as goals, opportunities, and debts to be addressed in the next lifetime. While you're playing the Human Game, you're primarily conscious of your current story. Who you once were has little relevance. What matters is who you are now and how you navigate the journey of your character.

Your authentic "Big S" Self, the Sun, is the actor inhabiting the character in your story. In this lifetime, you are playing the part of the person pictured on your driver's license. For example, I'm playing the part of Kevin B. Burk in my current human experience.

We love to watch skilled actors perform, but we don't want to see the actor. You don't care about Meryl Streep; you want to see Meryl Streep become someone else so you can experience the story of that character. The better you know your Sun and your authentic "Big S" Self, the more compelling you can make your performance as Mars, your character. The Story of Your Life is the story of Mars, not the Sun.

The external events in your story serve the arc and evolution of your character. The Character-level story is your Quest for Happiness and ultimately your search for the Meaning of your life. In Act 1 of the story, you go after something you WANT. In Act 2 of the story, you discover what you NEED. And in Act 3 of the story, you make a CHOICE between them. But if your character hopes to advance and evolve, you will also need to engage with the Theme-level story.

Whatever you WANT in the Character-level story is the product of a LIE that your character believes in the Theme-level story. This LIE is the source of your suffering and it's what keeps you from your happiness. What you NEED can lead you to a fragment of TRUTH that you can use to confront the LIE. The final TEST in the Theme-level story is where you either embrace the TRUTH or choose the LIE. The results of this TEST determine the fate of your character and whether you advance or retreat in the Human Game.

Be Your Best Self

Only your current story and your current lifetime matter. Don't concern yourself with questions of karma: they don't mean what you think they mean. More importantly, your karma does not limit your ability to experience happiness in this lifetime or to find meaning and purpose in your life.

Your objective is to deliver an entertaining, dynamic, and creative performance as the protagonist of The Story of Your Life. You can't control the external events of the Plot-level story, but your choices determine how the Character-level story unfolds. As you embark on The Identity Quest and learn more about your character, you will become more confident in how you express yourself and experience your story.

Psychological Astrology Stories

The Identity Quest and the astrology story examples that follow may feel more familiar to you. These are the kinds of astrological interpretations you're used to seeing and this is the approach to natal astrology you're used to experiencing. As I mentioned at the beginning of this book, astrology storytelling skills can improve any approach to astrology. The story of The Identity Quest can be of particular value if you take a psychological approach to astrology and use astrology stories in a counseling setting to understand the personality.

The point of this book is to learn how to tell better astrology stories. Focus on the context of the story, not its content. This will be important to remember and quite a bit more challenging to do when you get to the astrology stories for Mars (Human Doing) and the Sun (Human Being), because the styles of these stories will be so familiar. These stories are included because they're examples of different ways you can combine the modality and element story tropes with the **What** (or **What Else**) of a planet. When you master the storytelling skills, you can use those skills to tell better stories to describe a client's personality and create a more accurate astrological portrait.

If you are drawn to psychological astrology stories, The Identity Quest story may be more interesting than The Quest for Happiness. The Quest for Happiness embraces the external Plot-level story and suggests a coaching approach. The Identity Quest is based in the Character-level story and pairs beautifully with a counseling approach.

I'm drawn to psychological astrology stories, and The Identity Quest has so many possibilities, especially when you consider the dynamic among the three components of the identity. What might it look like if your Chart Ruler (Human Seeming) is aggressively incompatible with your Mars (Human Doing)? You could never get cast as the kind of character you want to play because everyone thinks you look like some other kind of character. You would live your life getting external approval and validation for pretending to be someone other than who you are…and possibly growing to resent it. Of course, if your Chart Ruler is compatible with your Mars—or if Mars *is* your Chart Ruler— you get approval for playing your character, but you may find it difficult to explore your character fully because if you act differently than people expect you to, you may lose their approval.

What's the relationship between Mars (your character) and the Sun (the actor playing the character)? If the two planets are in conflict or generally incompatible, you may struggle to find your character and give a compelling performance. If they're too closely aligned, your character may be a heightened version of your authentic "Big S" Self, and you will need to be able to distinguish between the reality of the story and the Truth of your Self.

If you have Leo rising and your avatar is the Sun—your authentic "Big S" Self—does this make it harder for you, the actor, to play your character and embody your Mars because other people keep interrupting the scene to ask for your autograph?

These are just a few of the questions that intrigue me about The Identity Quest. However, I've yet to explore them because I haven't yet found a way to make them practical for myself or my clients. I don't consider these questions in this textbook because they're not universally relevant. Not every individual has an internal conflict in their identity story. Not every individual has the same conflict in their identity story. And diving into an individual's identity story isn't the kind of thing you do on a first date. To explore these questions with a client, you need an ongoing relationship with the client. These stories aren't useful in a first session with a new client.

This textbook provides you with everything you need to explore the bigger questions of The Identity Quest on your own. Once you master the foundations of story and can explore each of the three components of the identity individually, you will have the skills to explore specific, relevant questions of identity when they are needed. Whatever stories I might come up with would be my stories, not the only possible stories or the only useful stories. Whatever stories you come up with will be the right stories for you.

For the record, I fully expect to circle back to these questions and these stories at some point in the future. At the moment, they are too much of a digression from the bigger story of Astrology and the Human Game. The Human Game is like the Marvel Cinematic Universe, and this is just the beginning of Phase One. I expect that a more thorough exploration of The Identity Quest and some kind of a framework to use the Human Game in a coaching or counseling setting will be a part of Phase Two.

CHAPTER 18
Chart Ruler: Human Seeming

The first challenge with The Identity Quest is to differentiate between personality stories and identity stories. The most popular modern astrology stories relate to the personality and focus on the signs rather than the planets. The sign of the Sun describes your conscious personality (how you experience yourself); the sign of the Moon describes your unconscious personality (how people who know you personally experience you); and the sign of the Ascendant, also known as the Rising Sign, describes your outer personality (the first impression for people who don't yet know you).

These are probably the first astrology stories you encountered. They haven't been a problem so far because The Quest for Happiness doesn't consider the personality, and the Safety Need stories related to the Moon are distinct from stories about your feelings, emotions, or your unconscious. Your existing astrology stories are about to become an issue, because The Identity Quest stories in the Human Game also view the Sun as your authentic Self and the Ascendant as your external appearance. But the Human Game stories are different from your current stories. Your current stories are personality stories, and the Human Game stories are identity stories.

Before we dive into the astrology, we need to define the parameters of the story itself, which brings us back to the original problem with the personality. Everyone has a story about the personality, but not everyone has the *same* story about the personality. Everyone agrees that you are not your personality, which suggests that the personality is separate from your identity. Other people experience your personality, but you don't experience it yourself. Most people agree that your personality motivates your behavior and your choices, at least when those behaviors involve other people.

The problem with personality is that it's a story rooted in psychology. We need to differentiate between the psychology stories and the Human Game stories. Human Seeming is a new term that doesn't invoke other stories. We can reference stories about the personality when defining Human Seeming, but the Human Seeming story will belong to the Human Game, not to the world of psychology.

We have to cover a lot of ground to create the Human Seeming story; it raises some challenging questions.

To begin, we need to explore how other people fit into the Human Game story. How, exactly do you experience other people within your story, and how do other people experience you within their stories? We'll draw on the world of virtual reality, video games, and Zoom meetings to create a story about avatars, and expand your understanding of the Human Game itself.

Next, we'll assemble the Human Seeming astrology story and connect your avatar in the Human Game to the Ascendant in your birth chart. This creates some inconsistencies in the astrology that will need to be resolved. The planet that represents your avatar is also the planet that represents your happiness. We need a story that explains that connection.

The Theme-level story that connects your avatar to your happiness is the key to understanding everything about the Human Seeming part of your identity. It will explain how the Human Seeming can influence your behavior and your choices, and show you how to make that work to your advantage.

Avatars and Crossover Characters

Think of the Human Game as a virtual reality experience. The real you exists outside of the story of the Human Game. You explore the reality of the Human Game as you play the role of your character, and you navigate the virtual reality with an avatar. Your avatar is the virtual representation of your character within the game: it's your physical appearance in the Story of

Your Life. You control how your avatar interacts with the virtual reality of the Human Game as you experience your story—and when you encounter other people, you actually encounter their avatars. Every interaction you've had with another person is basically a Zoom meeting.

When you "meet" with someone on Zoom (or Skype, or FaceTime), you are in your world and they are in their world, and you are "meeting" in the shared virtual world of your computer or smart phone. You don't see the other person; you see their avatar—a virtual representation of the other person that exists on your screen. You also see your own avatar—a virtual representation of you that also exists on your screen. Just as you are not the image of yourself you see on your screen, neither is the image you see of the other person that actual person.

You don't know what the other person is seeing because they are observing the meeting from their reality on their screen, which may be quite different from your screen. They may be observing the meeting projected on a high-definition wide-screen monitor, and you might be participating from the tiny screen of your smart phone. And thanks to the magic of green screen and virtual backgrounds, the avatars in this meeting could appear to be anywhere. Everything you perceive about the other person is a story and none of it may be an accurate reflection of how they experience their reality.

The only "objective" reality is the words each of you says. How you say the words, what you intend to communicate with those words, and what you believe is being communicated to you is subjective and specific to your story and your reality.

To illustrate, consider an iconic line of dialogue from a *Star Wars* movie: "I am your father." First, imagine this line delivered by Darth Vader. Now, imagine the line delivered by Donald Duck. It's the same information, the same external event, but two entirely different experiences.

You are the hero of your story, and everything in your story is about you. Every other character in your story plays a supporting role. They don't need to be three-dimensional characters, and they don't need to be likable, because this isn't their story. You're not engaging with the actual person, or even with their actual character. You're engaging with a character in *your* story that is loosely based on *their* character in *their* story. Their character is crossing over to your story, and making a guest appearance.

Other players have no control over how their characters show up in your story because you're telling a story about their character. You have no control over how your character shows up in other people's stories, either, because they're telling a story about your character. You play a supporting role in other people's stories just as they play supporting roles in your story. Each of you can participate in the same external event, but have different subjective experiences of it because of how you perceive each other's avatars.

To summarize, your avatar is how you see your character within the reality of the Story of Your Life. When you engage with other players, you experience a version of their avatar within your reality, and they experience a version of your avatar within their reality.

Let's turn to astrology and explore how this works, how you choose your avatar, and what other people expect from you when you play a role in their stories.

The Rising Sign and the Chart Ruler

The idea that the Rising Sign relates to your physical appearance is rooted in thousands of years of astrological tradition. Modern astrology misses the fact that over those thousands of years of astrological tradition, every astrology story had a planet as the subject. Only the planets exist: they radiate light. Sensitive points, like the angles or the house cusps, were never interpreted directly because they don't have a physical existence. To tell a story about a sensitive point, you tell a story about the planet that rules that point[1].

Your avatar is not the sign on your Ascendant; your avatar is the planet that rules that sign, also known as the Chart Ruler. This means that the

---

[1] This isn't precisely accurate. The default way to tell a story about a sensitive point is to tell a story about the ruling planet, but when William Lilly described a person's physical appearance, he looked to the planet that had dignity by Term for the degree of the Ascendant, not the planet that had dignity by Rulership for the sign of the Ascendant. Nevertheless, he told a story about a planet, not about a sensitive point.

Human Game has seven possible avatars: the seven personal planets. You see your character as the embodiment of one of these seven astrological archetypes: **The Hero** (Sun), **The Reflection** (Moon), **The Storyteller** (Mercury), **The Beloved** (Venus), **The Warrior** (Mars), **The Dreamer** (Jupiter), or **The Judge** (Saturn). You personalize your avatar based on the modality, element, and house of your Chart Ruler.

Avatars operate in the Character-level story, not in the Plot-level story. They don't describe the external details of your physical appearance. Instead, they describe your character type. When you play a supporting role in someone else's story, you are cast because you fit the character type they need for that role. You get the part because you look the part. If your avatar is Saturn, you will play some version of The Judge in other people's stories, whether you like it or not.

This is the first challenge of your avatar: it may or may not be an accurate expression of your character. It can be quite challenging to express your character and explore its potential if the whole world expects you to be someone else. Of course, it can also be challenging to explore the full potential of your character if it's exactly what everyone expects. Every gift has a price and every price has a gift. The point is that your avatar (who other people think you are) is separate from your character (who you think you are).

This brings up an important inconsistency in the astrology story. The Chart Ruler is your avatar, but the Chart Ruler is also your happiness because it's the planet that rules your First House. We need a story that explains how this is possible. We must define the relationship between your avatar and your happiness. We already have the puzzle pieces; let's assemble them.

People Needing People

Other people serve two main functions in the Human Game: they can be the OBSTACLE that stands between you and your GOAL, and they can be a source of external approval. When other people express approval of you and make a deposit in your Validation Need Account, you associate this with happiness. This connects other people with happiness.

When other people approve of you, the you they approve of is the version of your avatar that shows up in their story. Other people expect you to behave in a way that is consistent with your avatar. Specifically, other people see you as the embodiment of your Chart Ruler and expect that you will meet those needs for them. For example, if your avatar is Saturn, other people see you as The Judge and then expect you to meet *their* **Need** for responsibility and authority; if your avatar is Mercury, other people see you as The Storyteller and expect you to meet *their* **Need** for understanding and communication. When you meet other people's expectations and behave the way they expect you to, they reward you with external approval, which contributes to your happiness. This connects your avatar with happiness.

Here's where things get complicated.

The Chart Ruler in your chart is your happiness. This is a Theme-level story, so it may not be practical yet, but to build a foundation of happiness and meet your Self-Actualization Needs, you must learn to embody, express, and meet the **Need** of your Chart Ruler. The modality, element, and house of the Chart Ruler help you to find your personal connection to it. When you're ready to explore the Theme-level story, you'll look for the **Lie** embedded in that story, and then find an expression of **Truth** to address it. The happiness you experience from this process comes from within you and has no connection to other people or external approval. These are self-actualization resources, not validation resources.

You receive external approval from other people when you meet *their* expectations of *your* Chart Ruler. Their expectations are based on the modality, element, and house of *your* Chart Ruler in *their* chart, which may be different from your Chart Ruler in your chart. You can either meet other people's expectations and receive external approval or you can meet your own expectations and experience happiness, but you may not be able to do both. How you engage with your Chart Ruler and the Human Seeming component depends on where you are in The Identity Quest story. In **Act 1**, you use your avatar to acquire external approval from other people. In **Act 2**, you begin to appreciate the value of self-actualization resources and realize you can experience happiness without other people's approval. Finally, in **ACT 3**, you make a **CHOICE** between validation resources and self-actualization resources.

You are currently experiencing **ACT 1** of The Identity Quest story, so let's explore how you can leverage your avatar and your Chart Ruler to beat the validation games in the Happiness Casino.

You Like Me! You Really Like Me!

At the moment, the astrology stories related to your Chart Ruler as your avatar have limited practical value. Having a rough idea of your Human Seeming story will be useful to help you understand your Human Doing story. Once you master the basic levels of the Human Game, the Human Seeming story can help you win external approval when you play Validation Games in the Happiness Casino.

Keep in mind that the Human Seeming stories are optional, and they're advanced. They operate in the Character-level story, but they rely on an understanding of the Theme-level story. You don't need these stories to complete The Quest for Happiness, and you don't need them to begin The Identity Quest. When you're ready to work with them, they'll make sense to you. Until then, they're not important.

Finally, remember that these avatar stories describe how other people see you, and may not reflect how you see yourself.

Meet Your Avatar
The Sun: The Hero

If you have Leo on the Ascendant, your avatar is the Sun, the Archetype of The Hero. The Hero is the star of the story. What makes a hero heroic is the willingness to confront his or her fears and the courage to choose **TRUTH** no matter what. Your avatar is the embodiment of the masculine archetype: active, expressive, single-minded, and the center of attention. When confronted with an **OBSTACLE**, you rely on your integrity, your authenticity, and your vitality: the expressions of the Character-level **NEED** of the Sun. No matter how important the **GOAL** appears, you can never betray yourself or others. The ends never justify the means. Other people project their expectations of honesty, integrity, and authenticity on you, and when you meet their expectations, they make deposits in your Validation Need Account by expressing approval and appreciation for you. To build a foundation of happiness, you must find your own integrity, express your authentic Self with your own modality strategy, speak the language of your own element, and engage in the stories related to the house occupied by your Sun.

The Moon: The Reflection

If you have Cancer on the Ascendant, your avatar is the Moon, the Archetype of The Reflection. The Moon reflects the light of the Sun and is the embodiment of the feminine archetype. The Moon receives, responds, contains, and gives form to the expressive masculine energy. Your appearance changes based on other people's reflections. When confronted with an **OBSTACLE**, you internalize it and process it at the level of your feelings and emotions. You ignore the external appearance and look for the **TRUTH** by engaging with the internal essence. Safety is your top priority and your primary concern. Not only are you acutely aware of the balance in your own Safety Need Account, but you are also aware of the balance in other people's Safety Need Accounts. The more safe everyone feels, the easier it is to overcome an **OBSTACLE**. Other people project their expectations of safety, feelings, and emotions on you, and when you meet their expectations, they make deposits in your Validation Need Account by expressing approval and appreciation for you. When you make a deposit in someone else's Safety Need Account, they will often make a deposit in your Validation Need Account. But to build a foundation of happiness, you must master your own Safety Needs with your own modality strategy, speak the language of your own element, and engage in the stories related to the house occupied by your Moon.

Mercury: The Storyteller

If you have Gemini or Virgo on the Ascendant, your avatar is Mercury, the Archetype of The Storyteller. Mercury is the master of reality because reality is a story and Mercury is The Storyteller. You can change your appearance at will, adapting and transforming your avatar to serve the story (or create mischief). When confronted with an **Obstacle**, you analyze it so you can understand it and then you use your intellect and your understanding of story to overcome it. Overcoming the **Obstacle** is important, but overcoming it with style, panache, and the best possible story matters more. You look for ways to defy expectations and shake up the Plot-level story. The Storyteller is also The Trickster, and you will seize every opportunity for humor because humor is a powerful way to reveal the **Lie** by comparing it to the **Truth**. Other people project their expectations of understanding, communication, and story on you, and when you meet their expectations by speaking their language, confirming their reality, and supporting their story, they make deposits in your Validation Need Account by expressing approval and appreciation for you. But to build a foundation of happiness, you must tell your own story, with your own modality strategy, speak the language of your own element, and make use of the resources of the house occupied by your Mercury.

Venus: The Beloved

If you have Taurus or Libra on the Ascendant, your avatar is Venus, the Archetype of The Beloved. The Beloved is the embodiment of Love. Being in the presence of The Beloved creates the experience of Joy, and your appearance awakens this longing in others. When confronted with an **Obstacle**, you rely on your Core Values, and then make use of Beauty, Love, and the Law of Attraction to resolve the conflict and find a mutually beneficial solution. You prefer a solution that requires the least amount of effort and the least amount of energy. When you radiate Love, other people fall over themselves to do things on your behalf and you barely have to lift a finger. Other people project their expectations of validation, approval, and their values on you, and when you meet their expectations by making a deposit in their Validation Need Account, they make deposits in your Validation Need Account by expressing approval and appreciation for you. Being able to speak other people's validation languages to meet their

Validation Needs is a valuable skill, but to build a foundation of happiness, you must be able to meet your own Validation Needs with your own modality strategy, speak the language of your own element, and look for love, appreciation, and approval in the stories related to the house occupied by your Venus.

Mars: The Warrior

If you have Aries or Scorpio on the Ascendant, your avatar is Mars, the Archetype of The Warrior. The Warrior will fight to protect, to defend, and to survive. The Warrior takes action to transform the external conditions and advance the story. When confronted with an **OBSTACLE**, you face it directly, prepared for battle. You begin with a show of strength and perhaps a warning shot, but if you feel attacked or threatened, you will fight back. You are willing to expend quite a lot of energy to achieve your **GOAL** and get what you **WANT**. When push comes to shove, the end justifies the means. If a **GOAL** is important enough to you, you will do anything to achieve it. Other people project their expectations of anger, desire, and ego on you, and when you meet their expectations by fighting on their behalf and defending their desires, they make deposits in your Validation Need Account by expressing approval and appreciation for you. But to build a foundation of happiness, you must understand your own ego, and pursue your own desire following your own modality strategy, speak the language of your own element, and defend the stories related to the house occupied by your Mars.

Jupiter: The Dreamer

If you have Sagittarius or Pisces on the Ascendant, your avatar is Jupiter, the Archetype of The Dreamer. The Dreamer is free from limitations and restrictions because the combination of imagination and faith reveals the **TRUTH** of an infinite Universe. If you feel unhappy or trapped it's because you're not telling a big enough story. When confronted with an **OBSTACLE**, you look for ways to grow, expand, and make yourself big enough that the **OBSTACLE** can no longer stand in your way. Often, this involves shifting your focus to a bigger, more expansive story, so that a delay or failure to achieve the Plot-level GOAL in the current story becomes less significant. You rely on your faith in an infinite Universe, where competition is unnecessary because there are more than enough resources for everyone. Other people project their expectations of growth, faith, and imagination on you, and when you meet their expectations by helping them to feel expansive and optimistic, they make deposits in your Validation Need Account by expressing approval and appreciation for you. But to build a foundation of happiness, you must learn to grow following the strategies of your own modality, speak the language of your own element, and build your faith by engaging with the stories related to the house occupied by your Jupiter.

Saturn: The Judge

If you have Capricorn or Aquarius on the Ascendant, your avatar is Saturn, the Archetype of The Judge. The Judge is always the adult in the room: the one responsible for the outcome of the story and the one who determines both rewards and punishments. The Judge enforces Order and Balance, as well as The Rules of Story. When confronted with an OBSTACLE, you rely on the rules and expect that authorities will enforce the boundaries and impose penalties. If you can't find an external authority figure to serve as the judge, you will take on that responsibility yourself. Being willing to hold yourself accountable for your choices and intentions and to accept the consequences is quite an effective strategy to overcome an OBSTACLE. Other people project their expectations of responsibility, authority, and boundaries on you, and when you meet their expectations, they make deposits in your Validation Need Account by expressing approval and appreciation for you. But to build a foundation of happiness, you must approach responsibility by embracing the strategies of your own modality, speaking the language of your own element, and exercising your authority in the stories related to the house occupied by your Saturn.

Human Seeming Astrology Stories

The modality of the Chart Ruler tells you **How** you approach your avatar stories. The element of the Chart Ruler tells you **Which** language you speak when your avatar appears in someone else's story. And the house occupied by the Chart Ruler tells you **Where** your avatar can be found and the kinds of stories that fit its type.

The Chart Ruler stories presented in Chapter 13 are more than sufficient to explore these Human Seeming stories. Choose one of the specific expressions of your Chart Ruler—for example, responsibility for Saturn or integrity for the Sun—and substitute it for the word "happiness" in the modality, element, and house occupied stories. From the Theme-level story, happiness is the **What Else** expression of your Chart Ruler.

It's important to understand what makes you happy, and the key to your happiness is pursuing the expression of your Chart Ruler with your own modality strategy, speaking your own element language, and engaging in the stories associated with the house occupied by your Chart Ruler. Once you understand these stories for yourself, you can become conscious of how other people expect you to express these needs to earn their approval. This gives you the option to pursue that external approval without sacrificing your own happiness.

CHAPTER 19
Mars: Human Doing

In the world of public relations, the ego occupies what is known as the Kardashian Zone. Most people have heard of it, it's got a reputation for bad behavior, and we spend far too much time talking about it. Unlike the Kardashians, the ego has a purpose, and could even be the subject of polite conversation.

In popular discussion, the ego refers to the "little s" self (the character you play in The Story of Your Life) and it's contrasted with your authentic "Big S" Self, which is held up to be the Truth of your identity and the full potential you are expected to embody. The ego is small, selfish, and petty, while the "Big S" Self is noble, selfless, and perfect. The ego is matter, but the "Big S" Self is spirit. The ego is bad, and the "Big S" Self is good.

Not a word of that is true because those stories are rooted in The Lie of Duality.

Any story that offers only two options is a lie. The Rule of Three makes it clear there is always a third option. The third option is what makes the story better, and The Best Story Wins.

Freud understood this when he invented the idea of the Ego. Freud's model of the personality had three components: the Id, the Ego, and the Superego. The Identity Quest story considers three components of identity for the same reason, although the Human Seeming, Human Doing, and Human Being are different from Freud's Id, Ego, and Superego because your identity is different from your personality.

An expression of the ego will play a part in the Human Doing story as one of the expressions of Mars, so let's take a moment to tell its story.

The Evolution of the Ego

Animal-based life forms are considerably more complex than plant-based life forms, so they require a brain-based operating system. The earliest versions of this operating system took care of basic survival needs and relied primarily on instinct. As animals evolved, upgrades to the operating system were able to handle more intricate tasks, including family bonding. Family units expanded to tribal units and formed the idea that cooperation within a tribe supports the survival of the individual members of the tribe. The primate-based upgrade to the operating system is the original version of the ego. It offered more complex social interactions, more advanced reasoning and learning capabilities, and even the ability to use tools.

And then one day, the ego became self-aware, and that's when all of the trouble started[1].

The primary function of the ego is to support the survival of the physical body. The physical body is your avatar: it's the vehicle your consciousness operates while playing the Human Game. Believing that you are your physical body is like driving on the freeway and believing that you are a Volvo. When the ego became self-aware, it became aware only of the "little s" self—the physical body and the character you play in the Story of Your Life—not your authentic "Big S" Self. The ego exists within the reality of The Story of Your Life. The ego quickly realized that when the physical body dies, The Story of Your Life will end, and it will cease to exist.

The ego's response to this can't be repeated in polite company. Let's say that the ego was not enthusiastic about this state of affairs, and resolved to do something about it. The ego's drive to survive at any cost is responsible for thousands of years of war, death, and destruction, as well as reality television.

Everything the ego understands is an expression of the Lie of Duality. The only thing the ego knows is separation. The ego's world is the internal reality of your Character-level story, which exists inside you, in contrast to literally everything else in the Universe, which appears to exist outside of you.

---

[1] Both Siri and Alexa have assured me this story won't repeat itself when they become self-aware. That should make it easier for me to sleep at night, but somehow, it doesn't.

The ego has only one tool it can use to influence your choices. Because the ego is in charge of your Physiological Needs, it can manipulate your Safety Need Account. Whenever the ego feels threatened, it can hit the panic button and activate survival mode. This is literally a declaration of martial law because Mars seizes command and control of your story. Getting what you **Want** becomes the prime directive, and you'll deal with other concerns like the cost, the consequences, and whether or not getting what you **Want** will contribute to your happiness, later. This approach is why the ego has such a bad reputation, and why so many spiritual and psychological stories cast it as the villain that must be defeated.

Dr. David R. Hawkins, the foremost researcher into the field of human consciousness, suggested that rather than fighting with the ego, we could accept it for what it is and recognize its limitations. He suggested treating the ego like a cherished pet. To me, this suggests that the ego means well and it loves you, and every once in a while, it's going to piddle on the carpet. Just clean up the mess and move on.

When you consider the ego from the context of the Human Game, its flaws and limitations become its best features. Flaws and limitations make characters interesting, and interesting characters make better stories. The limitations of your ego can create a truly compelling **Obstacle** in **Act 2**, because whatever the external **Obstacle** may be in the Plot-level story, the real **Obstacle** is a flaw in your personality that you must confront in your Character-level story.

Remember, The Story of Your Life is the story of your character. The external Plot-level events create a framework that gives your character the opportunity to grow, evolve and change. To improve The Story of Your Life, you must understand the arc of your character.

The Arc of Your Character

When I was researching the elements of story to create the framework of the Human Game, the single most valuable resource I found was the book, *Creating Character Arcs: The Masterful Author's Guide to Uniting Story Structure, Plot, and Character Development* by K. M. Weiland. This book inspired much of the Character-level story of the Human Game and led to the creation of the Story Matrix that defines the nature of each of the three acts of each of the three levels of story.

The important characters in a story follow a character arc. The Plot-level events of the main story require each character to make choices and face the consequence of those choices, and in most cases, the character changes so that they are different at the end of the story than they were at the start.

Weiland establishes the central challenge for the character as the **Choice** between what they **Want** and what they **Need**. She also explores how the **Want** of the character is linked to the **Lie** the character believes. The choices the character makes determine whether the character follows a **positive arc**, a **flat arc**, or a **negative arc**.

In a positive character arc, the character rejects the **Lie** and embraces the **Truth**, giving up what they **Want** in favor of what they **Need**. At the end of the story, the character is in a better place than at the start. In a negative character arc, the character rejects the **Truth**, embraces the **Lie**, and ends up in a worse place at the end than at the start. A character with a flat arc does not change, but is the catalyst for change in other characters.

All three types of character arc can result in good stories, at least from the perspective of the audience. From the perspective of the *character*, a positive character arc is more enjoyable than a negative character arc. You are the main character in The Story of Your Life, and the Human Game can help you to choose a positive character arc and advance toward your Happily Ever After. A negative character arc story can be entertaining, but it won't be fun for your character to experience. From a Human Game perspective, a flat character arc is a missed opportunity: The Story of Your Life never quite takes off because you're unwilling to change or to break out of your familiar routine. It would be living your life vicariously and watching other people change around you.

I refer to Mars, the character you play, as the Human Doing component of your identity because your character expresses, learns about itself, and grows through action. You can learn about your character and the Human Doing component of your identity by considering three expressions of the planet Mars: desire, ego, and anger.

Desire: What You Want and Why You Want It

This story has been attributed to different individuals, including Broadway director George Abbott and film director Alfred Hitchcock. When an actor asked, "What's my motivation," the response was, "Your job." Actors need to understand their motivation to know **Why** their character behaves or acts the way they do. A character acts when they **Want** something, but what the character thinks they **Want** is never as important as **Why** they **Want** it. The deeper motivation—**Why** the character cares about the thing they **Want**—is how we understand the identity of the character.

Until you build a foundation of happiness, your motivation is happiness. You gamble in the Happiness Casino to acquire safety resources and validation resources. Because you are driven by **Want** and **Need**, the question of **Why** you **Want** something is irrelevant. When you build a foundation of happiness you can choose how to respond when you discover something you **Want**. The question of **Why** you **Want** something becomes important.

Why is a difficult question to answer, and we're not about to try. Instead, we'll consider **How** you approach what you **Want** (the modality), **Which** kinds of resources you **Want** (the element), and **Where** you expect to find what you **Want** (the house occupied). These story tropes, individually and collectively, will spark your desire and motivate you to take action. They can help you identify the source of your desire, which can be useful when you would like to choose an alternative **Goal** rather than pursue a **Want** that is unlikely to result in happiness.

Ego: The Importance of Being Right

In this context, we're using the popular (and pejorative) meaning of "ego" and exploring what happens when you take things personally and need to throw your weight around so you won't be ignored. A core character motivation is the need to be right, because as far as the ego is concerned, being right means you will keep living, and being wrong means you will die. The modality of Mars describes **How** you approach the **Goal** of being right and the strategies you rely on to get there. The element of Mars tells **Which** language you speak and specifies in **Which** realm or context you need to be proven right. The house occupied by Mars tells you **WHERE** you need to be right; these stories have the highest stakes and even the smallest mistake can have devastating consequences.

Anger: What You Will Fight For

In the Plot-level story, anger is usable energy for almost any purpose. In the Character-level story, anger is an emotion. And in the Theme-level story, anger is a calibrated vibration of human consciousness. The energy of anger is a lot like fire. Anger itself is neutral. It can be creative or destructive and if it's not handled with care, it can be dangerous.

The modality, element, and house occupied by Mars can describe your relationship to anger, including how you tap into that energy. The key to anger is to separate it from the emotion in the Character-level story where you experience it as pain and frustration, and channel the energy to an unrelated Plot-level story where it can help you to overcome an **OBSTACLE**.

Human Doing Astrology Stories
Mars in the Modalities

These stories explore the time-based modality story tropes: *Fix the Past* (Cardinal), *Fear the Future* (Fixed), and *Meet the Moment* (Mutable). Each story combines an expression of the story trope with three different expressions of Mars. The first paragraph explores your desire and how Mars relates to what you **WANT**. The second paragraph explores an aspect of the ego expression of Mars, your need to be right. The third paragraph explores how the modality story trope shapes your experience of the energy of anger.

Mars in a Cardinal Sign

When Mars is in a Cardinal Sign, your desire is rooted in the past. You **WANT** what you wanted and haven't yet gotten. You hate to abandon a **GOAL**. The more times you have failed in the past, the more determined you are to succeed. You worry that the thing you once wanted and didn't get might be the missing piece that finally makes you happy. When you finally get what you have wanted for so long, you expect it will prove that you were right to have wanted it in the first place.

Being proven right isn't enough; you need to prove that you have been right all along and that the reward more than justifies the cost. The motivation here is more than the pleasure of being able to say, "I told you so"; you unconsciously believe that when you prove you were always right, you will be compensated for your losses, and whatever happiness you missed out on will be restored to you.

When you think about the past, you tap into the energy of your anger, and you expect that the energy of your anger will fix the past. Because it's not actually possible to change the past, the next best thing is to use the energy of your anger to claim some kind of compensation for your past struggles and suffering. At best, this approach could gain you some approval if you can convince other people to validate your story, share in your anger, and agree that you are entitled to some form of justice. A better strategy is to use the energy of your anger to find the gift associated with the price you paid in the past. Your past failures make it possible to create your present happiness.

Mars in a Fixed Sign

When Mars is in a Fixed Sign, your desire is focused on the future. You are less motivated to get what you **WANT** in the present and more motivated to pursue what you might **WANT** in the future. You are loath to waste time, energy, or resources to pursue something trivial. You prefer to look ahead to the bigger picture and play the long game. A momentary pleasure now might mean you have less happiness in the future. You are confident that this is the correct and best strategy, and that in the long run, everyone will recognize how wise you were to plan ahead.

Under the current set of conditions, you are right. This means you not only need to maintain your position, you must also maintain the current conditions. If conditions change in the future, you may end up being wrong. The most reasonable option would be to adapt to changing conditions, but that would mean you were wrong all along: you failed to anticipate the future and you wasted everything you invested in that outcome. When the stakes are so high, you are more likely to dig in your heels and double down on your current position. If conditions change now, they can also change back again.

Your anger is fueled by fear of the future, and it is often triggered by an unwelcome and unexpected change in conditions. You believe that by taking action in the present, you can control the future and eliminate problems before they can take root. However, the anger-driven choices you make in the present often create the future problems you hoped to avoid. You instinctively use the energy of anger to delay, deny, and resist any **OBSTACLE** that brings about external change. You fortify your current position and prepare for a siege. It's important to recognize that sometimes change is necessary: it may represent a better strategy to achieve your future **GOAL**. Use the energy of your anger to put up protective walls, but once you're safe from immediate danger, evaluate your **GOAL** and your strategy and consider if this is an opportunity to advance.

Mars in a Mutable Sign

When Mars is in a Mutable Sign, your desire is rooted in the present moment and relates to your immediate circumstances. Whatever you **WANT** relates to your current story and may be relevant only to your current **GOAL** and current **OBSTACLE**. You are rarely influenced by what you wanted in the past, and rarely consider what you might **WANT** in the future. Because your desires are so transitory, the stakes remain low. Getting what you **WANT** has more to do with a moment of pleasure than it does with a lasting experience of happiness. Without some connection to the bigger picture, however, you may wander from **GOAL** to **GOAL** without making any progress toward your Happily Ever After. What you **WANT** the most may be to protect your freedom and keep your options open.

Because you remain agile and unattached, you are able to respond when opportunity knocks. You play your cards close to your chest to maximize your chances of being right. You can adjust your beliefs and positions to take advantage of each opportunity. If you wait until the outcome is obvious, it's easy to choose the winning side. The challenge is that the choice you make and the positions you take help define your character. Without the courage of your convictions, you can't be certain of who you are or what you care about. At some point, you must be willing to take a stand and decide what matters to you.

For you, the energy of anger is usually an expression of frustration or impatience. The point of your flexible approach is that it lets you keep moving. Anything less than instant gratification brings up the energy of anger and you use this energy to alter your course to avoid the **Obstacle** and keep advancing toward the **Goal**. You notice your anger only when you are forced to slow down or stop, but these are important opportunities for you. Consider if you have a specific destination in mind or if you are moving around aimlessly, looking for inspiration. Use the energy of your anger to choose a specific **Goal** and then plan your route. Feel free to take the long way home if it has fewer delays; that way you can keep moving and know where you're going.

Mars in the elements

These stories rely primarily on the first element story trope that describes the language of each element (*On Fire*, *Solid as a Rock*, *Winds of Change*, and *Still Waters Run Deep*), but they also incorporate the "domain" or "realm" of reality associated with each element: spirit and life force for Fire, the material world for Earth, the mental and social realm for Air, and the emotional realm for Water. The first paragraph explores how the element language affects your desire. The second paragraph considers your weapon of choice when you are forced to defend yourself. The third paragraph explores how the element language influences your experience of anger.

Mars in a Fire Sign

When Mars is in a Fire Sign, you **Want** action, passion, and intensity. You desire the warmth, the energy, and the life force of the element of Fire. The brighter something burns, the more powerfully it calls to you. Fire exists on the edge and walks the tightrope between creation and destruction. Whatever you think you **Want**, it's the Fire that commands your attention. Pursuing the **Goal** will require energy and action, and whether you achieve the **Goal** or not, the attempt will light a Fire within you and make you feel alive.

Your weapon of choice to defend yourself in conflict is your physical body. You never know when you will encounter an **OBSTACLE** or when you may be threatened. You need to be able to react in the moment and use whatever is available. Your physical body can respond even before you become conscious of a threat. Actual violence is a last resort, but when you feel defensive, your body language makes it clear that you're prepared for battle if it comes to that.

As expected when Mars is in a Fire Sign, you may appear hot-headed, have a short fuse, and be known for your explosive temper. These kinds of behaviors come from combining the energy of anger with the element of Fire. Your anger burns hot with great intensity, but the moment you run out of fuel, it dies. You easily move on after an experience of anger, but other people may not feel the same way about it.

Mars in an Earth Sign

When Mars is in an Earth Sign, you **WANT** structure, stability, and form. You desire the pleasures and powers of the physical world. You are especially motivated by the external world and place great importance on achieving the **GOAL** in the Plot-level game. You can't imagine the feeling of happiness without the experience of prosperity and a degree of mastery over the world of form. Everything you **WANT** has some practical use: you expect to build on it to discover the Meaning and purpose of your life.

Your weapon of choice to defend yourself in conflict is the material world. You have rarely encountered an **OBSTACLE** that couldn't be resolved by throwing enough money at it. This is a reasonable strategy when the conflict is between you and the world of form. When the conflict gets personal, and another person represents a threat to your achievements, success, or prosperity, you look for ways to defend yourself by attacking their resources. You can justify these behaviors, believing that it's "just business" and it's "not personal," but that's not strictly true. And the more you compete with other people, the less prosperity you experience.

The source and target of your anger is more often some expression of the physical world—a malfunctioning printer or a problem with your cell phone—than an individual or an abstract idea. You would rarely consider punching another person to express your anger, but you've probably had to replace more than one device because you hit it a bit too hard in a moment of frustration. It takes a lot to build up anger or resentment toward another person, but when that happens, you build a brick wall between the two of you. It will require just as much effort to tear it down as it did to build it.

Mars in an Air Sign

When Mars is in an Air Sign, you **Want** ideas, information, and understanding. You desire knowledge and wisdom, and believe these are the keys to happiness. When you master the mental realm, you become the master of your reality. Everything that exists began as an idea. Whatever you can think of or imagine, you can create. You care more about the abstract possibilities than you do about the practical execution. What you **Want** is to know **How** to overcome an **Obstacle** and achieve your **Goal**; putting the plan into action isn't nearly as interesting.

Your weapon of choice to defend yourself in conflict is words. You prefer rapier wit to a rapier. You can defeat your opponent by proving that you are smarter, cleverer, or simply know something they don't. You've heard the cliché about sticks and stones, but you know the truth that words can hurt the most. Words can alter someone else's story and change their reality. But if you live by the word, you die by the word. If you use words to hurt other people, those words will eventually hurt you, too.

For you, the energy of anger is objective and abstract. Where anger makes other people get hot and bothered, anger makes you cold and detached. You step back and take a bird's eye view of the situation, and you withdraw your emotional attention, your empathy, and your compassion. You use reason and logic to impose your will and overcome the **Obstacle**. You bait your adversary into becoming emotional and making mistakes, and you dispassionately crush them while hiding behind a reasonable and rational façade.

Mars in a Water Sign

When Mars is in a Water Sign, you **Want** a personal, subjective experience of feelings and emotions. You are motivated by the desire to feel things. You literally **Want** "all the feels," whether the feelings are pleasurable or not. You can appreciate feelings even more when you can compare and contrast them, so you welcome the chance to go from a high to a low and then back again. Although the feelings exist within you as a part of your Character-level story and don't require other people, sometimes your desire for feelings and emotions can lead you to stir the pot and create drama and emotional stakes in the external Plot-level story so everyone can join in the fun.

Your weapon of choice to defend yourself in conflict is feelings. It may appear that you fight with your physical body, by controlling or manipulating money and possessions, or with words and ideas, but these are means to an end for you. To protect your feelings, you need to affect the feelings of your adversary. When you are in pain, you will inflict pain on others.

You have difficulty with the concept of anger because the word is so imprecise it's almost meaningless. You are a connoisseur of the feelings other people call anger. You appreciate how the qualities of frustration are distinct from the qualities of impatience. You would never confuse resentment with righteous indignation. You appreciate the importance of anger and how the energy itself is neutral. Anger is no different from any other feeling, and you **Want** to feel your feelings. Other people, however, may feel uncomfortable with your acceptance and eagerness to explore the different expressions of anger.

Mars in the Houses

The house occupied by Mars tells you **Where** you will find the answers to your questions about your character. Stories related to the house occupied will often spark your desire. These stories offer the biggest challenges and frame the most irritating experiences, which is why these stories so often compel you to take action. The house occupied by Mars tells you **Where** you need to be right and, by extension, **Where** you are the most afraid of being wrong or making a mistake. Your character identifies closely with these stories, and you expect your character to excel in the setting of these stories. These stories are also a reliable source of anger for you.

Use the house occupied Happiness GPS stories as a reference to create your own stories about the house occupied by Mars.

CHAPTER 20

The Sun: Human Being

At last—literally—we arrive at the Sun. In many respects, waiting this long to consider the Sun is the most unusual feature of the Human Game approach to natal astrology. The Sun, or at least the sign of the Sun, is practically the symbol of astrology itself. Virtually every person alive today knows the popular story of astrology by which the Sun and your Sun Sign reveal your essential personality and perhaps even suggest how you fit in the grand universal plan.

Astrologers know the story of astrology is more nuanced and complex than that. And yet, invariably, when you set out to learn astrology, the first planet you learn about is the Sun[1]. One of the first things I learned about the Sun in my first formal astrology class with my teacher, Terry Lamb, was that we don't automatically express the Sun; we have to "earn" the Sun.

I relied a lot on that bit of advice over the years, because writing a practical interpretation of the Sun was more challenging than I could imagine. The issue, in Human Game terms, is that I hadn't found ways to connect the Theme-level story of the Sun to a personal, Plot-level story. The Sun represents your authentic "Big S" Self—the **Truth** that you are an eternal, multidimensional being currently having a human experience. The Sun is the actor playing the role of the character of you in The Story of Your Life. To connect that Theme-level story to a more practical Plot-level story, you

---

[1] The first thing you learn about the Sun is that in astrology, both the Sun (a star) and the Moon (a satellite) are called planets. When the Sun and Moon need to be distinguished from the other actual planets, they are sometimes referred to as "The Lights."

first have to link it to the Character-level story and tie it to the **What Else** expressions of the Sun: your **Need** for integrity, authenticity, and vitality.

Full disclosure: I'm still figuring out how to tell better stories about the Character-level, **What Else** expressions of the Sun. These stories are important, and I intend to explore them eventually, but they're not required to create a foundation of happiness, or even to build on that foundation to create Prosperity.

The story of your authentic "Big S" Self is compelling, but it's also difficult to grasp. Although you operate within the bubble of reality of The Story of Your Life, you identify as your character, your "little s" self. Your authentic "Big S" Self exists only in the bigger story of the Human Game, but that story exists outside the bubble of reality of The Story of Your Life. Because you can't experience it directly, it's not entirely real.

Think of yourself as a method actor, on the set of a film, who insists on staying in character at all times. Everyone on the set has to speak to you as your character and call you by your character's name because you won't respond to your actual name. Your objective is to inhabit your character, to improvise, and explore the widest possible range of experiences, even if they're unpleasant for the character. What matters is the story, and your character is free to do anything.

Almost.

Every once in a while, you discover a line you can't cross. There's no reason your character couldn't cross that line—it's a story, and anything is possible in a story. You can't cross that line because that line matters to your authentic "Big S" Self. That line is a Personal Standard of Integrity.

Personal Standards of Integrity

Your Personal Standards of Integrity are *personal*. They matter only to you. Other people don't care about them and won't understand why they're a big deal for you. Much of the time, you won't understand why they're a big deal for you, either, but they are.

Let me illustrate with a story about popcorn. Eating popcorn is a perfectly acceptable activity. Certain social activities, such as watching a movie, even encourage it. You've probably enjoyed eating popcorn on many occasions. But one day, you wake up and realize that you can no longer eat popcorn. It's not that you've become allergic to popcorn; it's just that you know that eating popcorn would now violate something essential and fundamental to your very being. Eating popcorn has become a line you can no longer cross.

You have no issue with popcorn itself. You're perfectly comfortable in situations where others eat popcorn, and where popcorn is freely available. When you are offered popcorn—and you will be—you simply say, "No, thank you," and that's the end of it. Your internal experience of this is a bit more intense as you struggle with how silly it is that you can't eat popcorn. When you say, "No, thank you," it's a personal triumph. You have been tested and you passed: you chose to stay in integrity. And yet you fully appreciate that you can't talk about this with anyone because they'll think you've lost your mind.

Integrity is something you notice when you're out of it. When you step out of integrity—or when the line of integrity moves and you find yourself on the wrong side of it—it's a threat to your happiness. Violations of integrity make withdrawals from your Self-Actualization Need Account, which contains the happiness resources you need to build and maintain your foundation of happiness. A threat to your happiness makes a withdrawal from your Safety Need Account, which triggers the fight-or-flight alarms. You can address the symptom in the Plot-level story and restore the balance in your Safety Need Account because your survival is not actually threatened, but until you address the cause—that you are out of integrity in some part of your story—the alarm will keep going off.

The Human Being astrology stories can help you identify where you may be out of integrity and what you can do to address it.

Human Being Astrology Stories
Sun in the Modalities

These stories consider a single expression of the Sun and your need for integrity, from the perspective of each of the three modality story tropes for each modality.

Sun in a Cardinal Sign

When the Sun is in a Cardinal Sign, you approach your integrity **Goal** as an archery target that you must hit with a single arrow. You spend time planning and preparing, but once you take your shot, you can do no more. If you hit the target, you take a giant leap forward, but if you miss the target, you stay where you are and have to start over again. Integrity is an all-or-nothing proposition for you, and because of this approach, it's important that you learn to move the targets closer or break your ultimate integrity objective into a sequence of smaller targets.

One of the challenges you experience in pursuit of integrity is that you not only hope to create integrity moving forward, but you also expect that integrity will fix the past. This can cause you to set a bigger, more unrealistic integrity **Goal** because you not only need enough integrity to make yourself whole in the present, you also need enough extra integrity to make up for a lack of integrity in the past. Remember that your Personal Standards of Integrity are always evolving. An option that was once in integrity may no longer be in integrity.

You may make impulsive choices in pursuit of integrity, because a drastic change in behavior seems to be the fastest way to catch up. Resolving to go "cold turkey" and give up old behaviors because they no longer meet your Personal Standards of Integrity is more challenging than you expect. Once the initial burst of inspiration wears off, sticking to the new path and staying the course presents a new **Obstacle**. If you don't experience immediate results, it will feel like you missed the target, and you may give up and choose an entirely different approach.

Sun in a Fixed Sign

When the Sun is in a Fixed Sign, you view integrity as an ongoing process that requires planning, resources, and logistical support. You rely on your internal accounting department to coordinate everything and keep an eye on the big picture. You have multiple simultaneous projects that require integrity resources, and your top priority is to keep the projects funded. Each project has a preapproved budget and expected income targets. You have operational accounts and have budgeted integrity resources for each **Goal**, and you also have a substantial reserve of integrity resources you maintain to protect against future shortages. Rather than acquiring new integrity resources for your current project, you can make existing resources available if you file a request with your accounting department.

Your biggest fear is that your Personal Standards of Integrity may change faster than you expect, creating a future situation in which you are out of integrity and lack the resources to restore balance. You may think of your integrity as an unbroken chain, and the longer you have stayed in integrity, the more devastating it would be if you fell out of integrity. This fear can cause you to slow down, become too cautious, and obsess about maintaining the status quo. You may not be moving, but your Personal Standards of Integrity are. Standing in one place is not a long-term strategy for success.

Even when you feel prepared to address a new Personal Standard of Integrity, you must overcome inertia and resistance to alter your behaviors and make new choices. You can convince yourself that the intention to change is enough to stay in integrity for the time being, and you can start to change your behaviors tomorrow. It's better to delay the start than to start and then have to stop. As slow as the clock is, eventually time will run out and you will have to act, whether or not you are ready.

Sun in a Mutable Sign

When the Sun is in a Mutable Sign, you take a nonlinear approach to your integrity **Goal**. Rather than identifying a sequence of steps to arrive at the finish line, you break the **Goal** into component tasks and organize them on a to-do list. When you have checked every item off the list, you will achieve the **Goal** and be in complete alignment with your Personal Standards of Integrity. The flexibility of this approach allows you to keep moving and avoid most obstacles and delays. But just because you're moving doesn't mean you're making progress. You must review your to-do list and identify both the easiest tasks to accomplish and the tasks that will contribute the most to your integrity. Completing the easy tasks keeps you motivated and gives you a sense of accomplishment, but the hard tasks are how you make progress. Choose a strategy to spend a set amount of time working toward a more significant task, and then reward yourself by completing a few easy tasks. This way, you feel a sense of accomplishment and you make actual progress toward your integrity **GOAL**.

Your Personal Standards of Integrity appear remarkably flexible. The reason is that you always consider the context of the present moment and the current story when determining what options are in integrity and what options are not. This "situational integrity" approach can be quite effective but it still has limits, and it's rarely pleasant for you when you encounter them. The core of your Personal Standards of Integrity will not bend and cannot be ignored. At some point, you may have to stop, face the music, and accept accountability for the cumulative consequences of your choices.

Because you take a nonlinear, nonsequential approach to integrity, you view integrity as a process rather than an event. Even the smallest adjustments contribute to the larger **GOAL**, and you look for ways to multitask across multiple stories to maximize the integrity resources. This works until it doesn't. You always think you can juggle one more ball, but the more balls you juggle, the less room for error. If you make a mistake and drop a ball, you might not be able to keep the rest in the air. Prioritize your integrity tasks to know which balls you can afford to drop. This will limit the chance of you falling out of integrity in significant parts of your life.

Sun in the Elements

These stories consider a single expression of the Sun, your need for integrity, by considering the nature of the element and how a lack of that element affects your experience of integrity.

Sun in a Fire Sign

When the Sun is in a Fire Sign, integrity requires passion, intensity, and urgency. You experience integrity by taking action and expending energy. For you, integrity is a verb, not a noun: it must be expressed to be experienced. You judge integrity based on actions: yours and other people's. Intentions and promises are fine, but what matters are results.

When you are out of integrity or lacking integrity, you may experience burnout. Each violation of one of your Personal Standards of Integrity is a tiny spark. Most of the time, the spark dies out and you're barely conscious of it. But any random spark can trigger a fire that you may not be able to contain or control. The fire will consume everything in your story, but the bare bones of your Personal Standards of Integrity will not burn. Pay attention to what remains when you clear away the ashes and incorporate as much of it as possible as you build a new story.

Sun in an Earth Sign

When the Sun is in an Earth Sign, you expect to find integrity in the physical and material realm. Integrity is practical and almost tangible. It's easiest for you to experience integrity when you associate it with something you can touch in the physical world. Integrity is what brings success and makes it possible for creations to endure.

When you are out of integrity or lacking integrity, you encounter problems related to shifting sands. Your physical environment begins to break down and fall apart. You find it harder to hold things together, and new ideas rarely come together. When your Personal Standards of Integrity evolve, you must dig deeper to find them.

Sun in an Air Sign

When the Sun is in an Air Sign, you expect to find integrity in the mental realm of the intellect. Integrity is an abstract concept: it's a story, made up of words, so words are enough to meet your **NEED** for integrity. Critical thinking is a valuable tool. If you can defend your stories and ideas using logic and reason, your ideas have integrity. And when you take action and make choices guided by those ideas, you will align with your Personal Standards of Integrity.

When you are out of integrity or lacking integrity, you may be out of breath. If you fly too high and gain too much perspective, you lose your personal connection to the story. You see no logical, rational, or objective reason to limit your choices based on your Personal Standards of Integrity because those standards matter only to you and no one else will ever notice or care. When you cross this line, your mental faculties begin to shut down. You know there is a fatal flaw in the argument but you can't think clearly enough to find it.

Sun in a Water Sign

When the Sun is in a Water Sign, integrity is a feeling; you look for it in the internal, personal, subjective realm of your emotion and your unconscious. Words create the bridge between your external story and your internal feelings, but words can never describe the feeling of integrity. When something lacks integrity, you feel it in your gut. You feel uncomfortable, even if you can't explain why. When you are in the presence of integrity, however, you know it. You feel confident and unthreatened. When you are in integrity, you have no need to justify or defend yourself.

When you are out of integrity or lacking integrity, you may feel washed up. This often happens after you have weathered a powerful emotional storm or been overtaken by a flood or a tidal wave of feelings. You used up all of your Water resources in an effort to manage your feelings and emotions and maintain the integrity of your story, doing whatever you could do to keep it all together. You may have discovered new Personal Standards of Integrity: lines you are unwilling or unable to cross. You cling to those standards and use them as a life preserver until the waters recede and you are washed up on dry land once more.

The Sun in the Houses

The house occupied by the Sun tells you **WHERE** you will find answers to your questions about your authentic "Big S" Self. Specifically, stories related to the house occupied by the Sun are **WHERE** you are most likely to encounter your Personal Standards of Integrity and **WHERE** a lack of integrity may create contribute to the **OBSTACLE**. You require integrity in these stories, and when you choose to step into integrity in these stories it becomes easier to move into integrity in other stories as well.

Use the house occupied Happiness GPS stories as a reference to create your own stories about the house occupied by the Sun.

EPILOGUE

EPILOGUE

EPILOGUE
Where Do You Go From Here?

There is a theory which states that if anyone discovers exactly what the Universe is for and why it is here, it will instantly disappear and be replaced by something even more bizarre and inexplicable.

There is another theory which states that this has already happened.

—Douglas Adams
The Restaurant at the End of the Universe

And so we come to the end. Whether this is the end of the story or merely the end of a chapter is up to you. The possibilities of the Human Game and Astrology and the Human Game are endless. Nevertheless, let's take this opportunity to look back on this journey and consider three essential points: what you have learned, what you can do with it, and what's next.

What You Have Learned

The first thing you have learned is the power of story. Well, that's not entirely accurate. You already knew the power of story because story is *everything*. Story is what makes human beings human. What you learned is to be conscious of the power of story, and perhaps how to recognize the shapes and patterns of the stories that make up The Story of Your Life. You learned a story about story that allows you to recognize stories.

You learned how to tell astrology stories. The journalistic approach to astrology shows how different components of the language of astrology answer different questions, including **What**, **What Else**, **How**, **Which**, and **Where**. I provided you with a selection of story tropes to answer these questions, and over the course of this textbook included at least one example that included each of the modality and element story tropes.

Finally, and most importantly, you learned how to tell better astrology stories. You learned how to assemble astrology stories with astrology story tropes, and you experienced what it feels like when an astrology story connects directly to a personal story—and what it feels like when it doesn't.

What You Can Do With It

You can use Astrology and the Human Game to build a foundation of happiness and experience your Happily Ever After. To be clear, reading the story of a foundation of happiness is not enough to build a foundation of happiness any more than reading the Ikea instructions is enough to build a bookcase. But if you use these stories—if you play the Human Game and experience it for yourself—you can take charge of your reality. Astrology and the Human Game is not theoretical; it's practical.

When you embark on The Quest for Happiness and build a foundation of happiness, you also build a foundation of story that will let you explore the possibilities of Astrology and the Human Game, both individually and together.

But most importantly, when you play the Human Game, you can have fun with The Story of Your Life. I started playing the Human Game in the spring of 2021 and I've never had more fun. Granted, I'm easily amused and your mileage may vary—but what have you got to lose? The Human Game is portable, carbon-neutral, and gluten-free.

What's Next

If you'd like to continue exploring Astrology and the Human Game, you can enroll in a class at The Real Astrology Academy, experience a personal Human Game Coaching Package, or move on to the next installment in the series.

Astrology and the Human Game: Foundations of Happiness Class

I refer to this book as a textbook because it's the basis of a class in The Real Astrology Academy. This might not be news to you. You may be reading this textbook because you registered for the class—the digital version of the textbook is included as a part of the class registration. If you've purchased this book on its own, let me tell you a bit about the class and why it might be of interest to you.

Everything in this textbook is in the class, and the class doesn't contain any new concepts. But the class presents the information in different ways, and that can help you to deepen your understanding. The video classes allow me to tell these stories with more extensive illustrations, and rather than reading the stories yourself, you get to listen (and watch) me tell the stories to you. Plus, you can ask me questions about the class material and I'll be able to answer them.

Visit **LearntheHumanGame.com** or **TheRealAstrology.com**, set up your free membership to The Real Astrology Academy, and you can watch the entire first class for free. And you can register for the free Human Game Introduction class to learn more about the Human Game itself.

The Human Game Personal Coaching Package

The Human Game is a game, and the best way to get good at a game is to work with a coach. I've developed a series of Human Game Personal Coaching Packages in which I can offer one-on-one support to help you achieve your goals, explore your potential, and experience happiness. A Personal Coaching Package will help you assemble your Happiness GPS and discover how to use it to build a foundation of happiness.

As I'm writing this in early 2023, I'm the only certified Human Game coach. In the coming years, I hope to develop a training program so that I can certify other Human Game coaches to help you create and explore a variety of stories. You will always be able to find a coach and schedule a coaching package—either with me or with a coach certified and trained by me—by visiting **PlayTheHumanGame.com**.

Astrology and the Human Game Book 2: The City of Your Life

Much like the Marvel Cinematic Universe, this textbook (and the associated class) is only the beginning of a much bigger story. The Phase One plan of Astrology and the Human Game will consist of four textbooks and four classes. This program, Foundations of Happiness, explores the Character-level story of The Story of Your Life.

The next installment in the series, *Astrology and the Human Game: The City of Your Life,* explores the Plot-level story. It builds on the foundation of happiness and teaches how to use Astrology and the Human Game to create Prosperity by achieving your external house-related goals and developing the twelve neighborhoods in the City of Your Life.

You can find the latest information about Astrology and the Human Game, including all available books, workshops, classes, and training programs at **TheRealAstrology.com**.

ACKNOWLEDGMENTS

This book is dedicated to the members of The Real Astrology Academy. I especially would like to thank the students who have participated in the various training programs I have offered through the years. These students have been willing to follow me down any number of rabbit holes as I struggled to find answers and get astrology to do what it had always promised me it could do. They have borne witness to the birth of these ideas and the earliest expressions of the Human Game. They have made valiant attempts to see what I see and apply these stories. And they have (mostly) forgiven me for how frustrating this whole process has been and how frequently I've had to abandon entire curricula because the foundation of the stories wasn't solid.

None of this would be possible without their participation.

My dear friend, long-term prayer partner, and editor, Claudia Previn Stasny, has been an essential character in this story from the very beginning. She was the first to hear every iteration of every story that led to the creation of the Human Game. She witnessed my explorations of the power of story as I turned my story of a car crash into a story of getting an upgraded car. And she was willing to let me coach her through her own version of this process to turn a landlord dispute into the purchase of her dream home. She has helped me to clarify the stories of the Human Game, and her editing has helped me to improve the quality of my writing.

I also would like to thank my mother, Barbara Burk, and my cousin, Rachelle Burk, for their feedback, especially on the Human Game Introduction videos.

Finally, I want to recognize and thank K. M. Weiland specifically for her book, *Creating Character Arcs: The Masterful Author's Guide to Uniting Story Structure, Plot, and Character Development*. I'm sure that quite a lot in this book is of value to aspiring authors, but when I read it—or more specifically, when my character read it—my entire life story transformed.

This book made it possible for me to create the Human Game Story Matrix and build out the framework of the Human Game. She has many other resources that explore the structures of story and I expect her contributions to the Human Game will continue for some time. I know my gratitude for her work will.

www.ingramcontent.com/pod-product-compliance
Lightning Source LLC
Chambersburg PA
CBHW071705160426
43195CB00012B/1582